Facts Need Not Be In Evidence

Facts Need Not Be In Evidence

✦

The Politically Correct's 'Social Fascist' War On Classic Whig Liberalism

Craig P Boulton

iUniverse, Inc.
New York Lincoln Shanghai

Facts Need Not Be In Evidence
The Politically Correct's 'Social Fascist' War On Classic Whig Liberalism

iUniverse, Inc.

For information address:
iUniverse, Inc.
2021 Pine Lake Road, Suite 100
Lincoln, NE 68512
www.iuniverse.com

ISBN: 0-595-33402-4

Printed in the United States of America

To Alan Colmes of Fox News and Chris Mathews of MSNBC who spew on without ever seeming to have read a history book and those 'liberal' political operatives with their 'talking points' who inspired me to write this book.

Contents

Riots and overall general violence were the norm of the day as two visions of the 'will of the masses' competed for dominance. The core of one was nationalistic and that of the other was internationalist. The goal of each was to rule the nation according to the vision of the party elite, irrespective of what the actual 'will of the masses' might be. To obtain power a Rousseauan appeal to emotions was utilized to an unheard of extent without regard to fact as reality was replaced by fantasy.

Eventually the lands concerned became ungovernable, thanks to a continuum of violence engineered by conflicting totalitarian visions until existing elites turned to the least offensive masters of propaganda who'd promised an utopian paradise, if only they were in power. Thinking that they could control the Robespierres of the day and thus indirectly control the actions of the Sans Coulettes de jure, the elites constitutionally accepted Adolf Hitler as Chancellor of Germany while Italy's king bowed to the inevitable by appointing Benito Mussolini to be Italy's Prime Minister.

Today, as America's politically correct run amok with their propaganda and assumptions devoid of dependence upon fact to re-acquire power at all costs short of violence and the country struggles to prevent more terrorists attacks, visions of post World War One Germany's Weimar Republic dance in my head.

Introduction

Back when Ronald Reagan was in the White House, a white haired Republican lion of the House of Representatives from Illinois, Henry Hyde, came to Redding, California where I heard him speak before a GOP gathering that I helped assemble. Two items stood out from what he had to say that day.

The first was that, although raised a 'yellow dog Democrat', he started reading Eleanor Roosevelt's daily editorials while a law student at Chicago's De Paul University. As the first lady of American socialism and matron of world government by the United Nations continued to write, he felt that he was slowly being pushed over the edge of a cliff and into the Republican Party. Even though I was 'baptized' at birth into the Grand Old Party, I understand his progression as I've observed the politically correct become ever more shrill and divorced from reality.

The second came when he moved on to a discussion of the then current 'Iran—Contra scandal' where he'd been a key member of the Joint Congressional Committee conducting the investigative hearings. Despite the impropriety and questionable legality of the instigator's actions, if Congressman Hyde ever ended up in a North Vietnamese prison, it was the two key perpetrators looking for a way to escape that he wanted to share a cell with. His point being that when 'push comes to shove', it's the politically correct who try to cut deals for expediency rather than sucking it up and going for freedom.

This has been a particularly acute as terrorist activity has built up in recent years, especially after the Clinton Administration did only the minimum necessary to keep the wolves away from the door with its emphasis on legalism. Now we're in the midst of a three front war in an effort to put the genie back in the bottle and many Americans are ill at ease with the measures that need to be taken.

When coupled with a pervasive sense of fear that normally comes with a world that's changing faster than most people can adjust to, the door has been opened for those who pander to that fear by maximizing the use of disinformation. Their objective is to reassure the populous that if they were in power, we could go back to more comforting times. However, in the process of kissing the 'owwie' like our mothers did when we were all children, this has risen to an unparalleled level of propaganda and vitriolic rhetoric.

This was not a book I wanted to write at this time since it severely detracted from the investment web-site that I operate. However, given that the political climate in America continues to deteriorate to levels we probably haven't seen since Jefferson left the reservation in 1800. I feel that the country I fought for as a Marine Corps combat officer and the core values that casued the 'greatest generation' to confront 20th Century totalitarianism are at risk.

Until this point I've been attempting to fight the ideological once a month—two hundred words at a crack; this is the limit imposed on me and others who write to the editor by our local Gannett owned daily newspaper. Given the volume of 'misinformation' that's propagated as if it were truth without any substantiation, it's obvious that this limited effort leaves too much unchallenged to what I deeply feel is the detriment of the political process. Thus its time for this old 'Goldwater Republican' to rise to the occasion; especially after years of being spit on, screamed at, and discriminated against just like African-Americans in the pre-civil rights south because of my unrepentant service in Vietnam.

The problem before now is that I never understood why liberals were so vehement in their denunciation of people like me. After years of reading countless pundits from Jean-Francis Revel *(How Democracies Perish)* to Ann Coulter *(Slander: Liberal Lies About the American Right)*, I could never come to grips with the why. I've also spent hundreds of hours studying totalitarianism as part of my graduate work on planned economies going back to when I attended George Washington University while on active duty at Quantico, Virginia.

I just couldn't grasp the motivation of those people who seem so hell bent on undermining our country because of seemingly irrational hatred. Recently though, my thinking has 'jelled' and the mental slicing of the Gordian Knot occurred once I'd recognized that liberals are not liberal. Eureka, now things fell into place and the writing about the linkage behind the edifice of liberal hostility and their behavior with its relationship with 'current events' is the subject of this book.

My objective has been to stay with what I know—my own experience as a 50 something with a blood count, half of which has been spent as an investment professional, and my education as a trained economist and 'board certified' securities analyst. Additionally I've spent a lifetime becoming a self-educated general historian that when coupled with over a decade as an elected GOP functionary in the real Northern California, ought to provide me with a reasonable foundation for the following text.

Believing that every thesis has a context and exists to establish perspective, I've used chapter one to point out what basic Republican values are from the point of view of independent self-employed core America using my own and family experiences as the platform. Chapter two continues these perceptions and contrasts them with the attitudes and behavior of those who later became America's politically correct.

Since the Vietnam analogy, based on ignorance of the subject by most American's living today, serves as the rationale for taking the position that our effort in Iraq is axiomatically doomed to failure, chapter three discusses that war as a prelude for what follows. Chapters four through six cover the War in Iraq and the one in Afghanistan from several perspectives that continuing rhetoric strongly suggests that the politically correct fail to grasp. The remaining chapters cover those current economic and social issues that my background suggests I can discourse on with some competence, plus the nature of today's politically correct's behavior and rationale behind it.

I should note that the text of this discourse reflects my own unique style. Once, back in college, I had fantasies that every paper I submitted would be full of Churchillian eloquence, but as I usually found myself struggling around 2 AM to meet a 10 AM deadline, Churchill got fired and whatever showed up in print had to do. Having had to plow through God knows how many SEC filings and public offering prospectus's during my stockbroker years, I'm still well aware of the need for verbiage that keeps the reader from nodding off. Ergo, I write the way I do and try to be somewhat conversational and include occasional stories and what not to enliven what can be a droll exercise.

I'm also bi-polar and thus my prose can become a little disjointed, but so was Teddy Roosevelt. Since he pulled it off in his written work, this shouldn't be too much of a handicap. Hopefully I've at least met the standard Senator Zell Miller set in his 2004 book, *A National Party No More* and, exceeded the minimal bar of former Vice President Gore in his published rantings about the environment.

I trust that I stuck with the expository format of thesis, findings of fact, and then conclusions supported by the same. If I've PO'd those liberals wound too tight for their own good—great. Hopefully I've converted some of them to the extent that we'll still have a republic where Cato won't be murdered and Cicero can chime on for eternity. Click here to input your introduction, if any.)

The Root

1

Republican Values

Common Values

One day I had the pleasure of listening to Tim Russert of MSNBC's '*Meet The Press*', a liberal Democrat and former Senator Daniel Moynihan staffer, discuss his book about what he learned from his dad—'Big Russ'; a proud veteran of World War II who worked two jobs to support his Irish Catholic family in Buffalo, New York. In 'big Russ's' life, the American Legion was an important focal point and Tim was required to have his first book signing there, along with having to buy a keg of beer for his dad's fellow vets.

This story tends to cause this old grunt's eyes to well up a little for it is one that's also part of my life. When I was first commissioned in June 1968, I'd gone up to Sacketts Harbor, NY to visit my grandparents. The next morning my grandfather woke me up and made me put on my dress Marine Corps khakis with their brand new gold bars for a trip down the road to the local Legion Hall. Since he'd missed WWI, probably thanks to my 'black belt alanon' grandmother, he'd never been allowed in.

Anyway, that morning we arrived at the Hall to have a drink with old Buster and he showed off his oldest grandson and second-generation American military officer to those present. Later on in life I too became a Legionnaire, rising to become a three time post commander and now past chef de guerre, and like former President Reagan, I've maintained my membership—along with being a life member and periodic post officer of the VFW, hardly 'hip-slicking' cool.

However they reflect core American values that have helped hold this country together since Washington's officer corps coalesced into a cohesive professional body at Valley Forge. It was the Revolutionary War officers' Order of Cincinnati who became a critical force in ensuring that the Old Northwest Territory was barred to slavery; yet today that organization's successors are subject of ridicule in film because they still foster the values of democracy and '100% Americanism'.

3

Another Democrat's book I read at the same time was Georgia Senator Zell Miller's *A National Party No More,* where he decries the loss of values that once represented the Democratic Party while describing how Harvard scions have turned it into a body that looks down on its southern brethren. Despite the fact that he's an unabashed 'yellow dog Democrat'. (as in I'd rather vote for that yellow dog than vote for a Republican) I easily relate to the values he was taught by his mother that ultimately led to his earning his Phd and multiple terms as Georgia's Lieutenant Governor, Governor, and finally a seat in the United States Senate.

Even though I'm originally from the Upper Midwest and the product of what David Hackett Fisher termed the 'Yankee Migration' in *Albion's Seed,* these are also the values I was taught growing up. It was little ole me straining to push my family's primitive lawn mower across the grass and picking up after all the neighborhood dogs (ours included) in an era when neither kids nor pets were kept behind fences.

After we'd moved to another somewhat high rent district overlooking the Rose Bowl. I still had to cut the lawn with the added task of digging up all the dying orange trees (some 20 of them) with their massive taproots. Since Dad wasn't the one who had to do that, he felt that the family's simple hand saw could do the job when anyone in their right mind would have instantly opted for a chain saw.

Today too many kids have never touched a lawn mower since the job throughout Silicon Valley has been relegated to Juan Valdez and his team of 'illegals'. The same can be said for just about every other region of America as basic suburban grunt work has been relegated to the teeming masses of Mexico lucky enough to make it across the border; leaving today's kids free to play all the video games Japanese imagination can dream up.

Obviously something's been lost in the intervening years since I got my first fanny whack in a Cleveland Ohio hospital in the summer of '46. Today, when families get ahead of the game economically they become liberalism's chosen people. Back then one was born and became a Republican after moving to the suburbs; or in my case, got baptized at birth into the 'Bob Taft GOP'—which wasn't quite the 'silver spoon GOP'.

'Brick'

My grandfather on dad's side was born in Sacketts Harbor, on the northeastern end of Lake Ontario in the real upstate New York near the St. Lawrence River. Brick, so named because of his red hair and his six foot, 212 pound frame, came from a line of Yorkshiremen who came to the US in 1828, ultimately becoming dairy farmers—some of whom are still milking cows.

As a kid, Brick helped my great-grandfather run sturgeon lines out under the ice during the winter once the lake's bays had all frozen over and the other small businesses that he'd migrated in and out of. Along the way he managed to cop an attitude and dropped out of high school to go fishing, as he put it. But Brick was like many Americans of his era who spent much of their free time later in life becoming self-educated.

With or without a diploma, depending on the story de jure, he did land a job with a major concrete construction company. Following stops at Ogdensburg, NY where my uncle was born and then Massena, NY where dad was born, Brick had worked his way up to live in Rochester, NY during the Great Depression. This was the time he had to leave his kids and my grandmother at home while he took his concrete crews to Washington, DC to pour floors for many of he government buildings along Pennsylvania and Independence Avenues. Despite this, both he and my grandmother remained rock-ribbed Republicans; although there was rumor of an unpardonable family secret that she once voted for FDR.

While they were living in Rochester, summers were still spent on the family homestead on the point where the British landed during a critical American victory during the War of 1812. Overtime what had originally been a campsite on the lake was turned into a cottage—stone by stone, most of which were manhandled by my dad and uncle. Finally, after Brick had a few free-bucks to his name, the cottage got in-door plumbing in 1954.

Like many of his generation, my grandfather had his share of prejudices. When I was a kid, one of his favorite jokes coupled the Pope's nose with the part of a turkey that was last over the fence. Considering that around the St Laurence River, it was the Catholic French Canadians who weren't highly thought of and that my grandmother was raised a staunch Methodist on a farm just south of Ottawa with twelve siblings and her Scotch-Irish father, this was understandable.

Prejudice towards Blacks was on the 'back-burner' since there weren't that many living along the St Lawrence and this was definitely Scotch-Irish territory and their prejudices go all the way back to the days of 'King Billie' and the 1690 Battle of the Boyne. My other paternal great grandfather was a hardcore member of the Orange Lodge and every 12th of July he banged on the big drum as his fellow Orangemen marched through town.

These were the 'original drunken Irishmen' whose ancestors had been forcibly ejected from Scotland and replaced with sheep during the 'Highland Clearances' following the Rebellion of 1745. The prevailing theory was that sheep were less trouble and if the 'French and Indians' killed off all the transplanted 'Scots', who'd care. The same premise was at work when the rest of my Celtic ancestors were 'Fed-Ex'd' to Appalachia prior to moving to Ohio. Fortunately the 'Green' showed up to take the 'Orange' off the hook and made us respectable.

From a politically correct perspective, though, this is 'unpardonable thinking' and the 'cause' of all the problems minorities face today. But it's an attitude that overlooks generations of skillful negotiation between the races, particularly in the slaveholding south, and accompanying entrepreneurialship by African Americans despite the prejudices they faced, something that's amply documented in the references I've listed in the references.

What the politically correct apparently do not choose to understand is the nature white-black relations often took during my grandfather's generation in the north. All through the 'New Deal' years when unionization and various 'prevailing wage' acts became the bar that precluded black employment in the skilled trades, Brick's main man was 'Nigger Hayes'. He doesn't seem to have ever been called by any other name—even by the African—Americans who worked for him.

When dad and my uncle were old enough to work during the summer, Brick would ship them out to work as manual labor for Hayes as part of his African—American crew. Additionally when times were tough and Hayes's crew was out of work, my grandmother would do what she could to help sustain them and their families with food, clothing etc.

Years later after we'd moved to Evanston, Illinois, it was a much older Hayes that Brick hired to build a retaining wall to keep our front yard from sliding into the street. It would seem that for almost three decades, Brick basically took care of Hayes and his boys while they took care of him. Having lived awhile myself, I know that most professional relationships don't last that long without strong ties of mutual respect.

Finally in 1969, after retiring as the regional manager for the rust belt states and countless floors poured for factories in myriad places between Chicago and Pittsburgh, we buried Brick in Sacketts Harbor—not outside the North Shore Country Club in Glenview, Illinois where he'd lived his last 15 years.

Roughly thirty years later a group of local boys from Sacketts Harbor bought a horse and almost won racing's 'triple-crown' with him. I'm not sure that the politically correct from the Westside of LA really understood the phenomena of 'Funny Cide', but there is no question that my grandfather would have. Had he still been alive, he probably would have bought his way in as a partner over the objections of my grandmother, as would his male descendents.

Mother's Family

Conversely, my mother's family was more refined with some of them the products of Ohio Wesleyan. Like my paternal side, they came from the original settler families of Upper Lake Champlain, and they too were hard-core Republicans from the day the party was started. In fact former President Rutherford B Hayes is somewhere in the family tree. They were also a clan that believed in self-employment, although my great uncle ended up as the city editor of the *Cleveland Plain Dealer* after his magazine for that city's betters was buried by the 'crash of '29'.

Both my mother's Dad and her uncle got their start working for Warren G. Harding when he published his newspaper in Delaware Ohio. It was probably because of this experience, when Harding ran for the White House, that my grandfather ended up voting for a Democrat for the only time in his life. Otherwise he was a die-hard Republican and avid Roosevelt hater.

I suspect that this was partially because he'd gotten his first real break thanks to the Standard Oil Company. Back in 1910 there wasn't such a thing as an industry trade magazine reporting on a specific industry's issues. It was also a time when Standard Oil was receiving a lot of bad press. Ergo, my grandfather was suddenly the founder, owner, and publisher of *National Petroleum News*. A magazine that he eventually sold to MacGraw Hill in 1954 for really what was a million dollars; juxtaposed to the equity value of a Silicon Valley home that many luckily bought during the early years of the Valley.

Despite the apparent glamour of *Time, Newsweek,* et al magazine publishing is not an easy business. Most rags or books as insiders refer to them, require the publisher to drum up his own content while selling enough advertising to economically sustain them through the next issue. Having grown up in that industry, I can assure you that magazine owners can get sucked into a 24/7 existence and in 1910, the whole idea was new and therefore suspect.

This didn't stop my grandfather as he packed his thirty-eight and headed off to the oil patch every year to collect stories and more importantly, sell 'space' in his magazine. My aunt, mother and grandmother were all left in Cleveland to fend for themselves for weeks on end as he built his business. Eventually, by the crash of '29 he was making enough money at it to move to the new upscale subdivision recently built in Shaker Heights.

At the age of 50 something, when World War Two and the Landings at Normandy occurred, he left a minimal staff behind and went to France to report on the war's oil logistics for his magazine; something not many of either party his age were willing to do. After selling his 'books' in 1954, he retired to the Pacific Palisades—just down the street from Ronald Reagan and spent his last years writing letters to me about what I needed to know in life while furthering his education as another self-taught American adamant about the value of knowledge.

Values Carried Forward

Mother was born in 1920, as was Dad, making them both part of what newscaster Tom Brokaw termed the 'Greatest Generation'. Unlike her sister who would have preferred remaining in the middle class life of East Cleveland with its public schools, mother grew quite comfortable in neuvo upper class Shaker Heights—private school at Hathaway Brown and dating the 'fellows' from Country Day. Summers were spent deposited at the Country Club of Cleveland under the supervision of the resident golf pro or several weeks at camp in New Hampshire with the Kennedy scions.

Despite being to 'the manner born', she still learned that if one wanted to play good golf, one had to work at it. Rules were important since golf required 'hitting the ball where it lay' and keeping an honest score—concepts that would later infuriate me when my ball would hit the macadam cart path and bounce halfway to Mt Wilson. Life is 'unfair'—tough.

Mother never became an 'ace student'. Even with this self imposed handicap she managed to graduate from Northwestern with a BS in psychology—statistics and all. How she pulled that off I don't know, yet she did—maybe it was because dad was out soldering with Douglas MacArthur her senior year.

She also believed in service work, as did many of her generation, which she did through the Junior League and the Republican Party where she rang doorbells for Bob Taft in 1952 and later as a precinct chairman after we'd moved to Evanston, Illinois. When we moved again to La Canada, California, she again picked up the reins as a GOP volunteer precinct chairman and when I turned 21, she was the one who drove me up the mountain and made sure I was properly registered to vote—GOP of course.

As per the rules, her Junior League activities came to a halt when she turned 40, but during those years in Evanston she ran the League's thrift shop and organized the effort to acquire mothers milk for premature babies along Chicago's lower North Shore; hardly garden parties. Later in La Canada, when the need arose for a junior golf program at the local country club, she was the one who dragooned dad and others into making it happen.

When dad's magazine went under, having never worked a day in her life beyond the war years spent in Alcoa's personnel department, mother became La

Canada's 'Welcome Wagon Lady' on a direct commission. That's where one is only paid when something gets sold; no sales—no money. Finally she moved on to supervise all the other 'Welcome Wagon Ladies' in Los Angeles's San Gabriel Valley and finally earned a modest salary. This wasn't exactly how life was supposed to turn out and she did complain about why it worked out this way. Still she rose to the occasion and did what was necessary.

More Values Carried Forward

Dad's early years were a bit rockier because concrete foreman pouring floors for the country's industrial expansion could get one close to the upper middle class, but not rich. Then there was the Depression. Following a childhood on the St Laurence and growing up in Rochester New York, he landed in Evanston for high school as Brick moved up the ladder. Although they were by then suburban middle class, his family still didn't really have a 'pot to pee in'.

This meant that he and his older brother were going to have to finance their own way through the local college that fortunately turned out to be Northwestern. (Stopping with a high school diploma was not an option) It also meant that 'straight As' were a necessity and the conduit to the scholarships that both of them received. Once coupled with monies earned working in the University Library and mild subsidies received as fraternity house officers, both were able to graduate in four years—dad with honors from the B-school.

Having been active in student government during their high school years, both dad and my uncle became presidents of their fraternity chapter. Dad subsequently took that a step further and became a campus political leader. There is no question that he enjoyed these activities, but they also embodied a culture where one was supposed to step up to the plate and do what needed to be done for the 'good of the order'—almost like a now maligned Mickey Rooney and Judy Garland movie.

Graduating with the Class of 1941 and with war on the horizon, he 'putzed' around as a trainee for Aetna Insurance before the bombs fell on Pearl Harbor. His brother was already in the Army thanks his job with IBM and my other uncle had already pulled a tour with the Royal Army, serving as a paratroop trained medical officer before eventually transferring back to ours once War was declared.

Dad turned out to be a less than enthusiast soldier; but he still volunteered early in 1942 and after OCS, ended up as a staff officer with the Army Air Corps in New Guinea. Two and a half years later and after every one of MacArthur's landings in the South Pacific, he found himself just outside Manila with Captain's bars and orders home. Recognizing the potential need for a war with the

Soviet Union, he stayed on the rolls until Korea and three kids convinced him to give it up.

Once again a civilian, dad went to work as the general manager and marketing director for his father-in-law's magazines. The job carried the impressive title of 'vice president' but what he actually did was go out and make sure the ad salesmen were making their calls and getting space sold. When they weren't successful selling it themselves, he had to do it. When I became a stockbroker, the operative phraseology was 'hustling up the business'. Fortunately, by this time the need to pack heat when venturing down to the oil patch had passed—dad wasn't good with guns.

After my Grandfather sold his magazines, dad went to work for another publication in Chicago doing essentially the same thing and though we were living in a high rent district, the deal was the same—hustle up the business for a percentage of the revenue generated plus salary. It was always the words 'for a percentage of the revenue' that made life interesting since it meant that Dad's income was prone to volatility, as it is for everyone who's livelihood is based on direct sales.

It also meant that one periodically stared the 90% income tax bracket right in the eye and wondered how to avoid the direct confiscation of the fruits of their labor. A concept I'd later come to understand when I'd make a third of my annual income in one month, only to have over 80% disappear into the withholding vat.

Eventually dad worked up the courage to do what he really wanted to do—own his own magazines. This led him to buy *Pacific Oil Motive* and *Automotive Dealer News*, moving us all to the hillsides overlooking Pasadena, California in the process. Now instead of just being the guy that brought in all the revenue, he was also the one who had to write all the text needed to fill the blank paper.

This ain't easy, particularly when the guy you bought the rag from was being subsidized by the west coast oil companies because they really liked 'old Wayne' and felt a need to keep him afloat out of personal loyalty. After 'old Wayne' bailed by selling out to a hustler from Chicago, these ties of loyalty were broken and the ad space they represented evaporated.

So despite the appearances represented by a country club membership and a house on a hillside overlooking the Rose Bowl, life was economically precarious. Every fall when the next year's ad budgets were being put together, dad spent six weeks driving all over the eastern half of the United States drumming up business. It also meant that the 'family hobby' was counting all the paid pages in his and the competitions monthly issues.

Another important drill was verifying each publication's subscription list. For *Dealer News* it was fairly easy. Tarawa Gene (he'd been a Marine Corps corporal during the war) and a couple of others went out and called on every gas station they could find in Southern California selling subscriptions. In return for building the circulation list, they got to keep the subscription money—$6 per year per subscription.

This was hard core selling and I had to do it the summer I did penitence for flunking physics my freshman year and temporarily blowing my NROTC scholarship. It took everything short of a gun to get the crusty bastards who operated service stations at the time to break into the till and fork over the six bucks for a bi-weekly rag. Given this, one had to give credit to guys like Tarawa Gene. Years later dad finally owned up to the fact that he knew he couldn't do it and I had ample proof that I'd failed.

POM was another story since its orientation was towards the executive side of the industry. Here dad opted for 'controlled circulation', meaning he picked who he sent the magazine to. However they had to be real marketing executives in the oil industry and required a circulation audit to prove it. For half a buck an hour I counted and cataloged each of the number codes dad used four times a year for all ten thousand 'subscribers' spread out amongst the thirteen western states. So much for the silver spoon enjoyed by kids in Silicon Valley. If it's a family business, mother kept the books and did the billing, while the kids did what they could.

Another problem with the family business is that times change and in the 1960s the way tires, batteries, and accessories were marketed did change. The oil companies went to central purchasing of the capital equipment that went into gas stations and developed company brands for all the peripherals that gas stations sold. This meant that all the 'jobbers' (wholesalers) who had been the intermediaries for all this stuff were out of business.

Along with their demise went the need for advertising and the publications that served that part of the industry. Thus, after a few years of a slow death spiral, dad had to fold his 'books' and look for other options at 50 something. A way of life was over for him and a lot of others, but they didn't run to the 'Feds' for readjustment payments, nor did the government offer any. They just sucked it up and went on to plan B, however inferior that might have been.

For dad, plan B meant driving all over the Pacific Coast selling space for *Golf Digest*—a magazine started by a couple of his fraternity brothers back in the1950s and one where he'd once been a member of the board of directors. Fortunately old favors were returned, but a couple of years later *Golf digest* was sold to the

New York Times and they wanted Dad to make isolated calls in the Pacific Northwest. Ones that were productive for *Golf Digest* but not for dad since he had to spend several hundred on each trip up there in return for a minimal commission.

It was now on to plan C since Dad couldn't afford to subsidize the *New York Times*. However plan C involved a partner as he stepped in and recapitalized a small struggling golf glove manufacturer located in Azusa, California—USA from A to Z. The project had promise and once the partner, who had quietly stolen 5,000 gloves from the partnership to pay gambling debts, was forced out after a painful lawsuit. Dad's glove company made very good golf gloves from the best leather one could get from Gloversville, New York, but selling them was another issue.

Once again my father was on the road calling on pro-shops all over the land. In the process he discovered that most golfers didn't want the best glove, they wanted the cheapest and with the way my grip wears them out, I'm in the cheapest camp. Another problem was cost competitiveness. Gloves made in Korea were always going to be cheaper to make so there was no way Dad could ever compete on price. As logically as Harvard's Michael Porter lays this out in his famous 'Five Forces Model' beloved by B-schools everywhere, it can be heartbreaking when you're on the receiving end.

Thus it was on to plan D—printing and dad got good at it. He went to the auction sales and bought his equipment, made his own light table and darkroom, then he discovered that he was the wrong color. Being white in the nascent world of affirmative action meant that the new Miller Brewery next door had to use an African-American print shop. Next the chemical plant with its expensive safety labels that had to be attached to each bottle, blew up and moved to the wilds of Arkansas. Because of subsequent insurance issues, the others in and around the western San Gabriel Valley followed.

By this time, the nights spent running his press when his illegal help failed to show up and blotting out the white dots on the plate negatives were getting awfully long for a sixty year old guy. With annual positive cash flow deteriorating by the year and following years of periodic IRS audits because he was self-employed, he finally died in that shop at the age of 68. For mother's sake and the benefit of the IRS, I tried to sell his printing business, but that didn't work out which is reasonably typical.

One thing the politically correct forget in their haste to impose estate taxes is that businesses like dad's represent the 'retirement assets' of their widows. Often too, family businesses constitute sweat equity of those kids who spend half their lives helping their parents build it. This is their equivalent of stock options etc and when the IRS grabs its 'fair share', plus all the working capital, the value of their life's work and career's to that point disappear with the money needed to pay estate taxes.

Finally, the point of this long tail is that dad died a Republican, never asking the government for any help, nor thought that he was entitled to it. When it came time for the average American to step up and do his duty, dad raised his hand and took his turn. He knew that Communism was wrong and that both the Japanese and Hitler had to be stopped. Once that was done, he made his way through life the best way he knew how, doing the things that his spiritual forebears in the Order of Cincinnati would have understood.

When Everyone Liked 'Ike'

So it was into this upper middle class world of basic Republicans that I joined on 14 August 1946. World War Two was over, the 'baby boom' was starting, and the Indians were capable of winning a pennant or two. After two years of living in a dinky East Cleveland apartment, as mother told it, dad bought a house next door to the 'future home of John Carroll Football' over in University Heights, Ohio.

Besides a few family memories, I remember two things from that time. The first was that I was the minority. The Scotch Irish kid with blond hair, thanks to a Viking who crawled under the fence and into the family gene pool, woke up one day in the first grade and found that he was one of six kids who had to go to school on Jewish holidays.

Since that initial exposure to 'different people' I've lived with, worked with, and served with people from all walks of life, religions, and colors. From that I've learned that diversity isn't having a mixture of skin color governed by 'group think' as it is amongst the politically correct like the denizens of the *New York Times*. It's the different capabilities and perspectives we all bring to the table to accomplish common goals, whether it's winning football games or staying sober in the rooms of AA.

Like most everyone I've ever been associated with, I grew up understanding that some of the most ominous words in life were 'wait until your father comes home'. In my case that usually gave me the rest of the afternoon to decide whether running away to Milwaukee wasn't the optimal choice. Others thought about hiding out with a relative in Orange County.

Before I moved up to Idaho from Southern California I sponsored a Chicano who'd grown up in Baldwin Park California—the then barrio in the suburbs. After a while I finally got tired of listening about the disadvantages of growing up in an 'Anglo world'; especially since he'd earned his masters from UCLA and had siblings and cousins that were doctors, psychologists, and successful businessmen.

Evidently his father had done a pretty good job of raising a family on his wages as a skilled mechanic and I eventually told him to quit complaining about how he'd been brought up. From my perspective there didn't seem to be much of a difference and both of us had to cut the grass as kids. Then I'd rib him about his Spanish because it wasn't much better than the residual German I'd learned in school; which is also where he learned Spanish because back then the third generation from Mexico didn't acquire it from their parents.

The other significant memory was the advent of television—not the early shows because mother refused to buy one since it would interfere with her kids learning to read. Instead it was being drug down the street to her best bud's house to watch MacArthur's farewell speech to Congress ('old soldiers never die, they just fade away') and the McCarthy Hearings.

This was during the Korean War and the 'bouhaha' surrounding Truman's refusal to let MacArthur fight for a victory. In the background there was the issue of communist infiltration into the highest levels of government, something Ann Coulter explained in detail with extensive specific references gleaned from 'Nexus—Lexus' in her book *Treason*, and later justified after the opening of KGB archives following the collapse of the Soviet Union.

About the same time I became involved in my first political campaign. Since my family were all Bob Taft supporters (then known as 'Mr Republican), mother volunteered for grunt work during his primary fight with Eisenhower and of course she volunteered me. So at age 6 I diligently colored the precinct maps so everyone would know who voted where and as mother rang the doorbells, I pulled the campaign literature down the street behind her with my little red wagon.

Ike won of course and looking back at it from the perspective of age and education, it was probably just as well. One of the GOP's problems was that the party had never quite gotten over the First World War and under Taft's tutelage, tended to cater to the isolationist wing of the party. Had Taft rather then the eventual nominee Wendall Wilkie gotten the nomination and beaten Roosevelt in 1940, we'd be living in a much different world. America needed an anti-fascist to sit in the White House in the days before Pearl Harbor. By 1952 the foreign threat was much more dangerous and the White House was no place for a debating society, no matter how learned Adlai Stevenson might have been. Ergo, Ike with his command experience was the only choice.

A few months after Ike had been sworn in, I was ensconced in the second grade at Evanston, Illinois' Orrington School where classes were overcrowded and by today's rhetoric, it was impossible for me to learn anything. We had only one principal, a librarian, and a part-time school nurse for the administrative staff. This was the baby boom school system and even a town like Evanston couldn't keep up with the necessary construction needed to accommodate the demand—not that this really bothered the parents becasue we still learned.

Today, under these conditions we might not have, and given the tendency for today's educators to blame everyone but themselves for the problem, one might have thought that I grew up in a town of 'schleps'. This was hardly the case. Orrington School was within short walking distance of Northwestern and we often played ball on its campus. Additionally my classmates had some of the country's most eminent academics for fathers.

One father was President of Kendall College. Another's dad was the premier Woodrow Wilson scholar, having written several volumes on the 28th President. A third's dad was a full professor of physics and when we were in the fourth grade, his son recited the whole of *Huck Finn* in class in lieu of us having to read it. The rest of us merely had parents who worked as executives in the 'Loop' or were professionals scattered around other parts of Cook County. Even the then Illinois Attorney General lived on the next block and his grandson was one of my running mates.

This then was not a community that gave short shift to educational standards and at that time Evanston Township High School was then rated amongst the top 10% in the country according to the annual rankings published by General Electric. Even today ETHS manages to show up in the *Wall Street Journal* as one of those public schools that manages to shunt a significant portion of its graduates off to America's premier universities.

In school we joined the Audubon Society or the Red Cross and didn't think anything about it. As Cub Scouts we all marched in three parades a year—Memorial Day, the 4th of July, and Veteran's Day. We also knew what 'buddy poppies' represented, something I recently discovered today's kids don't know when I sold them at my local supermarket for the first time in my VFW career.

Evanston was also integrated, with the only exclusions being the Catholic kids who universally seemed to attend one of the numerous parochial schools. This was a world where the kid who got all the answers right on the endless number of tests all kids take got the 'A'. Those who didn't 'failed' and had to discuss the 'problem' with the school principal. There weren't any 'special adjustments' for social disadvantages.

Ergo, another dynamic had to be at work and I suspect it was along the lines of academic standards and the requirement that kids had to meet them whether we wanted to or not. These were the days that we all dreaded parent teacher conferences because that usually meant a family discussion about personal failings—ours, with undefined consequences if we didn't start working up to our potential.

One spring vacation dad with his accountant's precision decided to make me achieve the same. This came after he'd visited my teacher and saw that the papers I'd turned in were full of inkblots and generally lacking in 'neatness'. Despite the teacher's declaration that such was acceptable, he grabbed the lot and made me recopy them until they'd met his standard. Looking around my desk today, his cure obviously didn't take and in retrospect, the only reason I pay any attention to detail is due to the efforts of a couple of USMC drill instructors and their immediate superiors.

The beauty of this, whether Republican or Democrat, my experience wasn't unique. We might have been the Dr Spock generation but there were many moments when our parents said 'Spock be damned, the little bastard needs to clean up his act'. We got into our fair share of trouble and when we did, Ward Cleaver wasn't there to reason us through what we did wrong. We had freedom but getting caught put one beyond the pale.

When a few extra bucks were needed, we went out and hustled. This wasn't 'gansta' stuff—we actually earned it. Every time it snowed I charged out into the neighbor hood with snow shovel in hand to make sure I was to first to mark-up the fresh snowfall and shovel everyone's walk for a quarter. Additional cash flow came from raking levels throughout the neighborhood when the region's once ample supply of majestic elm trees shed their plumage. Today these trees are all gone thanks to the ravages of Dutch Elm Disease.

Warmer weather brought the 'carnival'. We'd buy penny candy that came in five distinct packages and set-up a few games—like tossing a coin into a dish filled with water for a penny—success brought our younger siblings a 'new penny' as we succeeded in turning one cent into five cents. Too bad such opportunities didn't turn up later in life when I really needed the money.

Finally there was the 'children's paper drive' for cash. In those days schools had periodic paper drives to fund student activities and many around town would accumulate newspapers for these annual drives. We however always beat the school to it by marshalling our wagons and canvassing the neighborhood collecting these caches for sale to commercial trash collectors. Periodically there'd be a big truck parked in the family driveway loading up the haul for a buck a ton while business savvy 10-year olds double-checked the weighing to ensure they weren't being screwed.

Politically everyone liked Ike and Norman Rockwell ruled the covers of the *Saturday Evening Post*. Baseball meant the Cubs at Wrigley and Ernie Banks—the ultimate baseball hero we all shared despite Mickey Mantle and those playing for the 1957-58 Milwaukee Braves. The latter won games but it was Ernie who signed our programs when players would do it for free. There's a good reason Ernie has gone down in Americana as 'Mr. Cub' and the game lost a lot when he finally retired.

We were not really Sox fans because at that time the Southside seemed as close as Cleveland, but once I did get Dad to take me down to the Southside to see the Yankees and sit in center field to catch one of the Mick's homerun balls. Besides the fact that Mantle went hitless that day, the thing that stood out from that trip was the desolation all around Cominsky Park.

The first Mayor Daily then ruled Chicago and he'd finally decided to replace the Southside slums with public housing. As far as the eye could see, there was brick rubble. Whatever it was he replaced these slums with, they too met the wrecking ball and replaced with more slums—probably a couple of times over as a testament to the futility of 'subsidized housing' programs that Jack Kemp latter tried to correct over liberal objections when he became HUD Secretary.

Professional football was the Bears, still monsters of the midway under 'Mr. Bear', George Halas. No one really cared about the Cardinals except for the annual 'north-south' game in the snow because they played in Cominsky and hadn't won since 1949. Then there was the college all-star game where the great Otto Graham coached 'stars' from the prior season would get beaten up by the reigning NFL Champs at Soldier Field.

Because Evanston was home to Northwestern, it was 'Big Ten Country' and the Wildcats was the team that really counted. These were the years Ara Parseghian coached them and we assiduously attended games at Dyche Stadium—15 minutes away on foot. As Boy Scouts we got paid to usher as decisive victories were won over Woody Hayes and Ohio State, Michigan, and a Bud Wilkinson coached Oklahoma team. The annual highlight, however, was the NU homecoming parade—frequently before Indiana received a thumping.

Then there was 1959 when the White Sox won the pennant. The night they clinched, air raid sirens all over Cook County went off. Two World Series games on the south side of which the Sox won the first. The rest went to the Dodgers with several pundits noting that the scandal plagued Black Sox of 1919 managed to do better. Try imagining this happening today throughout San Francisco's East Bay or down in San Jose where they're more sophisticated.

We also had the Cold War and its very real threat of nuclear annihilation. Every Tuesday the air raid sirens would go off to test the system. Of course we had the ubiquitous drills where we had to hide under our desks; but by 1959 we'd gotten use to the routine and had long since put aside the fear that personal vaporization was just around the corner. Probably the only thing that actually caught our attention was sputnik and the fact the US was not going to be the first in space.

So until moving to California, mornings brought the *Chicago Tribune* when it was still ruled by Col McCormick's rabid Republicanism, with the evening bringing the more sedate but still Republican *Daily News* delivered by my friends while I tried selling *TV Guide* subscriptions door-to-door. However I don't think we were really aware that there was a difference between the parties since our reflections of our parent's views never really showed through. The big issue was how to efficiently mange the New Deal.

The Golden State

Besides the shock of actually moving, finding myself in 1960 at the age of thirteen living in California wasn't that different than being in the Midwest. True there was the ocean and the 'surfing culture' soon emerged, but we were located north of Los Angeles in the Glendale—Pasadena area. This was where the executives from the oil and other traditional industries lived.

Politically the bias was strongly Republican with several 'safe seats' in the legislature and Congress wasted by the likes of Frank Latterman and Carlos Moorehead. The former's specialty was noise abatement when he should have been more pro-active on behalf of the self-employed. Moorehead seemed to be the classic back bench vote that the 'Ev & Charlie Show' could always count on when he could have been more original without risking his career.

Movies and Hollywood were over on the West Side—Beverly Hills etc and that was a different world, although my cousins living in Brentwood were just as 'Kingston Trio' as the denizens of Pasadena's John Muir High School. My aunt and uncle however were a little more 'FDR' than my folks, but the big statewide issues of the day evolved around Governor Pat Brown's various mammoth infrastructure projects and their affordability. Everyone wanted freeways, water, and quality school systems.

Like the affluent of Chicago's upper North Shore, Pasadena had its equivalent in the Tournament of Roses Committee and the Valley Hunt Club. Dancing lessons, as they were in Evanston, were held weekly, etc. So in many respects moving from the Midwest to Pasadena was more a matter of changing locales than cultures. Even the school systems were comparable since Pasadena was often cited as a leading example of progressive educational practices.

There was one difference though. While Pasadena was integrated as a city with a broader range of other minorities, particularly Hispanics, Japanese, and Koreans, its school district ultimately lost a civil rights case over the matter of segregation. La Canada—Flintridge, where I lived, and the west-side of the Rose Bowl were white and attended La Canada Junior High School. Altadena was also still white with its kids going to Elliot. Washington Junior High School encompassed Pasadena's ghetto and took in most of the Asians. Except for a few exceptions where neighborhoods blended together, the other three junior highs were basically white.

In theory, allocating three junior high schools as feeds to one of the city's high schools would seem to be 'fair and equal'. As it turned out, 'fair and equal' meant that minorities went to John Muir and Pasadena High ended up white and larger by roughly 1500 kids. When a third high school, Blair, was built after I'd moved on to college, the skew towards a more lily white PHS became even more pronounced and the Supreme Court finally felt compelled to step in to readjust the distribution.

However, these were the 'Days of Camelot' and the civil rights battles hadn't broken out yet. Yes Ike had sent the National Guard into Little Rock, but being Yankees none of us quite understood why Southern Whites had a problem over integration beyond the issue of schools being a local responsibility—not Federal. The same was true for other aspects of the segregation issue.

Coming from families of businessmen, professionals, and even a football coach or two, the general feeling was why would someone be so dumb as to cut himself off from a large segment of his potential market. Also, why would someone not want to hire a black if he could do a better job? After all my grandfather had spent years with Hayes as his main man and had turned his two sons over to him to teach him many of life's necessary lessons.

Additionally the Constitution states that one has the right of association; ergo, we're all free to choose who we want to hang out with. By inference that also meant we each have the right to choose who we don't want to associate with and trust me, in my life the criteria for the latter is lengthy but race, creed or color hardly comes close to the top 10. Thus if someone wants to use race, creed, and color to choose his customers, friends, and business partners, that is his right however dumb and indicative of 'deep seated' personality problems.

On a daily basis, none of this mattered. We went to school wearing our 'Kingston Trio' oxford button down shirts and went about getting an education with behavior variances typical of teenagers anywhere. Race in the ninth grade seemed to be more reflective of a lack of self-esteem because my teammates reacted as players tend to do when they're up against a perceived superior opponent—eg: the black kids at Washington JHS. The surprise was that we won.

At John Muir we were all on the same team and the best guy for the position got to be a starter—no complaints, and Muir was a Southern California athletic powerhouse; still is. Classes were integrated and again, he who got the most answers right on a test got the best grade. Generally that meant my Nisei teammates on the golf team who were more 'Tommy Trojan' than I could ever be—'fight on for old SC'.

I specifically remember learning two things from my Afro-American teammates. When Clyde joined the team after moving from Louisiana, he tried out for quarterback and then gave up on the idea. After I asked him why, he said that he was African—American and that blacks weren't allowed to play quarterback. At the time I wasn't programmed to understand that. The second was when Ron told me to never step into the huddle unless I knew exactly what play I was going to call. As the QB, it was my job to provide clear direction and any indecision in front of my teammates would undermine their confidence that I knew what I was doing—basic Leadership 101.

In fact, leadership 101 is why high school athletics are so important; not that it's an incentive to stay in school, although that too is important. Using football as an example because I played it, football teaches some of the most important things one later needs in life—stating with learning how to 'suck it up' when one has to and then learning that one can.

My junior year, the first 'two-a-day' drills involved a general practice with pads in the morning. That afternoon, after the infamous layer of Pasadena smog had rolled in, we scrimmaged. That was an unpleasant experience because by the time we were done, each of us was gasping for air like asthmatics having an attack and collectively sick to our stomachs. The next morning, half the team had turned in their gear because they weren't willing to pay the necessary price for glory on the gridiron. As Bear Bryant once put it, he never had to cut a player—they just disappeared, leaving the remainder as the real deal.

This is what athletics helps kids develop; the moral courage to hang in when the going gets tough. Learning true teamwork, where each member's unique abilities are meshed together to strengthen the unit develops the faith that if one does his job to the best of his ability, others will do the same. This is the essence of survival in combat and reflective of leadership by example and something I later found to be just as important in a Wall Street brokerage office.

Something that is markedly different from the false exercise required in schools all the way up to the university level today, where all participants bring the same thing to a problem and end up with a few carrying the load while others get a free-ride. This latter approach teaches the virtues of 'free-riding' and that one can get something for nothing provided one ends up in the right group.

Finally, one learns from athletics that it is not what one thinks one is that matters. Everyone knows how to talk the walk and I hear it often at the 'no drinky' club. It's walking the talk that counts and in football that's means actually making the tackle. Apparently, despite a general lack of athleticism, I managed to pull that off. At the end of my senior season I got a special award for team leadership and that little plaque is still on my wall while all the medals and ribbons from Vietnam are in a box stashed somewhere in the closet.

Years later my youngest nephew was a high school linebacker in San Jose. It was his last year and his was a senior laden team that was expected to win the district title. However they lost a couple of games early on and his fellow seniors decided to start mailing it in. Naturally they lost more games and ended with a losing season. When I asked him why no one stood up and starting chewing on everyone, he just shrugged his shoulders.

This was something I didn't understand because when I was the only senior on Muir's JV team that was getting badly beaten in our first outing in San Bernardino, I stood up and ripped everyone because that was not how John Muir teams were supposed to play. By the time I was done, halftime was over and our poor Coach hadn't gotten a word in. It was all about standards and values—the ones that I had been taught by those who'd worn 'blue and gold' before me.

Before moving on there're a couple of other points I need to touch on. My generation seems to have been the last that was told that if one wanted a car, one had to earn the money to pay for it. For me this meant menial labor as I periodically went around the neighborhood knocking on doors looking for grunt work at fifty cents an hour. This led to learning how to trim citrus trees while getting my skin scratched, dodging black widow spiders cleaning up brush, and finally scrapping paint off of greenhouse windows and stripping years of wax off of some lady's floor.

As mother put, that last gal sure took advantage of me and my partner; another 'yellow dog Democrat' and Jewish. For roughly twenty dollars each, we did a job I think even today's illegals would turn down. Manual labor is not a function of race creed or color and it can be bi-partisan; but it is something I suspect many middle class kids plus the likes of the current Democratic nominee for the White House are unfamiliar with.

Finally it came time to graduate and by then I'd acquired a high school education loaded with intangible lessons learned from both golf (play the ball where it lies, even if that isn't 'fair') and football. I'd even picked up college credit for four history courses thanks to scoring well on the advanced placement tests. This was unusual at the time since the concept of advanced placement courses with their automatic GPA hike didn't exist. In fact the only reason that I even took the tests was that one of my teachers picked up on the idea that I might pass.

Consequently I filled out the forms and showed up at Muir's library to answer a coterie of essay questions. I passed so that all the history that I'd taught myself to that point ultimately had a value. It obviously helped that history has been an avocation since childhood that surprisingly has been a definite help in understanding where the financial markets are likely to head and in picking stocks as I've usually found a way to generate what investment professionals refer to as a 'positive alpha'.

One of the last things I did in high school was to join the Navy Reserve. I'd always thought that a military career was a viable possibility and there was something romantic about the Navy. More pragmatically there was the draft and because my scientific aptitude was limited, I'd ruled out the academies and their degrees in general engineering so that left either reserve officer training or NROTC as a path to commissioning. The benefit of the latter was that the Navy paid tuition and books, plus $50 per month in return for 4 years of service as a regular officer—just like 'Boat School'.

It was also the right thing to do given the geo-political situation at the time and dad agreed. So on 3 December 1963 I took the oath and started wearing my blue jump suit once a week. Later I went through the interview and testing process that was akin to that for Annapolis and ended up with a midshipman appointment. Then it was a matter of getting into one of the 55 schools that had NROTC. For a number of reasons, the match turned out to be the University of Rochester, Rochester NY—with one drawback, I was a 'Goldwater Republican'

2

Clash of Values

Culture Shock & the Breaking of Academic Balls

Following graduation I spent the summer doing enlisted service with the Navy including a stint on the USS Yorktown where we replaced blank ammunition with the real stuff during the 1964 Gulf of Tonkin Crisis. At the same time the Turks had invaded Cypress and the 24-hour radio news stations were repeatedly stating that Russian planes were on their way to intervene. After hours of listening to it while switching the ammunition, it became clear that those Russian planes were never going to reach Cypress and the whole story had been a hoax, re-enforcing the need for what the military calls 'presence of mind'—the ability to maintain perspective under chaotic conditions.

So after being released, there I was—a bright freshman and midshipman on the campus of the University of Rochester suddenly discovering that there people brighter than I was in the world. Being born in 1946, I was part of the point cohort of the baby boom that was going to flood America's colleges for the next 20 years—the leading edge of the 'pig in a python', as one author has put it. Institutions like the University of California system had already exceeded capacity and had adopted a policy of flushing out at least 50% of every incoming freshman class. Thus if one managed to make it to the sophomore year at UCLA, one was already assured of being in the top half of the class.

One of the reasons I was there, besides NROTC, was that my test scores had shown that I was up to the task of graduating, despite a less than stellar academic performance at John Muir. It was still a shock to find classmates who'd actually 'maxed' the SATS with perfect 800s and that my 650s were back in the pack. Despite the 'Pasadena' reputation, there was quite a difference between its schools and the products of institutions like New York City's Boys High, Brooklyn Poly, and some of the country's premier private schools like the ones that pumped out the likes of Al Gore, John Kerry, and George W. Bush.

Finally I was also the sole student from west of the Mississippi once Sundance moved back to Wyoming. Turns out that the U of R had evolved into a heavily Jewish institution, some 49 to 51%, juxtaposed to the ethnic population mix of Western New York demographics that my father and grandfather remembered. Where integration to me and my Pasadena peers meant joining to achieve collective goals, to my new found colleagues it seemed to mean singular achievement; ie: New York City values transported.

Fortunately the U of R was not UCLA or Berkeley, but its faculty still had an unfriendly attitude towards undergraduates—a grouping that even today constitutes only 40% of the U of R's student population. The rest are either in Med School over at Strong Hospital, lodged in the Simon School of Business getting MBAs that hopefully would prove as valuable as those earned from Harvard, and a few thousand seeking Phds in myriad fields. Chico State it ain't!

The problem that the university faced in the 1960s with every incoming freshman class was its skewed interest in becoming doctors, physicists, engineers, etc. At the time one didn't go to Rochester to major in business or psychology, it's just something that tended to happen as the school used introductory courses to start weeding people out.

After 50% of those taking biology 101 received a failing grade, the number of pre-meds dropped dramatically. The same was true for math, physics, engineering and the other hard sciences. Even the department of economics limited itself to less than 25 degrees per year by establishing D+ as the average grade handed out in both micro and macro-economics. Nobel prize winners were not big on grading lots of papers and so the number of enrollees in my upper division economics classes were rather sparse. I think one could have counted the number of us taking international economics on both hands, so the policy worked.

We were graded on the curve, unlike today's practice, and the curve was pyramidal, meaning that when I walked into class on the first day and saw Dr. Peter Drucker's daughter sitting there, expectations of maybe earning an A dropped to hopes of a B+. Often this led to a competitive atmosphere where one found that key articles that were required reading had been ripped out of the periodicals stored in the library.

One problem that I found both the Cal State Universities and the University of California hypersensitive to in the 1990s that we did have back in the 1960s, sans the occasional missing reading assignment, was cheating. Egos were big enough that everyone did their own work when preparing term papers and the three hour final exams were either complicated enough or only had three or four essay questions on them that cheating was nigh on impossible.

Not so in the 1990s, as I learned when getting my graduate degrees and from articles in the *LA Times*, where professors act as if they expect it as the norm, implying that something has gone severely wrong amongst today's generation. Another sign of the times is the current requirement that business schools have an ethics component inside every course in order to maintain accreditation. Unfortunately this can't be taught because one is either ethical or one is not, but the inclusion is indicative.

Back then if one didn't shift into a survival mode early, one was clearly in trouble and after four years, this got old. As I told some of my younger fraternity brothers one night during my senior year, we might not end up with the college experience we thought we would have, but we'd sure know how to suck it up and rise to the challenge by graduation day. This presupposed of course that we were amongst the 60% who eventually made it the finish line.

Today when I look at the tables in the *US News & World Report* rankings, I still see that the U of R runs a 'retention rate' around 65% compared to rates approaching 90% for the other private 'category one' schools. This seems to have impaired Rochester's national ranking compared its peers and one my sister-in-law recently explained to me. She and my brother both work in Silicon Valley, drawing down their six-figure salaries in a world heavily populated with Stanford grads. According to them, even through Stanford is extremely hard to get into (something I and my brother are both well aware of since Stanford had once perfunctorily '86th' our applications), once in, the university busts a gut to see that one graduates.

This is a concept I can't relate to since we fully understood that it was our responsibility to make sure we graduated. Our job was to take notes and learn how to cull out the important stuff. The professor lectured about whatever he wanted to talk about, often cutting edge stuff as in the case of Drs. Engermann and Fogel when they laid the groundwork in class for what turned out to be the new field of economic history based on statistical minutia. In recent years I've read more of their stuff and it's fascinating what one can learn from comparing height and weight records maintained by our military services over the past 150 years, etc.

When I went back and got my MBAs from the California State University system years later, the standard operating procedure was to provide both undergraduate and graduate students with learning objectives and lecture outlines. Thus alleviating them of the responsibility of taking notes and processing information to discern what was important and what wasn't. Several times these were accompanied by power point presentations necessitating a darkened room and I raised a few eyebrows every time I walked in with my flashlight.

At the U of R, what was left out during class lectures was made of for by the multi-page reading list. In the case of Russian History with Michael Cherniavsky, the only textbook was his still published *The Icon & The Ax* where he laid his theories about the 'princely saint and saintly prince' being the legitimizing force behind Medieval Russia's monarchy. It was to the library that we marched to read all eleven volumes of Yale's eminent George Vernadsky's history of Russia that was the basic textbook.

For Shakespeare it was a play every other day, not five plays in 10 weeks that now represent the California State University standard. English novel was the killer with seventeen of the beasts ranging from Defoe to Conrad. I only made it through 15 of them and burned out somewhere in *Middlemarch*. In economics, if any of the great theorists wrote something—we had to read it and in the 1960s it was all written before television when brevity wasn't a virtue.

Today, even in graduate school amongst the below category one's as per *US News & World Report*, its all shoved together in one textbook with multi-colored graphs and sidebars to illicit further interest in the subject. When I went back to tidy up unfinished business by getting the MA in economics, I think I was the only one of my classmates who'd read the entirety of Keynes's *General Theory*. The last time I wandered through a Cal State bookstore, it seemed that a undergraduate could walk out with less than what'd fill a backpack. The message is that there is something missing because part of getting an education is learning how to process and prioritize information.

In the process one learns how to take information from one field and usefully apply it to totally different fields, something I've had to do my entire life. I never took a course anywhere where there wasn't something that I haven't used in another context. Yes it is difficult to understand why the musings of Aldus Huxley might apply to the world of finance, but after years of trying to understand markets to make a buck I've found that some of the stuff Huxley wrote about does just that. When kids are just handed stuff on a platter and told to learn it for a test and then forget about it, they never develop associative thinking skills and there's a price we pay for that in all endeavors today.

Politically Incorrect Greek Letter Societies

Both my dad and uncle were Phi Kappa Sigmas at Northwestern and that experience had to have been of enormous help to my uncle as he climbed the ladder to become IBM's treasurer. Mother was a life-long 'Theta' (Theta Kappa Pi) and thoroughly enjoyed the experience for all the traditional reasons. Even my sister's an initiated Alpha Phi and lived the sorority life until she copped an attitude—seems her values ended up conflicting with those of her 'sisters' because she had to work her way through UC Santa Barbara and they didn't. In my case I pledged Sigma Chi and still am a life loyal member. The initial reason was to follow in my parents footsteps and enjoy campus life under the illusion that I was participating in an old 'Andy Hardy' movie—Mickey Rooney and Judy Garland et al.

Despite the fact that life isn't filmed on an old MGM set, most of those expectations were fulfilled; but there was something more. What the old movies left out was the fact that since people ate and slept in the 'house' someone had to do some work. There had to be house leadership and of course all this led to bills having to be paid. Knowing that we were a fraternity, the local breweries and food service companies often wanted to be paid on delivery. We also had an open kitchen and the brothers could snack as they pleased and somehow we needed everyone to pony up for what they ate. When it was party time, local rock 'n roll bands weren't doing gigs for free.

Ultimately this came down to the fact the Gamma Pi Chapter of Sigma Chi was a business with the house itself owned by a house corporation run by the alumni—of which I'm still a member by virtue of being an initiate. On top of this, with a running membership of roughly 55 guys, there was the need for disparate personalities to get along. The running gag from the movie 'Animal House' about the cookie cutter 'smoothies' on fraternity road is fiction. Every fraternity chapter that has ever existed has issues that need to be refereed through consensus.

Learning how to keep the zoo running and the inmates under control is a microcosm in life and good practice for what comes next. In my case, after a stint as alumni chairman where I hit upon the novel idea of re-linking the undergraduate chapter with its alumni (nascent public relations), I spent two years being the one who ensured that there was food on the table and snacks in the fridge.

Food had to be affordable for two reasons. The first was that those with houses on the 'Quad' partially competed on cost, ie: meals would be cheaper in the 'houses' for those of us who became Greeks than it would be if eaten at one of the university dining halls. This was a significant selling point for fraternity membership since most of us were usually broke, but one that only worked if the food was palatable.

The fiction that us fraternity types were rolling in dough is mostly an illusion. Only the 'Sammies' and 'Phi Eps' had the bucks for their own cars. Generally I and my brothers had to walk unless one of our brothers with families in town showed up with his dad's Chevy. I've already mentioned that the Navy paid tuition and books plus $50 per month. Dad subsided me to some extent, depending on his ongoing relationship with the IRS. The rest of my bills were covered by what I earned as a Gray—Y counselor and during my two-year term as 'kitchen God' the chapter paid for my room.

In essence, in my late teens I found myself running a multi-thousand dollar food service company dependent upon the volunteer efforts of my fraternity brothers for a modest stipend—some of whom were not remotely interested in doing their part. Consequently I had to learn the art of moral suasion integral to getting the unwilling to do what needed to be done for their own best interest as I perceived it. This wasn't bad training for a future combat platoon commander and later stockbroker.

The 1960s however was the era when being a 'Gamma Delta Iota' became a dominant force in campus life. Greek letter societies came under attack for a multitude of sins ranging from discrimination to allegations that they stifled individualism by fostering excessive conformity and thus undermining the egalitarian underpinnings essential for campus life dependent upon a 'free market place of ideas'. Leaving aside the fact that many 'GDIs' back then didn't gave a hoot about the last item, much of the allegations reflected conjecture based on only a modicum of fact.

Under Inter-Fraternity rules at the time, every student at the U of R had free access to every party on the quad. Amongst the different fraternities, the free-riding benefits tended to balance out over time. But this also meant that non-Greeks could wander into parties at Sigma Chi, Delta Kappa Epsilon, and/or Tau Kappa Epsilon at any time to dance to the band we paid for and drink all the beer they wanted at our expense. To the politically incorrect, this is called freeloading; but to 'GDIs', this was their right under the entitlement mentality then forming.

That said, there's the matter of discrimination and this subject tends to get complicated. Especially during the 1960s when civil rights issues were so extremely contentious. However, that is what social organizations do—discriminate; as does everyone on the face of the earth as individuals. This is the way it has to be or we'd all be trying to marry Julia Roberts and leaving millions of other women to die of spinsterhood.

In the fraternity context, 'GDIs' mostly self-selected themselves out of the process, for whatever personal reason they had. There clearly was racial discrimination, the severity of which depended on where on went to school and with large national fraternities like Sigma Chi with its substantial southern base, these issues impacted the rushing policies of their northern chapters as we found out.

However the 1960s were not the 1920s when Catholics were barred from membership in a majority of fraternities under Protestant only policies. In the 1950s one could still forget about Jewish brothers in the chapter. Thanks in part to previous U of R 'Sigs' who'd help remove the 'mug shot' from pledge applications, when someone called from national to ask about a 'John Grossman', we could tell them that he was a Catholic of German ancestry whose father was a prominent Connecticut physician.

This was true by the way and he also was a legacy since his father had been initiated before the war. The rest of the brotherhood was an ethnic mishmash with a sizeable proportion being Jewish, some from NYC and others from west of the Hudson. Then there were the Anglos from various places and finally the Italians from Western New York who seemed to be related to just about every other Italian who'd escaped northwards from New York City's 'Little Italy'.

The only thing missing were African-Americans and Hispanics, not that the latter reflects a homogenous grouping despite politically correct assumptions that Hispanic means Mexican. This was a University problem because African—Americans and Puerto Ricans just didn't end up at the U of R except for a couple of local athletes who didn't succeed academically. Because their skins were a little darker than the rest of ours doesn't mean they were excluded from the fraternity system. Henry was initiated a Psi Upsilon and Eddie was a Theta Delta Chi—both of whom had bigger and nicer houses than we did.

The Sigma Chi problem with African—American brothers was the racist attitude of our southern chapters where integration wasn't an accepted concept until after Coach Rupp's all white Kentucky Wildcat basketball team lost to Don Haskins's all black Texas Western Miners in the 1967 NCAA championship game. Further acceptance came following the thumping John Mackay's USC Trojans gave Bear Bryant's all-white Crimson Tide in Tuscalusa.

As far as integration was concerned, these were quite possibly the most significant events in the civil rights battle. Its one thing for a bevy of US Marshals backed up by a battalion from the 82nd Airborne Division to force the University of Mississippi to admit one black student with a court order in hand. It's quite another when segregated teams from the Southeastern Conference work up the stones to play integrated ones from the North and get their clocks cleaned. When the final gun went off the day USC clobbered Alabama, integration was a done deal.

That day in Alabama though was a few years down the road and the university was insisting that we pledge an African—American, despite the U of R's inability to get any to come there or stay for that matter. The campus newspaper, radio station, and local SNICK chapter plus a host of 'GDIs' were demanding that our campus privileges be revoked irrespective of property right considerations or common sense.

The house corporation legally owned our modest facility and had a ninety-nine year lease allowing use of our plot on the quad. The problem was that we were the target of a moral crusade that even our most liberal brothers couldn't understand. Another problem was that had we pledged an African—American, we would have lost our charter as the Sigma Chi's at Stanford and Cornell ultimately did. The fact that our chapter had done much to eliminate ethnic discrimination against other ethnic groups and probably was more ethnically diverse than other houses on the quad didn't matter. We were the fascist enemy de jure in a holy crusade.

Discrimination also naturally occurs in more micro contexts. When everyone was expected to graduate in four years and those who hadn't in six probably never would, every fraternity had to replace roughly 25% of its membership during the fall 'rush'. As elsewhere, this was a structured process established by the Inter-fraternity Council and the university. For the existing brotherhood this meant finding 10 to 20 new pledges that were personally compatible with most of the brotherhood to fill the ranks. The one or three man 'blackball' process wasn't reality since the economic viability of the organization depended on maintaining an adequate level of membership in the face of competition from the other fraternities.

The only time I remember that a pledge was successfully blackballed was when our sophomores opposed the initiation of two other sophomores that had been pledged the prior winter. To prevent this, since we felt that it was a violation of trust to 'blackball' someone we had pledged, I and my roommate proceeded to blackball my fraternity 'little brother' almost all night. Finally we recognized the futility of our efforts and gave in, letting the underclassmen eject the two 'unwanteds'.

The point we raised was that the sophomores shouldn't have pledged these guys to start with and fairness dictated that after subjecting them to a year of being pledges, they had earned the right to be initiated. That was a very unique situation and value systems were clearly in conflict. Once a brother, even if only in candidate status, one doesn't arbitrarily break that contract no matter how 'uncool' the rejected ones are and the two individuals weren't cool, but they were decent guys.

The other side of the coin is discrimination by the prospective pledge himself. After knowing all the houses on campus, in retrospect it's clear that I never would have fit in with several houses on the quad—two of which because they were Jewish and they didn't often pledge gentiles. Neither did a couple of fraternities that didn't have a house—they had their own dorm wings and weren't inclined to assume all the burdens having a house entailed and they had a point. However I wanted to live in a fraternity house, which I did for two years as space opened up, so the non-house fraternities were out for me. Other colleges have enough African—Americans on campus to have strictly black chapters and many of their brothers like it that way. More power to them, their choice no matter how much it might infuriate the politically correct.

As far as fraternity life stifling my individualism, I think I sustained that by selecting Sigma Chi over my other options—I chose a house where I felt that I could belong and share some common values. That I was one of only five campus Republicans ringing doorbells for Goldwater during the 1964 election should've established some intellectual independence. Watching me and 'brother PE' and no one else lifting cold ones every time the results appeared on the tube for one of the two states old Barry carried ought to confirm it.

The fact that all fraternities, starting with learning to recite the Greek Alphabet, do some indoctrination does not negate this. Every organization needs to develop some group values as a means to bond all its members to achieve a common goal. The military does it and so once did IBM when all its employees had to sing 'IBM We Hail Thee' in the elevator on the way to work. In the brokerage industry, every time I walked into an EF Hutton office all the inmates wore vest and tie with their jackets hung on the backs of heavy wood chairs.

At one time Merrill Lynch used to have bells and buzzers go off when news came over the 'broad tape' concerning a company that Merrill's analysts followed. The theory was that upon reading the news, all of Merrill's brokers would call clients and prospects to bring them up to date on their stocks in hopes of generating more transactions. To make this work, each broker had to follow in 'lock-step' the recommendations published by the firm. As Ross Perot found out, when he tried to resurrect DuPont Walston using what he thought was Marine Corps methodology, this usually doesn't work.

Probably more insidious in preventing the development of productive individualism is the creation of campus thought police that now apparently overpopulate today's campus's and the academic requirement that one must parrot the professor in answering test questions as a prerequisite to passing a course. This is something best left to the 'cable news channels' with their countless files and extensive film archives to document. But when I was an undergraduate I didn't particularly notice this, quite possibly because I lacked the knowledge to raise a stink and more likely because it wasn't as prevalent at the time. However, the late Professor Bloom of the University of Chicago wrote a scathing indictment of his fellow academics in the 1980s called *The Closing of the American Mind*. In it he essentially equated the then current state of undergraduate education with the process that led to the 'dark ages' of Western European thought.

More recently 'Fox News Channel' has gotten into it with Duke University's political science department after receiving reports that 'conservatives were too dumb to add anything of intellectual value to the department', or words to that effect from the department chair. The theoretical premise behind Duke's 'poly sci' faculty's denigration of 'conservative' thought was that in trying to 'protect or conserve' the past, these lightweights were demonstrating an inability to cope with 'progressive ideas'. Students admitted from Duke's demographic base supposedly need to be intellectually challenged out of their mental comfort zones and by definition, 'conservative political scientists' were incapable of doing that.

Apparently the Chairman is unfamiliar with Dr Thomas Sowell at the Herbert Hoover Institute of War and Peace. I've read several of his volumes and none of it has been easy reading as he formulates ideas based on his extensive research in the context of the frontiers of knowledge as a true political—economist. I once had the pleasure of watching him being interviewed on Fox's *'Hannity & Colmes'* when the liberal half rephrased what Sowell had said before asking him if that was what he meant. The good Doctor's retort was that if he meant to say what Colmes was putting in his mouth, he would have said it. End of discussion.

Another apparently lightweight political economist by the Duke standard was Fredriech Hayak who wrote the *Road to Serfdom* in 1994 to explain to his British colleagues how a Hitler could emerge as part of the natural evolution of a socialist society. The very pointed message that he made was that one key difference between the 'Brits' and the Germans was the latter's twenty year head start thanks to Bismarck. Until Hayak received the Nobel Prize for economics in 1972, this tract was extremely difficult to get a hold of—almost as if one was trying to acquire a copy of the *Federalist Papers* inside of Stalin's 'gulag'.

Of course it is quite possible the good scholars inhabiting Duke's gray stone buildings had written Sowell off because he's an African—American off the reservation of acceptability and Hayak could be tainted because he was an Austrian who'd lived in the Third Reich before escaping to England. What's insidious to old Goldwater types like myself is that the attitude of Duke's political science department smacks of totalitarianism; as in Jews aren't allowed to teach at Heidelberg anymore, circa 1936.

'Do Not Fold, Spindle or Mutilate'

In the 1960s IBM had yet to fully develop the computers we're used to today, so most numerical tabulation was still done using the punch card systems developed before WW II. This was where my uncle served his country when all of the Seventh Army's logistical and personnel records were stored on these cards. Thus he was a 'light colonel' for command authority and the IBM's representative on premises ensuring that the IBM machines worked.

Because campus records and class assignment cards were also maintained this way with the ubiquitous phrase 'do not fold, spindle, or mutilate' clearly visible, students everywhere correlated that with efforts to make them conform to values they'd ceased to believe in. Ergo the spiritual effort to fold the cards to prevent them from being processed, spindle them to add erroneous data, or mutilate them to expunge the 'system' of any reference to the contents.

The 'why' behind this attitude still eludes me but I suspect in started with a reaction against the perceived need to 'conform' to the world of the *gray flannel suit* and *'Ozzie & Harriet'* during the Eisenhower years and its stark contrast with Jack Kennedy's 'Camelot Era'. This was long before all the stories of drug abuse (anphedimines dispensed by 'Dr Feelgood' to both Jack and Jackie), the use of IRS records to destroy political opponents, and Jack's sexual escapades, et al, came to light.

JFK had earned the Bronze Star in the South Pacific for what he did after his PT boat was sunk. Something the current Democratic nominee for the White House seemed to pick up on when he began to build a political resume, and entered the White House following an extremely close election. This was the election where JFK accused then Vice President Nixon of condoning the emergence of a missile gap between the US and the Soviet Union during America's first televised presidential debates.

Because evidence showing that such a gap didn't exist was classified, Nixon couldn't refute the charges and JFK's standing as a international affairs guru was enhanced. Once the Soviet Union collapsed, scholarly journeys through its old archives have shown that the gap was campaign fiction. Despite this 'advantage', it still took several thousand votes from some of Chicago's most reliable Democratic precincts (local cemeteries to be exact) to put Jack over the top.

At his inauguration JFK gave an inspiring speech where he stated that 'we'd go anywhere to fight for the cause of freedom' and told us to 'ask not what our country can do for you, but what you can do for your country'. Later he challenged America to be the first on the moon in ten years and for once the *New York Times* didn't waste column inches explaining why this would be impossible. Eventually we won this 'race' ahead of schedule with Armstrong landing on the moon that I saw on Armed Forces Television just before the VC showed up to take away my virginity as a combat officer.

My generation emotionally bought into this, albeit when push came to shove only those of us who served in Vietnam, the civil rights volunteers, and a few Peace Corps veterans actually took him up on it. Thus when JFK got shot, there had to have been a severe emotional hang-over that many of us on the West Coast never really picked up on. Ergo, thanks to Lee Harvey Oswald (maybe the Mafia, quite possibly both) the dream was gone and replaced by the reign of a Texas ward healer named Lyndon Johnson. Then came the 'John Birch society's pawn' from Arizona to represent the GOP in '64 and take us into World War Three had he won.

Concurrently the civil rights movement gained momentum with many students from Northern campuses joining SNICK to ride the 'freedom busses' and help with voter registration in Southern communities that clearly didn't want them around. Instead of defending America from foreign enemies, the fight was against perceived domestic enemies that soon turned against the values of 'the greatest generation' and those who believed that the ensuing race riots were the fault of white suburbanites. Any thoughts expressed that African—Americans might have had something to do with their own plight were soon treated as a high crime by the country's student liberals.

It quickly got worse—way worse and even though LBJ actually succeeded in getting much of JFK's proposals enacted with Republican help over the 'dead bodies of southern yellow dog democrats', there was little question as to who the real enemy was. In the minds of liberal student bodies, who'd quickly changed into the uniform of the day (disheveled, unkempt, and unwashed) to establish their individuality, those of us who thought otherwise needed to be 'controlled' for fear we'd undermine the rulings of their soviets.

The point these people missed in their superficial rejection of prevailing values is that personal neatness and attire is a reflection of self-esteem. What we wear is a declaration of how we feel about ourselves, which is why kids dressed up for school when I was a kid. If one looks like a 'crud', one often feels like one and is effectively expressing that to everyone else. This is why the military emphasizes personal appearance to the extent that it does. The theory is that the attention to detail one pays to the maintenance of one's uniform carries over to other activities.

This is also true of the military salute. When a Marine snaps one to recognize a superior officer, he's saying two things. The first obviously, is that he respects the officer's position in the chain of command and the responsibilities that go with it. The second and frequently more important one is that he respects himself as a 'squared away' Marine and because of that, he deserves the respect of others.

LBJ, Who'd You Kill Today

Then there was the war. In 1965 LBJ had sent the 9th Marines to Da Nang and our seven year 'in your face' confrontation with the North Vietnamese was on. For students who'd retained their draft deferment by not flunking out, this posed little risk. Starting with the class of '69, various professors began to improve the odds that some of their former students weren't going to die in the jungles of Southeast Asia by refusing to fail anyone—no matter how minimal their accomplishments. Thus began the grade inflation that plagues us to this day and one important reason that Al Gore's grades were better than mine or George W. Bush's.

Because the trick was to stay in college as long as one could, even going to graduate school when one didn't want to or God forbid, getting married, the 'lower classes' were the one's that 'bore the burden of war'—especially African-Americans, or so the mythology declared. The fact that statistics from the war have failed to bear this out and there were times I served in battalions where those of us from elite universities were over-represented amongst the officers had little to do with convenient perceptions.

There were other inconvenient facts that were shouted down because they were not what the unwashed in student mufti wanted to believe at the time; like there really were North Vietnamese troops in South Vietnam. This was dismissed as a valid response to America's entry into the war. Reason being that it would pull the rug out from underneath their mythology that American was participating in a civil war in violation of the Geneva Conventions of 1954 (the ones that had partitioned Indo-China in the first place and laid the behavioral ground rules for the signatories).

The propagated myth was that the South Vietnamese really wanted to be reunited with their northern compadres and that Ho Chi Minh wasn't really a communist. He had only turned to the Red Chinese because the CIA made him one in 1945 when its agents in the field were overruled thanks to pressure from that great right wing conspiracy. This one was right up there with the one about Ike turning Cuba's Castro into a 'Red' to appease the John Birch Society. Finally, since guerilla soldiers do not have base camps and that by the Viet Cong's following Mao's principle of 'becoming fish in the ocean', we couldn't win.

In the background there was the insidious acceptance of a moral equivalence between American principles and the practices of the Soviet Union. First, it appeared that the Soviet Union's economic growth was exceeding that of the United States—thus the Russians were doing something right and all remembered that we were once Uncle Joe's allies during world War Two. That this assumption was based on fiat values derived from faulty statistics never crossed their minds, nor later quite came up at George Washington University when I studied the economies of communist countries in graduate school.

Finally there was the possibility of 'mutually assured destruction' continually enhanced by the nuclear arms race. In several respects MAD was a dumb idea and it took Ronald Reagan to figure a way out of that strategic dilemma. At the time though, it was just about the only choice we had—particularly with limited troop availability due to our own and allied reluctance to maintain the ground forces necessary to halt a Soviet land attack against Western Europe.

When I remained on active service following my return from Vietnam, my associates and I knew that if WW III broke out that we were there to buy time and unlikely to survive. This almost came true during the 1973 Yom Kipper War when those of us assigned to various school commands at Quantico, Virginia were ordered to stay by a phone 24/7 as the USSR threatened to intervene using its paratroops.

However the thoughts of Marine officers on active service were hardly the emotional equivalents of students in mufti reacting to fear based emotions. Emotions leading to conclusions that, despite lessons that should have been learned from the attempts to appease Hitler at Munich, evolved into believing that the Cold War was America's fault and that if we were only nicer to Krushchev, he wouldn't have to act like a bully.

Besides Soviet society had been good to the Russians, leading to the USSR's advanced industrial economy. This attitude overlooked the fact that the foundation of Soviet industrial strength was the constant ongoing effort since 1928 to maintain a military force on a total war footing. Every other aspect of a normal economy was relegated to a very secondary position. However, there was that utopian quality to their alternative economic system based on mythology and that was the appeal despite all evidence to the contrary.

Therefore those of us inclined to say 'yeah right' and then attempting to rationally explain the true situation were accused of standing in the way of the liberal's right to be afraid and avoid feeling guilty over their clearly childish behavior. We were after-all opposing a great moral crusade and clearly deserved to have eggs thrown at us, which happened during at least two of our NROTC unit's spring sunset parades, and ostracized from society.

They even rioted to protest the choice of Richard Nixon, soon to become President, as the commencement speaker for the Class of 1967. This seemed to me to be a better choice than the one the university came up with for my graduation and there is something to be said for hearing what a former Vice President had to say in person. However the U of R bowed to the wishes of the protesters and replaced Nixon on the rostrum.

This was quite a contrast to the day President Nixon attended the official return of the 1st Marine Division from Vietnam. After the ceremonies were over and as the President was being driven around to be seen by the bulk of the troops sitting in the bleachers behind the parade, several thousand Marines piled out of the stands and charged his car. The officers, myself included, and the Secret Service had totally lost control. The next thing we knew was that the President of the United States was being carried around on the shoulders of the Marines like a football coach after a major victory.

These then were amongst the gentler forms of persuasion as the academic marketplace of ideas increasingly refused to accept any alternatives. This was particularly true of what were euphemistically called 'teach-ins'. These were often sponsored by Students for a Democratic Society that later evidence has proven was initially funded by East Germany's intelligence service at the behest of the KGB, where nothing was taught except vindictive propaganda directed towards American society in general and all things military in particular.

I attended one at the major's request at some personal peril given my military haircut and the attending mob made it perfectly clear that dissent was not appreciated. Finally the only way I could get to my 8 o'clock class with the major was to challenge right thinkers to stop me as I forced my way to the doors of Harkness Hall. I guess I usually looked determined enough that the sea of grungy mufti always parted before they'd let me make my day.

Besides that, these were adult children whose outlook on life seemed to be little different than that of oversized four-year-olds, aided to a limited extent by agent provocateurs from the Communist block. They didn't seem to grasp the difference between license and the responsible exercise of freedom, something that starts with respect for others that their behavior proved they didn't have despite verbiage to the contrary.

The idea of stepping up to the plate for the 'good of the order' evaporated under the threat that their lives might be disrupted by the requirements of war. Frequently, going all the way back to Valley Forge, this is how America has worked as only about a third of the population, according to historians, steps up to the plate to see the effort through to conclusion. The middle third tends to go with the flow, leaving the last third to continually raise objections while looking for ways for the country to 'cut its losses' whether we're winning or not.

This is poignantly displayed to every member of the American Legion who joins its '40 & 8' honor society during the initiation ceremony that goes back to 1919. Patriotism at the start of any war, or after an attack like 911, is cheap. But after awhile, people begin to lose interest and start questioning whether it is worth the effort. This was true during the Revolutionary War, the Civil War, and even to a certain extent—World War Two. Today mental fatigue is clearly setting in as the insurgency in Iraq continues with the number of people willing to admit that they supported the war from inception continuing to drop. Remember that the Vietnam era student protests finally came to an end with the demise of the draft. Ironically these victims of group-think would later complain about the 'me generation'.

My own feeling is that intellectual isolation had much to do with it. A intellectual isolation that is still proving detrimental to the political health of the republic that'll be addressed in another chapter. However, if one substitutes conjecture for fact and participates in discussions based on the same, then the ensuing conclusions are only as valid as those of 'Alice's Red Queen'. Off with their heads, trial later.

Chapter Footnote: As Dr. Payne discusses in his book *The Spanish Civil War, The Soviet Union & Communism*, Comintern decided in the late 1920s that in view of events that occurred in Weimar Germany, fascism was the counter-revolutionary use of force to thwart the establishment of a dictatorship of the proletariat. At the same time it classified Europe's socialist parties as 'social fascists' because of the split that occurred at the Second International when the Bolsheviks essentially went off in their own direction.

In the case of early 1930s Spain, when a fascist movement had yet to really materialize, the term was used to set up the existing constitutional parliamentary republican government as a straw man they could rail against. Moving forward some 30 years, this was the same tactic and rhetoric used by campus radicals to attack university administrations and anyone else who disagreed with the Students For A Democratic Society.

Another point Dr. Payne developed in his book pertained to the collapse of Spain's constitutional republican government into leftist anarchy during 1936. At the time the left of center Republican Party had obstinately eschewed an alliance with parties from the center and right so that they were forced to ally with the leftist Popular Front to form a government. Given that their majority in the Cortes was predicated on keeping their leftist allies happy, the latter were able to 'blackmail' the Republicans into using unconstitutional measures to eliminate right of center opposition.

This included the release from jail all the radical socialists who'd instigated the 1934 insurrection against Spain's republican constitutional government while those from the military and police forces who'd forcibly restored law and order were incarcerated. Because of this, Spain's political structure broke down to the benefit of the country's Marxists and civil war ensued. Having been there at the time, the collapse of university authority over the student body during the 1960s and early 1970s seems to have been a microcosm of what happened in Spain prior to the Spanish Civil War.

War & Peace

3

When Liberals Quit

It started Before Vietnam

On 12 April 1945 FDR died and by sundown it was probably clear to his successor that a piano had just landed on his head. The war in Europe was wrapping up but there still was a major struggle left to bring Japan to heel. A couple of months later at the Potsdam Conference, that 'good old boy' icon of the liberal media, Uncle Joe Stalin, shed his skin and proved that he wasn't the warm, fuzzy guy everyone wanted to believe he was.

Poor haberdasher Harry, once a plain senator from Missouri and protegee of the Kansas City political machine was in the deep end of the pool. But, given the old World War One 'cannoncocker' (artilleryman) that he was, President Truman sucked it up and did the best he could starting with the decision to drop the big nuclear rocks on Japan to bring a decisive end to World War Two.

From that point on Truman was to be vilified by the politically correct for being the one responsible for the only use to date of nuclear weapons on the battlefield. One would think that these intellectuals would've recognized that after the carnage of Iwo Jima and Okinawa, where the Japanese contested every rock, any military assault on Japan itself would entail the bloodiest fighting in the history of the world. Estimates at the time pointed towards the number of allied dead reaching at least a million soldiers and marines. Truman made the right decision.

Later when the 'iron curtain' dropped on Europe through means both fair and foul, he correctly formulated the Truman Doctrine calling for direct confrontation with any and all Soviet efforts to expand the curtain beyond the limits of the Yalta agreements and reality on the ground as of VE Day. When Stalin tried to starve out the Western presence in Berlin with a blockade, old Harry ordered the Berlin Airlift and pushed the Marshall Plan through Congress.

Unfortunately this stalwart opposition to communist expansion turned soft in the Far East as diplomatic inferences suggested that the North Koreans might be able to get away with unifying the peninsula with a blitzkrieg assault on their southern brethren. With the backing of both Mao and Stalin, amply proven since from the recently released Soviet documents that research teams from Yale University have ratted through, Kim Song Il's North Korean Army (NKPA) blasted across the 38th parallel and headed for Soul one fine June morning in 1950.

This was not a war that the United States was ready to fight and one that fortunately ended up maintaining the status quo. At the time Kim's troops headed south, the United States had effectively disarmed following World War Two. Since we had the nuclear bomb and enough airplanes large enough to carry these heavy rocks long distances, it was felt in most circles that we no longer needed either a navy nor an army. In Truman's eyes it also meant that we sure as hell didn't need a Marine Corps.

For all practical purposes the South Koreans didn't have an army and what little force they had was deliberately emasculated to avoid irritating the North Koreans and Chinese. The theory was that if the ROKs didn't pose a military threat to the north, despite the wishes of its president Sygmon Rhee, then war in Korea could be avoided. Terrific thinking that has since been replaced with two of the world's largest and best trained armies still staring each other down along the final truce line.

At the time, however, this left General MacArthur, plenipotentiary of Japan and Commander of US Forces Far East, with three minimally prepared divisions that had grown soft on beer and 'nasons' to stop them. Two of the divisions (24th & 25[Th] Infantry Divisions) were quickly fed piecemeal into the fray where they promptly vaporized in the fog of war. Finally the 1st Cavalry Division and the 1st Marine Brigade showed up and the NPKA was stopped around the Pusan Perimeter with the remaining ROKs jelling into some form of military organization.

Referring to the 1st Marine Brigade at the time as a brigade is a misnomer since that designation simply meant that ground troops went to war supported by their own airplanes. Other than that, the brigade was little more than a battalion landing team short one platoon of infantry per company and two battalions versus the normal three for the regiment it was built around. A regiment that had been assembled by grabbing just about every warm body dressed in khaki that could be found at Camp Pendleton, California. Eventually as more warm bodies were found, the brigade finally resembled a full regimental combat team just in time for Inchon.

Mustering First Marines was only a little more orderly. Instead of the press gang being limited to the confines of Camp Pendleton, it was nationally organized to include Marine Corps facilities everywhere. Seventh Marines wasn't even a regiment until it had arrived in combat as the Commandant rustled up reservists who'd long since thought that they'd heard the last shot fired in battle the day the last 'Jap' died on Okinawa.

This was the force that MacArthur led to the Yalu and the one that the Chinese jumped after Thanksgiving 1950. Surprisingly, this was one of the few times the CIA seemed to get it right. They had warned that Chinese were on the Peninsula and were ready to attack. Everyone else just shined off the warnings so that despite the Marine Corps stand at the 'Frozen Chosin', American forces ended up on the verge of being run out of Korea with MacArthur screaming about pulling back to Japan. The moment had come to fire MacArthur, but neither Truman nor anyone around him including the Joint Chiefs—World War Two generals all, had to moral courage to do it.

It wasn't for another couple of months and a dust-up between the two as to who was really in charge that Truman finally screwed up the courage to do what needed to be done the prior Christmas. By this time, thanks to the tragic death of General Walker in a car accident, General Ridgeway of 82nd Airborne fame had taken command of the Eighth Army and was kicking Chinese butt back to the North. With victory almost in hand, this was when 'Harry' lost his nerve, something liberals have conveniently ignored ever since.

The issues, besides one of personality that always came with MacArthur, centered around the strategic limits of the war. No one at the time or since ever advocated the direct invasion of Red China, although the Nationalist on Formosa (Taiwan) continually contemplated it. What MacArthur wanted to do was bomb the bridges over the Yalu and ChiCom staging bases just to the north to seal off the battlefield. Something that the geographic configuration of the area prevented him from doing if he was limited to just bombing the southern half of the Yalu bridges.

MacArthur also wanted to turn the Nationalist loose to cross the Taiwan Straight and invade the mainland. This should have been a 'non-starter', but the continual threat that it might happen had substantial strategic value. A point clearly missed by Truman when he made it clear to the world that the Nationalist would remain confined on their island, even if it took the Seventh Fleet to make them stay there.

The result was that, after being bled dry during the initial attack that had driven us south of Seoul and the pounding Ridgeway inflicted driving them back, the ChiComs were able to shift almost half million troops, here-to-fore frozen to protect the mainland from the Nationalists, to Korea as replacements for the million Chinese soldiers killed in just over six months of combat.

These Chinese reinforcements, however, didn't stop Ridgeway. Truman did that all by himself when the Chinese suggested that the parties begin truce talks to see if the war could be ended expeditiously. This was generous of them considering that they were low on troops available for combat in Korea at the time. But Truman and his advisors didn't pickup on this, figuring that truce talks were a good idea from a humanitarian perspective and that Communist China was as concerned about the contingent loss of life as we were.

Ergo, a year after the war had started Truman ordered Ridgeway to hold up and the talks started. The war however continued as the Communists dithered over one point after another until Americans got fed up and put Ike in the White House. A few months after Ike's inauguration and after inferences that he wouldn't rule out the use of nuclear weapons to end it, a peace of sorts came to the Korean Peninsula in 1953.

Interregnum

As the troops returned home from Korean to a mundane reception, the world drifted into Cold War equilibrium. The French had been fighting a communist insurrection in Indo-China but lacked the resources to ever win it. Particularly since French draftees could not constitutionally be sent overseas to fight in a colonial war. Because Algeria was legally an integral part of France with parliamentary representation, that war was a different story and outside of the American experience. However, it should be noted that militarily the French won, beginning with a cleansing of Algiers's Casbah using methods we don't have the stomach for in Iraq.

Concurrently, until the emergence of intelligence satellites by 1960, the US Air Force and Navy patrol planes continually tested Soviet air defenses to map their effectiveness. This led to some unfortunate events that occasionally surfaced on the public's radar screen; details of which are still coming out as cold war documents are gradually being declassified.

Along with the air reconnaissance campaign, there was the game of chicken played between our submarines and theirs that resulted in a few accidents as each side made strenuous efforts to track the location of the other side's boats so that they could be instantly neutralized when war broke out. Like the air reconnaissance campaign, details of this extremely tense 40 year conflcit are only now drifting into the public domain.

We also saw the abysmal effort at the Bay of Pigs to overthrow Castro that turned even more disastrous when JFK denied the insurgents promised air support. Based on JFK's reluctance to up the ante and drive Castro to his grave, plus

JFK's efforts to 'jolly him up' at a super power summit, Krushchev decided to put Soviet—American relations to the real test. The result was the Cuban Missile Crisis and the decision by some Americans that appeasement might not be that bad a deal and they did have a point. However an attitude of better red than dead virtually guaranteed red.

Most Americans at the time knew this, but dead if someone miscalculated was not palatable either so that some form of middle ground needed to be maintained. LBJ knew this when he branded Goldwater as a radical warmonger and drove the point home when his campaign ran that infamous TV ad showing a little girl picking flowers and then was slowly vaporized as an atom bomb went off in the background.

Still there remained the need to oppose Soviet aggression around the war as the latter turned to 'wars of liberation' to thwart the spread of 'American imperialism'. A nebulous concept based on the fantasy's contained in Lenin's writings that have been subject to some bizarre interpretations by politically correct leftists ever since and a genesis for the politically correct belief that everything the United States does in the world is motivated by evil intentions.

Vietnam: Korea Redux

The Vietnam War, contra to public opinion, actually started as the ink was drying on the 1954 Geneva Accords, it was just that we didn't know it at the time. According to these accords, Laos and Cambodia became independent under the rule of their traditional monarchies. Vietnam was split along the seventeenth parallel with Ho Chi Minh's communists getting the North and the South set up as an independent entity under the authoritarian regime of the Diem family. Not a perfect solution, but one that should have worked.

Ho Chi Minh and his politburo, however, never intended for the accords to work because the whole objective of the agreement in their eyes was to buy time to re-group before launching a major effort to bring the South under their authority. This is why they left ethnic South Vietnamese communist troops as VC, plus a cadre of Northerners to supervise the coming 'insurrection', behind when they withdrew their Viet Minh soldiers.

The only ones around that still dispute this, now busy ignoring the memoirs of General Giap and others, are America's now adult children yearning for the days they ran around as free-thinkers in disheveled mufti handing out flowers under the premise that 'love' would keep muggers from robbing them. Given their attire at the time, this spurious correlation probably held since the average mugger would take one look at them and assume there wasn't anything they had worth stealing.

At the time of the anti—war movement, I tried getting a few to read Douglas Pike's volume that clearly delineated the North's command and control structure—one that was quite comprehensive and the result of several years of careful research on Pike's part. In it he clearly debunked the myth that the 'National Liberation Front (Viet Cong in the vernacular) reflected a cross-section of South Vietnamese public opinion desirous of being freed from American dominance and the oppressive regime of the Diems.

That was the problem. One can't be self-righteous and use the moral high ground to camouflage rationalizations protecting one's rear-end when the evidence imploding the myth gets stuck in their face—just like an alcoholic in denial who gets tired of hearing about that stupid river in Egypt. Another point conveniently avoided at the time was the refugee flow—over 90,000 Catholic Vietnamese piled into US Navy landing craft to escape the North, with few leaving the South for the worker's paradise in the North. Even *Life Magazine* provided pictorial coverage of that northern exodus.

Another argument that should have ruined their day was the fact that a significant minority of Vietnamese were Catholic and those that weren't, were predominantly Buddhists. This eventually led to conflicts in the South akin to the problem of Sunnis, Shia's, and Kurds in Iraq today that led to the fall of Diem's government. But it should have been evident to the dimmest lightbulb in the crowd that neither has ever been compatible with the tenets of communism. The solution for the politically correct was to simply deny that Ho Chi was a communist only because the United States gave him no choice but to turn to Russia and China during his effort to eject the French.

Neat trick, but the Vietnamese knew better. They had enjoyed quasi Viet Minh rule during the war with the French where fellow citizens were arbitrarily executed if they'd shown any signs of cooperating with the French. The reign of terror employed by the Viet Minh, and communist regimes elsewhere, to force support and fill the military ranks with fresh cannon fodder in a war the average Vietnamese wasn't sure he wanted to support, was a fact of life the Vietnamese had lived with for years.

Finally there were reports of the mass executions of Vietnamese farmers in the North to clear the way for collective farming that percolated through the grapevine. Collectively this left a less than thrilled population in the South when VC agents showed up eliciting cooperation in the emerging war against the Diem regime. To over come this recalcitrance, VC agents started executing existing village chiefs and replacing them with VC operatives.

When the Cong needed money or material, they simply took it despite the fact that such appropriation would leave the local Vietnamese destitute. If more troops were needed they were simply conscripted from their villages and marched their conscripts off into the jungles bound together with ropes wrapped around their necks. It wasn't until the infamous 'phoenix program' was in full force and we started collecting the crop for centralized storage that this finally came to a halt.

Naturally this was well known to the administration and Kennedy had already dispatched Marines to the Upper Mekong River to block the North Vietnamese effort to subvert Laos. Unfortunately he didn't keep them there and the North Vietnamese had no intention of keeping the agreement they'd reached with JFK once the Marines were removed. He'd also upgraded the American advisory effort in South Vietnam in order to 'spiff up' the capabilities of South Vietnam's armed forces.

As always, including von Stueben's effort to turn Washington's army into a creditable force, this is a difficult task and it should have been self evident that there would be a few successes and many failures when later undertaken in Iraq. Even the vaunted 'ROKs' weren't up to the job in 1950, or 1951 for that matter, and they had officers more than willing to shoot and bash their own troops until they'd acquired the necessary military skills to win fire-fights. (personal knowledge: I've served with Korean Marine Corps officers) During the Korean War we even had to assist them using the 'buddy system' where 'ROKs' were integrated into American units on the firing line until they were skilled enough to provide a cadre for South Korean units.

In the case of the South Vietnamese, this task was both difficult and easy. The more difficult arose from the fact that the ARVNs had been at this for close to 20 years before American troops arrived in 1965. Furthermore, many of the local defense forces assigned the task of defending villages and regional centers had borne the brunt of the war against the Viet Cong with no end in sight. They were tired as I tried to point out to my Marines in 1969.

However the ARVN had an experienced leadership core since some of them had actually fought with the Viet Minh and many others had already served full careers with both the French and South Vietnamese forces. Thus they'd more than 'been there—done that', often with service in elite French parachute units and thus had a good grasp of what needed to be done on the small unit level. The problem is that once one has been in combat 24/7 for that length of time, the wear and tear of war grinds one down. When we appeared then, it was only natural that they'd take advantage of our presence to 'fade out' for a while.

Finally, although often competent on the company level, ARVN officers had never had effective command experience on the battalion or higher level and when it came to its generals, traditional problems of political advantage slipped in to disrupt the command structure. The opportunities available for graft and corruption and the fact that too many ARVN senior field grade officers took advantage of them further degraded the command structure.

Ergo, building up the ARVN would prove to be difficult and given that experience it should have been no surprise that it was going to take one step forward and almost two back to create effective Iraqi security forces. Additionally, during the War in Iraq the forces that should have been available to re-build on had evaporated during the conflict. They had simply walked away from the battlefield as those watching on the various cable news channels saw right before their own eyes. Secondly, there couldn't a real regime change had the old Iraqi Baathist officer corps been re-installed without altered values and the purging of those whose careers had been spent committing crimes against humanity.

Consequently time has been needed to find the troops who'd not only walked away, but those among them who were willing to return to the ranks under greatly altered circumstances. Next is the need to sort out those that could be effective NCOs and junior officers up to middle field grade. This is hard to do even within sophisticated American forces. Finally any reformed Iraqi security force needs competent senior officers effectively vetted so that the United States does not re-install the problem.

Because this hasn't happened within the 15 months that Iraq was under American occupation, the politically correct have exhibited their impatience by whining daily. You'd think that at least one of their more prominent spokespersons would at least read a general text about World War Two where they'd discover that even the US Army wasn't quite ready for 'prime time' against the Germans inside of that time frame.

Just over a year after Pearl Harbor, America's most combat-ready troops were thoroughly whipped by Rommel at the gates of Tunisia after almost 20 years of preparation with field commanders drawn from the ranks of World War One veterans. On the other hand, the politically correct don't need to do things like this because most of them have seen the old John Wayne movies and knew all they needed to know. Besides, to do so would surrender any political advantage that can be gained from bashing President Bush with the subject.

Vietnam & Its use to Justify Appeasement

Collective ignorance regarding Vietnam serves a purpose amongst the politically correct. Pontificating about the probability of success in Iraq based on what happened in Vietnam remains creditable only if the truth remains obscured. Since we all know how the Vietnam War ended after lasting seven years, it was obviously a quagmire that we should never have entered. Besides there's no way a western army like ours could ever defeat a popular insurgency supported by the will of the people.

Ipso facto, with the proper spin, this was the rationale used by the politically correct for opposing Reagan's campaign to overthrow the Sandinistas. Based on theology contained in Lenin's writings, the Sandinistas should have been allowed to remain in power following their overthrow of Samoza's regime and supporting the Contras was thus an immoral exercise in American Imperialism. The same logic is implied today when the invasion of Iraq has been declared a 'mistake' made by obviously stupid 'Bushies' looking for 'revenge' and oil profits.

Leaving aside issues of moral equivalency et al, these group think assertions simply aren't true. Despite all of our efforts to avoid 'winning', by the end of 1972 South Vietnam had a relatively freely elected government, supported by 62% of the electorate who'd willing re-installed President Thieu. Had these elections been rigged like the liberals claimed at the time, the Thieu—Ky team should have done much better; like something close to the 98% of the vote that Saddam Hussein got the last time he was re-elected.

More importantly, the South Vietnamese had succeeded in stopping the North Vietnamese cold in their attempt to overrun the country with a traditional cross border attack. Of course they needed our air power to do that. But their army had met and passed a very stern test during the NVA Easter Offensive, and through 1974 South Vietnamese forces even succeeded in keeping the Khmer Rouge out of Phnom Penh by conducting riverine operations up the Mekong River.

American objectives had been accomplished! Then the American liberal stepped in by denying them access to our air support while blocking all military funding for South Vietnam. Without ammunition the ARVN collapsed in 1975, as would anyone else's army—ours included. So how did we loose in Vietnam, very simply—Ted Kennedy and his colleague's appeasement of the adult children of the baby boom had engineered our surrender.

This is not to say that we fought the war brilliantly, far from it as NVA soldiers infiltrated their way south and into Viet Cong Battalions as the Johnson administration slowly fed American troops into the fray. Part of the reason for this piecemeal feeding of troops into combat had to have been due to our lack of the necessary 'logistic lift capability' that, when coupled with a lack of units ready to fight, led to many units belated arrival in country.

This was the primary flaw in our NATO strategy that was based in theory on re-enforcement's arriving from the US 30 days after any Soviet move through Germany's Fulda Gap. This couldn't be done as the Army confirmed during the six-month troop build-up prior to the 1991 Gulf War and later for the War in Iraq. Thus one very good reason General Franks adopted the 'blitzkrieg' strategy that he employed based on a two division march on Baghdad—later backed up with another to secure his lines of communications.

The second reason for the slow build-up of American forces in Vietnam was the Johnson Administration's alleged desire to fight the war 'on the cheap'. I believe that there's some validity to this charge, but more important was LBJ's failure to understand the nature of the enemy and how determined Ho Chi and his colleagues were to achieve unification before they died. For the latter, their military effort was accordingly aimed to conquer the south to the last Vietnamese left alive. In contrast, LBJ figured that if the price North Vietnam had to pay for victory on the battlefield reached a certain and modest threshold, they'd give up the attempt.

This disconnected perception obviously led to strategic problems as we conducted the war and the rate that the NVA died in battle as a result of the price Ho Chi and company was willing to pay never crept into the American psyche. Consequently the developing disbelief by the American people in the published body count during what quickly became a war of attrition.

The average American could not believe that NVA casualty rates could conceivably approach the total military aged manpower living in the North at the time. However that became the ultimate cost of the war for the North as General Giap eventually admitted in an interview with an Italian journalist in the 1970s—over one million dead troops that has later grown to closer to 1.5 million. The some 5, 000 plus (1,000 per year give or take a few) who eventually died during the bombing campaign seems inconsequential by comparison, yet the politically correct suffered considerable angst over that figure at the time.

Another prevailing rationalization at the time and since was that the War in Vietnam was different and represented a type of conflict we'd never fought before. When added to the myth that guerilla forces didn't have logistic bases that could be attacked and thus could operate as military free agents, the more knowing along New York's Upper Westside concluded that our effort was doomed from the start. Thus the war must be ended at all cost.

Apparently they'd never heard about how General Sullivan burned out the Iroquois in the winter of 1779 to put a stop to that problem. 'Mad Anthony' Wayne was a little more thorough after Fallen Timbers in 1796 and it took WH Harrison to finally terminate the Shawnee threat at the Battle of the Thames in 1813, but it was done. Indian conflicts on the plains followed similar courses with the addition of strategic encirclement from multiple directions to pin down the enemy.

Then there's the vulnerability American guerilla forces successfully dealt with during the Revolutionary and Civil War and the American military experience from Cuba to the Philippine Insurrection. Also the Marine Corps fought a number of small wars throughout Latin America which can be added to the lessons learned fighting the Japanese in Burma during WWII, so that it's apparent we've had ample experience successfully fighting insurgencies. Knowledge in how to do it therefore wasn't the problem.

The issue was in the application of that knowledge. When I read General Westmoreland's memoirs my basic thought was that he really didn't understand the nature of the war in which he was the commanding general. In it he talked about a wide-open strategic arena akin to the Civil War and the need to use large force operations to run down the Viet Cong. To a certain extent he was correct but instead of Grant in Mississippi, my mind turned to Sherman marching to the sea.

The result of 'Westy's' strategic vision was that as more American units arrived in county, they were assigned areas of operations covering strategic routes of attack on major South Vietnamese centers and told to go out and find the enemy. Once found, usually by some unlucky platoon or rifle company that just happened to bump into the NVA at the wrong time, destroy the enemy by piling on in what we termed 'main force search and destroy missions'.

These were multi battalion sized operations that usually left a lot of people dead, many of whom were ours and one hell of lot of them were theirs. It was ridiculous, considering the respective casualty rates to spout that the enemy continually evaporated into the jungle. Yes they eventually did, often retreating into the sanctuaries we allowed them to maintain inside Cambodia and Laos, but only after they were licked.

It wasn't Westmoreland's fault. The powers that be inside the White House had decided that Vietnam was to be a 'limited war', kept within the confines of South Vietnam. We were never allowed to pursue the NVA into the ground by continuing the fight until the last one had died inside his Laotian bunker; nor was the 3rd Marine Division permitted to chase the NVA back north across the 17th parallel.

This brilliant bit of thinking came from the mind of Robert McNamara, a Harvard man to the core, and resulted in many Marines getting killed with impunity while driving the bulldozers that cleared the brush for the infamous 'McNamara Line'. A sequence of electronic sensors, barbed wire and clear fields of fire available to shoot NVA only after they'd crossed a defensive line that never really was.

This was a war that also meant that dead NVA were strategically more important than hillsides in the 'boonies'. That's not to say that hilltops weren't important, but they were only important as fire bases for the artillery supporting other combat operations. Once combat operations had moved to other locations beyond the range of the guns, these bases were closed and the troops moved on. Tactical initiative in Vietnam was based on mobility and not the defense of static positions, albeit the latter was often important.

By the end of 1967 we'd clearly demonstrated that despite all the strategic restrictions imposed on the forces fighting inside Vietnam, the VC couldn't win unless we quit. There were lots of dead NVA and VC to support that thesis, but the problem was that there were a few million left to go—something no one in the lower 48 recognized. The NVA sure did though. That's why they organized the 1968 Tet Offensive based on a few erroneous assumptions. Starting with the thought that average South Vietnamese would rise up against the Americans and that the ARVN would disintegrate if they were surprised while many of its soldiers were on leave spending Tet with their families.

Didn't happen. In fact by the time the sequence of Tet 1968 related attacks were over, almost 200,000 VC bodies littered the countryside of South Vietnam. For them the Great Tet offensive was a suicide mission that made the Japanese sacrifice on Okinawa look petty. The NVA didn't fare much better as almost a full division perished at the hands of our Marines and the ARVN 1st Division in and around Hue City.

Of course CBS News made much of the VC flag that flew for days until 5th Marines finally took it down the hard way. But in the process, CBS never quite got around to emphasizing the execution deaths of 6,000 'American Lackeys' that filled the mass grave north of town. Maybe if these South Vietnamese, including the many on the faculty of the local university and other intellectuals, had been more receptive to the 'will of the people', they wouldn't have been murdered.

The Siege of Khe Sanh was also sucked into the cauldron of Tet. Operations around this outpost had been going on for some time before Tet since the position served as the western anchor of the McNamara Line and could potentially be used as a springboard for any offensive to cut the Ho Chi Trail. Eventually up to three divisions of NVA troops were committed to the mountains surrounding Khe Sanh and 'Westy' charged three battalions of the 26th Marines with holding the position.

There're several issues surrounding the battle and why it was fought. To the Marines that were there from those I know and what I've read, the big issue was survival. Not the kind presented in a John Wayne movie, but the most basic problem of sanitation, adequate food, and medical facilities. Except for a few probing actions, ambushed patrols, and the constant NVA shelling, Khe Sanh wasn't a bloody event from our perspective. The continual picture of destroyed aircraft on the airfield was just one plane whose picture was repeatedly flashed on the evening news for dramatic effect.

Down in Saigon at MACV headquarters it seemed that the issue was whether or not the NVA were going for a Dein Bien Phu reincarnate. That was the great battle in 1954 that saw the defeat of 15,000 French colonial troops and the trigger that induced the French to throw in the towel. Now it seemed like General Giap was going to repeat his tour-de-force, or at least that's what the American press worked hard to get everyone to believe despite significant differences between the two; ie: B-52s.

On the NVA side, it looks quite likely that they were using Khe Sanh to suck American forces away from South Vietnam's population centers so as to reduce opposition to their planned Tet offensive. If that was the goal, they failed. And that failure was compounded by the pounding our B-52s gave those poor bastards assigned to the three divisions surrounding our fortress. By the time the 1st Air Cav relieved 26th Marines, most of these troops were little more than hamburger. So much for the looming debacle predicted by the news media.

Finally there was the fall of our embassy in Saigon and the vicious fight that eventually regained it. At least that was the media's presentation. Actually the VC assault on the American Embassy was conducted by a solitary small sapper squad that only managed to make it onto the grounds. They never made it inside the actual building as the last one died just short of the front door. Another sapper squad managed to take over a local Saigon TV station and that too didn't last long. The limited scope of the actual attack on Saigon though, didn't stop the mass media from making a 'cause celeb' out of it as they all rushed unimpeded through the city to take their pictures for the 6 o'clock news.

When Giap's debacle was finished with the enemy in complete disarray, it was time for the US to take the strategic offense for the first time. In the White House's panic response to Tet, reinforcements were rushed to Vietnam—giving Westmoreland the troop strength to drive to the Ho Chi Minh Trail and turn north to the passes over the Annamite Mountains. Backed up by the 1st Air Cav securing the lines of communications, for the NVA this would have been like getting a fishbone out of one's throat that's wedged in forever.

The war would have had a far different result if the NVA to dig out a full American division fortified on top of the key passes on the 'blood road' linking the North with the South. Couple this scenario with an amphibious assault near the top of the panhandle, the mining of Haiphong Harbor before Nixon did it and the North would have been in a world of hurt.

Of course this wasn't going to happen as average Americans lost their nerve and its newly adult children, egged on by the news media, accelerated their temper-tantrum. Instead the North Vietnamese, just like the Chinese before them in Korea, suggested peace talks and LBJ took the bait. Once again, when it was the moment to exercise moral courage and finish the job, the country faltered.

When Nixon moved into the White House, we were stuck with plan B—Vietnamization. As the ARVN demonstrated an ever increasing ability to re-assume responsibility for beating the NVA, we gradually began to pull out our troops. By the end of 1971 we were just about out of there and the defeat of the NVA Easter Offensive proved that plan B had worked. December 1972, after finally becoming fed-up with the peace talks, Nixon turned the B-52s loose on Hanoi and mined Haiphong.

The North by then concluded that the game was up for at least awhile and signed the truce agreement in February 1973. Surprising we'd still won except for one problem—the American fifth column and their spiritual kindred on Capital Hill. Since the North couldn't win on the battlefield, as a gesture of sportsmanship we felt compelled to give them the South by Act of Congress that effectively disarmed the South Vietnamese and let the NVA walk into Saigon virtually unopposed.

My War

Another vision about how to prosecute the war was the USMC way. This was the war I participated in and reflected the 'lessons' learned by the Corps during the 'Banana Wars' it had fought around the Caribbean from Roosevelt to Roosevelt. It's also the segment of the war that refutes the politically correction assumption that we were 'baby killers etc' with visions of F-4s and napalm attacks dancing in our heads.

With the arrival of the first Marines in country General Walt's (the senior Marine commander) approach was to secure Da Nang and its surrounding environs to separate the VC from the native inhabitants. This soon led to patrols to the City's south, including the one where CBS's Morley Shafer filmed the torching of Vietnamese 'hootches' by the Marines. When shown on American television, his film editors left out pictures of all the under ground fortifications revealed after the 'hootches' were burnt.

More troubling was that Shafer had asked the Marines to set them on fire for more dramatic footage and even provided the cigarette lighter one of them used. This doesn't mean that the Marines weren't going to resort to the torch anyway considering the bunker complexes underneath, but it does point out the mass media's effort to turn factual reportage into mass propaganda at the expense of those fighting the war. The more pressing mystery is whether anyone gave Morley back his lighter.

As Marine troop strength gradually built up, Walt ordered his Marines to conduct cordon operations where one of our battalions would encircle a village complex to keep the VC out, while ARVNs would go into the village to secure the accumulated harvest, issue identification cards, and arrest VC cadres. The food by the way was never legally removed from the villager's, it was just transferred to warehouse facilities in return for ownership receipts the locals could use as they saw fit. Thus the VC ended up with little to extort and individual Vietnamese got to keep the fruits of their labor as they gradually released their crops into a free market.

Another Walt innovation was the formation of combined action groups. Here a command structure was created to oversee the operations of what became numerous eight man squads of Marines imbedded with local self-defense forces scattered throughout southern I Corps. One of these, by the way, was positioned for several years about two to four klcks away from My Lai where the Army's Lt Calley and his men conducted their massacre.

Given this dichotomy and my own experience, Calley was an aberration and not the norm despite efforts by the politically correct to portray it otherwise. This is why Massachusetts' Senator and current Presidential 'wannabe' John Kerry's 1971 testimony before Congress was so egregious. He took all the bar talk and isolated instances of 'war crimes' he'd heard of and portrayed that as the truth under oath. His condemnation of all of us who'd served honorably in country for his own self-serving purpose was clearly malicious slander for which he has yet to apologize.

With regard to my own experience as a Marine officer, by the time I appeared on the scene and was assigned to the first Marine Division's 9th Engineer Battalion, this rather successful war within a war was in full stride. Added to the CAGs were the 1st Marine Division's two independent engineer battalions, including mine. These units were given the task of keeping the main highway open between Da Nang and Chu Lai—once very unfriendly territory that for my battalion included the former battlefields around Tam Ky and the Que Son Mountains.

Whatever good or bad happened to that road was our responsibility as my battalion maintained platoons of Marines in 'rinky-dink' compounds spread north up the road from battalion rear at Chu Lai. Except for the Special Forces out on the Laos border, this was about as close to John Wayne at Fort Apache as one could get. Our mission was to maintain the road surface, eventually paving it, find every mine that might be buried in the road before someone else did, repair every bridge the VC destroyed and once repaired—defend it, which in the case of 'bridge 29' was a recurring exercise.

We were also supposed to stay alive. Accomplishing this which meant the usual experience of getting shot at and occasionally being allowed to return fire, taking out night ambushes in conjunction with local security forces and generally doing what we could to help others in their efforts to stay alive. I'm still breathing so something was done right, but the truth is that the military efforts of the much maligned local security forces and their touted unwillingness to fight probably kept me and my men alive as much as anything we did. These guys fought in good weather and in bad because they didn't want the VC.

One night I remember, just before the monsoon came in, a small platoon of them down the road across from an orphanage and local Catholic Church hammered it out with the NVA for hours separated by only two lanes of road and 10 yards of barbed wire. The next morning when we arrived on the scene, there was quite a mess indicating that our local boys had given back more than they'd received. The sad part was that the kids in the orphanage with its sisters and the padre that we'd befriended had disappeared—never to be seen again by us.

More pleasant was one miserable wet day during the monsoons when my patrol came upon an old 'papa-son' carrying his daughter while standing on the side of the road. She was not in good shape from pneumonia or whatever, so I had my corpsman bring in the medevac bird and off she went with her dad to a hospital somewhere. As things had unfolded over the years 9th Engineers had shared the neighborhood, the locals figured out who the 'good guys' were and they knew that if they waited patiently, a Marine patrol would come by and help them out.

That's what we did, no harassment of civilians on our watch and if some fool wanted to be cute and shoot one of their ducks I made them pony up many times the duck's market value as compensation. This in various forms was First Marine Division 'standard operating procedure' because it was the right thing to do! Yes there were 'free-fire zones' like Duy Xuyen, where few lived except allied small war fighters and the VC. Everywhere else, including Thang Binh where my company was planted, were subject to stringent rules of engagement and the Commandant was not a happy fellow if one violated those rules.

The last point before moving on was what I'd observed traveling the road between Chu Lai and Thang Binh. When I'd arrived in country and first rode northwards to check in with Alpha Company, passing Tam Ky proved relatively easy since the town had yet to expand out to the road. At the time its citizens were in the process of rebuilding what we referred to as the 'little people's bridge' the neolithic way.

On my last trip through Tam Ky, there were new multi-story living accommodations painted with the array of colors that's typical of Southeast Asia. A new and thriving covered marketplace was operating with considerable business. Finally, traffic through town was a real 'bitch' due to the congestion. In fact our morning mine sweeps had gotten to where we were backing up traffic as if Route 1 was one of LA's freeways during rush hour.

The country I left in 1970 was beginning to become a capitalist paradise, at least from the perspective of this Marine Lieutenant. Later that year an eventual candidate for the White House felt it was safe enough to drive alone to the coast to replenish his supply of 'mary jane'. A year later one of my friends who'd gone on the 'NROTC Bull Dog Cruise' with me in 1967 commanded a platoon in 1st Marines and after months of combat patrolling south of Marble Mountain, never found a fire fight. Yes children, we'd won the war.

Problems From Home

At least those of us in the Marine Corps knew we'd won it. Folks back in the world didn't seem to believe it, partly because of Walter Cronkite and his ilk who'd decided during the Battle for Hue that the war was unwinnable. Since Cronkite was the most trusted name in television news at that time, he was afforded a creditability that neither Presidents Johnson or Nixon could ever achieve. Ergo, when old Walter said we were losing, we were losing despite evidence on the ground to the contrary.

This perception ended up creating major command problems for those of us still 'in country'. Particularly when coupled with the whine from the children in disheveled mufti and the near treasonous efforts of radical black power groups to undermine the willingness of African—Americans to serve. It didn't help when Martin Luther King jumped in and declared that the war was immoral.

Thus African-American draftees arrived in country with the attitude that they were cannon fodder for the 'white man's war' that had already been lost, plus no one-whites included—wanted to the last one killed before the inevitable American surrender. The end result was an Army conducting combat operations almost in name only with many units simply 'mailing it in'.

Because the Marine Corps was still pre-dominantly a volunteer organization, the First Marine Division was spared the worst of the consequences. The Army, on the other hand, got 'nailed' and from Tet '68 on troop moral was precarious except in elite units like the 1st Air Cav and the 101st Airborne. For all practical purposes the Americal Division (Calley's parent organization) virtually ceased fighting as General Schwartzkopf's memoirs and other have noted.

This does not mean that the Corps was spared. By early 1970 my troops, regardless of ethnicity and geographic origins, didn't want to remain in battalion rear after sundown. All things considered they preferred to take their chances with the VC. We almost lost our battalion communications officer a couple of times due to 'fragging' and that was only because he'd taken to sleeping with his flack jacket on. Things had even gotten to the point where my battalion had a race riot in the enlisted men's club that triggered a needed change of command.

Fortunately Lt Col. K became our new battalion commander and the first thing he did was muster all of us, enlistedmen and officers, in Chu Lai where he told us what life was like growing up as a Czech or 'hunky' in an Anglo society during the 1930s. The point he was making was that at some time or another almost every American ethnic group had been subject to ill-rational prejudice with its accompanying discrimination and that it hurt.

This was something all hands regardless of racial background could buy into and iterated that our new battalion commander had some understanding of life on the other side of the racial divide. The next point was that every Marine was 'green' and would be treated as such with the understanding that all of us were obligated to make an effort to understand the ethnic sensitivities of our fellow Marines.

Since this was the way that most of us tried to run our subordinate units, the colonel's presentation had a creditable foundation and with his subsequent actions, the existing racial gap was effectively closed. This isn't to say that the problem was solved, but what remained was essentially the byproduct of other disciplinary problems that always exists amongst the 10% that habitually cause them.

However we were what Third MAF's Criminal Investigative Division called a 'targeted battalion' by the Black Mau Maus. This was a black power organization led by permanent riff raft found in any war, World War Two included when on any given day 15% of Ike's Army was over-the-hill. These were men who didn't have anything to do and didn't really belong to anybody. In 9th Engineers we had a couple, white and black, who were listed on the rolls, but hadn't been seen by anyone except CID since 1966 because financially the black market proved to be a better deal than earning a government paycheck in combat.

Anyway, the stated goal of the Black Mau Maus was to generate a racial uprising within the American forces in Vietnam. To accomplish this, its leaders would travel from firebase to firebase recruiting other African-Americans into their ranks as agent provocateurs. When caught, they were shipped off to the Third MAF brig, but not until they'd created considerable hate and discontent amongst those African-Americans in the rear with little to do. When one is bored amongst similar thinkers, the imagination can dream up 'wrongs' that no one would ever consider in saner moments.

One of the tragedies of this activity occurred when one of my Marines, the son of a Georgia preacher, finally decided that he'd had enough of the pressure and physical threats to join the movement. One calm day in a squad-bay on the LZ we shared with 7th Marines, he emptied a full magazine into the chest of his persecutor. A Marine corporal who'd also once belonged to me and one that we never would have suspected was a 'black mau-mau' recruiter without CID finally coming forth with the details.

The last time I saw the preacher's son, he was being kept in isolation so other black mau maus wouldn't kill him awaiting trial for murder. From what CID passed down to us, this wasn't the only black mau mau recruiting inside our ranks. Later back at Camp Pendleton, CA this problem was still with us as the base periodically went on 'terrorist alerts' to secure the facilities from those who were attempting to steal weapons and create other problems.

This was a little frightening since numerous National Guard armories had been broken into at the time with countless heavy weapons removed by America's militant underground. Additionally, we had tactical nuclear weapons on the base and some of them belonged to B Co, 7th Engineer Battalion commanded by me—something that heightened our sensitivity level.

Like all units we too had a drug problem, mostly with troops in the rear that weren't directly part of the war, which in most cases was the core problem behind many of the war's disciplinary problems—problems I could solve in the field with shovels and empty sandbags. On a scale between one and ten, we were still way short of the 11 reached by many Army administrative units.

But it created disciplinary problems none the less and these were mostly imported from prevailing American society back in the world. Once in country the 'casual draftee drug user' and occasional volunteer Marine had ample access to his drug of choice thanks to the in country drug trade that had grown out of the original French effort to finance special operations during their Indo-China War.

As the war progressed, this practice continued to do the same for the NVA/VC so in many respects, America's 'counter—culture' was undermining our ability to fight the war successfully and stay alive; ie: representing a form of passive treason by the politically correct.

4

When Defending Freedom Wasn't Cool

Aftermath

The big problem, once the First Maine Division returned stateside from late 1970 through the fall of 1971, was the need to assemble some semblance of a combat organization. This wasn't that easy to do because most of the division landed at Camp Pendleton as little more than trash piled up in a parking lot. The optimal solution would have been to have left this stuff at Da Nang's Red Beach for auctioning it off to scrap dealers. But we were told to make a 'go of it' with troops levels that made the survivors of Iwo Jima appear fully manned.

Typical of this is what I and my Marines had to go through to keep rolling stock of the road so that the Battalion Commander could keep his job and complete the battalion's assigned missions. These were numerous and seemed to reflect that HQ Marine Corps hadn't gotten the word that 75% of 7th Engineer's authorized strength had been stowed away in boxes. After being the CO of the battalion's only operating company for a while I finally made the command decision to put one-third of that unit into boxes and try to do the work of a full battalion with only two platoons.

The motor pool wasn't even that well off when I took it over. I had over 400 pieces of rolling stock and all of it was either broken or on deadline awaiting mandatory preventive maintenance. When the Marine Corps finally decided to dump the worst of the First Marine Division's trash into the salvage yard, my junior NCOs would take vehicles that were no longer salvageable but ones we weren't allowed to dispose of, to the yard. There they'd search amongst the vehicles other units had thrown away and when they found one in better shape than the one they'd brought, paintbrushes would produce a serial number switch and they'd drive home with another unit's trash.

This was what we did as kids when browsing through the neighbor's trash to see what delights we could take home. It's hardly a way to rebuild military units in preparation for the next war. Everyday represented a choice as to which Marine Corps order one would choose to violate because equipment status and manpower levels matched against mission requirements created unsolvable conflicts. Guess right and you'd done what was expected; guess wrong and there was a real possibility that a letter of reprimand would follow, or if one were lucky, one would merely be relieved of command.

An issue that wouldn't go away was drugs and after awhile I was on a first name basis with every drug dog on the base to no avail. About the only thing the dogs did for me was move the various stashes from wall lockers where the owner could be determined to the eves under the company barracks. At least I made it expensive for whoever it was that dealt the stuff.

Fortunately the problem didn't reach the severe levels experienced by the army, particularly in Europe where soldiers who complained about drug use in the barracks risked bodily harm and had officers literally afraid to crack down. Still we were losing roughly a Marine per month in the company to being caught with the stuff in their possession, usually by the North San Diego County Sheriff's station.

This meant a quick trip out the door with 'bad paper' in hand and thus the loss of VA benefits amongst other penalties. Over the course of a year, between those caught with drugs and the long standing AWOLs (a few had been over-the-hill for years), my guess is that the battalion eventually processed out almost 20% of its on board strength to everyone's relief. That's not to say that we '86st' everyone caught 'using'. One Marine the dogs alerted on in one of their forays to Bravo Company ended up with 60 days in the brig. A few months later, after I'd left for Marine Barracks Washington DC, I read that he'd been cited as the 'Marine of the Month' for Camp Pendleton.

Then there's the story of Marine 'S'. 'S' was part of a working party I'd corralled from the brig to bust tires the old fashioned way since the Corps never seemed to have a working hydraulic tire changer available. The deal I made at the time was that if these brig rats worked hard for me, I'd go to bat for them when their trial date arrived.

So one fine day I found myself testifying before 'S's discharge hearing where I was grilled by three full bird colonels about why I felt that keeping 'S' around was a good idea. When it was over I was firmly convinced that it hadn't gone well for 'S' and that I'd probably stepped in it 'big time'. 'S' however ended up serving to the end of his enlistment and turned out t be a pretty good Marine for the duration.

The real culprits, I've finally decided, behind the drug problem we had at Camp Pendleton were the daughters of America's Greatest Generation. They wouldn't go out with anyone who didn't smoke weed and buy into the prevailing culture of 'love and peace'. Therefore, if a Marine wanted any kind of female companionship in those days, he had to smoke weed and being products of that generation, they probably couldn't understand why the Corps made a big deal out of it.

We did have good reasons for our attitude towards pot usage and drugs despite the regular consumption of alcohol the Corps has been noted for beyond the issue of 'good order and discipline'. First it was illegal as per an Act of Congress and we had sworn an oath to uphold the law. Second, while booze creates problems, in a fire-fight the adrenaline takes over. Not so with pot where the abuser remains in a fog no matter what happens.

When Santa Ana raised the 'pucker factor' at the Alamo with his 'no quarter flag', the drunks inside might not have been in the best of shape, but they went down the 'hardway'. Had they all been high on weed, they more than likely would have wandered around the walls watching the phenomena, waiting to be rounded up and shot without putting up any resistance.

Considering the depths the Army had sunk due to drug use and the reported unwillingness of its officers to enforce minimal levels of order and discipline, the United States had reached the point where it lacked enough people with moral courage to defend it had the need arose. At least the Corps could field a force equal to the one shipped to the Pusan Perimeter, but the Navy and Air Force were also having major problems getting people to perform their duties.

Ergo, sans nuclear weapons, the United States was defenseless and the only way out was to turn to an all—volunteer military. This was the only way the country had to identify those who still believed in the values that led men to the Beaches at Normandy from those whose lives were based on making some other poor schlep do it.

Vietnam Combat Veterans Need Not Apply

I didn't stick around for what followed. After almost six years on active serve, 'one tour of duty', and 70 hour work weeks helping to put it all back together again, I'd had enough. Like roughly 40% of my fellow captains stationed at Quantico, Virginia at the time, I put in my letter effective 31 December 1973.

It was time for another life after spending quite a few years as a social pariah, being spit on and periodically barred from my nation's capital because I wore the uniform when some protest group came to town. This included 'the days of rage' and the one organized by the disheveled individualist in mufti and then navy LT John Kerry. This former though was the worst because they came to the Capital to shut down the government and given prior experience, they were a threat to life and limb of any serviceman that came their way.

Thus it was'nt paranoia by the military that resulted in standing orders precluding the wearing of uniforms except when duty demanded it while inside the confines of Washington DC. There was enough recurring proof buried inside the District's police blotters regarding military men murdered while in uniform merely because they'd worn that uniform.

One example I personally knew of occurred right after I'd checked into Qauntico after being commissioned in June 1968. Two lieutenants in dress whites and their dates in formals had stopped off at a hamburger shop in Georgetown on the way home after attending an official function. Apparently their attire had offended one of the locals so they were promptly gunned down on Wisconsin Avenue.

A worse shock was when I discovered how poorly former combat officers were regarded at the time. Besides being to told that we'd never worked before and made to answer questions about killing women and children by our stay at home peers, the whole idea that someone with my background had been through some of the best management training possible was an anathema to corporate America. (Chase Manhattan Bank amongst others in my case) I even had one WWII vet tell me in a job interview that those of us who'd served in Vietnam weren't worth shit and that the real leaders were the ones who'd fought in the 'Big War'!

We were also accused of being mannequins due to the politically correct view of military behavior. I also remember being told that private enterprise was based on the exercise of initiative and that being a former military officer, I was incapable of doing that. Besides all the preceding, this ignores the reason I chose the Marine Corps over the Navy when the choice was mine to make.

When I went on what's termed the 'Gator Navy' orientation the summer before my junior year at the Navy Amphibious Base, Little Creek, Virginia, we spent a day on an LST observing how it dropped its stern anchor before sailing up to the beach. This is necessary because it keeps the ship from being pushed by wind and current into a broach position on the shore. As we watched the senior chief petty officer direct the crew in running out the anchor cable, I watched the ensign in charge sleep on one of the locker boxes during the whole exercise.

It was clear in my mind that I didn't want to end up doing that as a result of a nothing job, nor did I want to become one in a mesh of officers without clear responsibilities and lines of authority. Because 2nd lieutenants in the Marine Corps command platoons of roughly 45 men each and later, following promotion, companies of over 150 men plus all the equipment that comes with them, taking the Marine Option would ensure that I'd be fully in charge of my own operation.

Ultimately that's the way it turned out. As a platoon commander I was given a mission and when it was accomplished, I reported back with the result—good, bad, or indifferent. As a company commander, with all the heavy construction equipment that belonged to the unit, I was running the equivalent of a multi-million dollar business and essentially had greater responsibilities than most of the corporate executives who interviewed me in 1974.

It also didn't matter. Because it was obvious that no one with a brain would serve in the military, Vietnam combat officers were considered the American equivalent of Germany's *SS* who naturally used coercion and threats to get subordinates to follow mindless orders. Leaving behind the rationale for a lot of traditional military practices, most of us looked for other ways to elicit subordinate cooperation.

From little tricks like initiating a salute first to make sure a junior always saluted their seniors, to going out of our way to foster initiative, the goal was to constantly groom subordinates for promotion and find ways to recognize those whose actions went beyond the norm. Even if that only meant buying the beer after a strenuous exercise exemplarity performed. One doesn't get people to do what they did for us at our behest without developing a positive environment to the extent the situation allowed.

Critical to this was 'leadership by example' and there were a number of times I recognized that my unit had too many chiefs and not enough indians; so the lieutenant picked up a shovel and went to work just like everyone else. Another rule was never to order someone to do something that we hadn't done or wouldn't do ourselves. This meant that our own personal performance set the standard subordinates were supposed to meet.

It's ironic that the Wharton School of Business now requires MBA candidates to go through the reaction course at Quantico. This was originally a German Army innovation used to test for a candidate's ability to step forward under induced stress and take charge without instruction. In the Quantico reaction course, the various problems were rigged to make them almost impossible to solve since the purpose was to identify developed leadership skills.

However when I left the Corps, this was long before the 'USMC management methods' of became best sellers so any representation I made to potential employers was moot at best. Thus all of us without specialized technical skills that could be converted into DOD contracts were blatantly discriminated against due to the prejudice de jure. Discrimination that today would produce substantial court settlements had our skins been darker than many of ours were.

I'd like to see any MBA do what we did day after day on little sleep with half strength units, getting the unwilling that often included ourselves to accomplish what we did. Even at peacetime Camp Pendleton I'd be out visiting my troops to show the 'flag' well after midnight as they were on various projects that needed to be done yesterday, just to hold it together.

Training candidates also came close to a 24/7 life that lasted from 0600 to well past 2200 once one considers all the counseling we had to do beyond being there for daily training. This was before one added up all the shin splints and knee cartilage that became liquefied. Somehow one would think that stepping down and managing civilian activities would be a cakewalk, but by definition we didn't know anything about effective leadership and management by many who've since proved that they probably wouldn't have survived the war because their troops would have shot them for self preservation.

Thus it became rapidly clear to me that I would have to 'invent' my own job or sell life insurance. This lead me to Dean Witter & Co back when there were still Witters around and for a minimum wage draw against commission, I started selling stocks and bonds for the next 20 years. For perverse enjoyment I started studying corporate proxies to see if one of us ever ended up on the boards of directors. Thirty years later I'm still looking and just like my father, if I wanted to eat I had to be 'inventive' and beat the bushes for business while hoping the IRS wouldn't clean me out after periodic successes that were interrupted by some financial dry spells.

I did once ask my ex IBM treasurer uncle for help in changing careers and his response was to use the 'GI Bill' and get an MBA—which I later did, but without government assistance. What my uncle and others of the Greatest Generation failed to understand was that the monetary amounts provided by the 'GI Bill' might have been more than adequate in their day, but hadn't changed in the ensuing thirty years.

Explaining to him that when I attempted to get my masters in economics at George Washington University while stationed at Quantico, it took the VA almost a year to process the papers and that I still had to make up a tuition shortfall out of my own pocket. Add to that the 'incompletes' resulting from the confinement to quarters while Kissinger resolved the Yom Kipper War short of a military conflict with the Soviets and then the need to make a living, completing graduate school was a nonstarter.

Because I'd already earned my BA, I wasn't as bad off as my troops. In their case it took the VA almost two years to get tuition money into their hands with room and board being out of the question. Consequently, many Vietnam Vets were never really given a chance to integrate back into society. Besides they were all 'druggies' anyway, or so the populous was led to believe. Hell, we weren't even eligible to join the VFW until 1981 so that my 23 year membership is just about as longstanding as possible.

Another source I turned to, not expecting much but it didn't hurt to ask, was the VA. The only advice they proffered was to simply leave references to Vietnam off my resume. Late in the 1970s, after getting extremely fed up with the general treatment I and other Vietnam Veterans were receiving, I called on Congressman Moorehead. After I explained the problem, he pointed out to me that he was a major in the National Guard. Next he asked me if we'd played Russian roulette in Vietnam like they did in the famous movie *'The Deer Hunter'*. I retorted by asking him how one could do that using a standard issue '.45 caliber' pistol with its magazine and walked out the door.

There's one final point before I get off the cross and let others have the wood. The day Saigon fell to the North Vietnamese I was on the phone with prospects all day as relief seemed to sweep the land. In the broker's 'bull-pen', many cheered and so did a number of the people I'd talked to on the phone. Apparently this was a good day for the United States as those who'd supported the war had finally learned their lesson. Later, when the Iranians grabbed our diplomats, these same people rose up to demand action and displayed yellow ribbons on their mailboxes.

This attitude was worse than the day Nixon resigned. That day I was still in the then six-month mandatory NYSE training program when one of my colleagues started worrying about a military coup. He wasn't the only one. In a book titled *The Anatomy of Fascism* by one of Columbia University's finest, he states on page 202 that he expected the American military to overthrow the government during the 'days of rage' riot by his fellow zealots in their disheveled uniforms. There could not be a greater insult to those of us who'd taken an oath to defend the Constitution of the United States of America because of the values emblematized by the 'Stars & Stripes'.

What he and the other peaceniks still do not seem to understand is that the greatest threat to the constitutional order at that time was themselves. True we had Nixon and 'Watergate' but the real problem was the prevailing violent unrest. The period from 1965 through the mid-1970 was punctuated by several race riots, the political riot surrounding the 1968 Democratic Convention in Chicago and recurring violence on the nation's college campuses including the 1970 protest at Kent State that led to the National Guard killing several students in self-defense.

I've already mentioned the underground movement's relatively successful efforts to obtain heavy infantry weapons, but they also were becoming knowledgeable in the use of explosives. These were used by groups like the 'Weatherman' to blow up research labs on college campuses and elsewhere. Then there were the shoot-outs between the police and coteries like the Symbionese Liberation Army that had abducted Patty Hearst and eventually shot it out with the Los Angeles Police Department after a siege in South Central LA.

From all appearances it looked like the country was coming apart with both the CIA, because of Soviet agents provocateurs and their seed capital planted to keep the unrest going, and the FBI charged with arresting the armed anarchists, active in domestic spying. As was the US Army for similar reasons. Throw in a few treasonous activities like releasing the names of all our CIA agents operating overseas and Daniel Ellsberg's theft of the *Pentagon Papers,* which when published by the press, did considerable harm to American foreign initiatives that were best left secret, and there were valid grounds for concern. All of this of course was ignored when it came time for the Democrats in Congress to pillory Nixon for doing what his two predecessors had done with impunity.

Finally we had the infamous Church Commission where liberal Senators Church, Kennedy, and their ilk emasculated the CIA and established the Chinese wall baring information sharing between the FBI and the CIA and the firing of many of the latter's covert operators. Thirty years later the United States would pay for this with 911.

Between War & Peace

There're better parts in the text to follow to discuss Ronald Reagan and our ultimate victory in the Cold War in the context of liberal fascism love affair with communism. The issues from the fall of Saigon and that of Baghdad that are important here pertain to the recovery of our military capabilities despite opposition from politically correct liberals. Before that recovery could begin though, things got worse.

Shortly after the fall of Saigon, President Ford directed the rescue of the SS Mayaguez crewmen from his desk in the oval office. It made strategic sense to rescue these men, after they were seized by Cambodia's newly installed Khmer Rouge regime, to establish a necessary point after we'd quit in Vietnam. Rampant piracy wasn't going to be tolerated!

However, when the raiding force coupled Marine Corps culture with that of the Air Force pilots who flew them to battle with the President of the United States playing platoon commander, casualties amongst the Marines who pulled off the rescue were inevitably going to approximate the number of crewman rescued. The same issue when arose again with the Corps providing the pilots during the aborted effort to rescue the diplomats from Tehran.

Here it seems that the problem was the Marine helicopter pilots flying aircraft they were unfamiliar with that messed it up. Besides that, this was a well-planned operation and to Jimmy Carter's credit, he succeeded in resisting the temptation to take charge. To the public though, it seemed that the aborted Tehran rescue was just another screw-up caused by the need for each of the four military services to participate and that our armed forces were grossly incompetent, which to many liberals confirmed their opinion formed during Vietnam. Military action by the US was pre-ordained to fail.

However the planning and his hands off relationship with the rescue operation doesn't get the Carter Administration off the hook. By the time he left office the logistic structure of our armed forces was a disaster with many of the Navy's ships lacking the repair parts needed to get underway and requiring the reallocation of whole crews to man those that could. Training and logistics in the other three services was hardly better so the belief that the US was still unable to defend itself unless it was willing to use the nuclear option retained its validity.

There was also a value issue involved. Though Carter was a Naval Academy graduate and had served in Admiral Rickover's nascent nuclear navy, his administration didn't share whatever inculcated values Jimmy still had. This was apparent when amnesty was granted to the draft dodgers who'd fled to Canada. They got the parades that should have been given the troops who'd toughed it out in Vietnam. Even more disgusting were the accolades showered upon them for moral courage by a 'grateful nation'. Lost in the shuffle and yellow ribbons was the fact that Vietnam Veterans were still society's pariahs despite the moral courage we'd exhibited and not given credit for.

The Reagan Salvation

Ronald Reagan, as we all know, reversed the flow despite strenuous objections from Democratic legislators every step of the way. First up were measures to restore the logistic base of America's military. Then came the build up to a 600 ship navy (actually 689). Finally 'good order, discipline, and professionalism' was restored to the ground forces led by my former associates who'd stuck around the Corps and army officers typified by Generals Schwartzkopf, Powell, and the others who've commanded our troops to victory in two wars with Iraq.

As part of his strategy to bring down the Soviet Union, Reagan, who probably understood the Soviet Union as well as anyone including Churchill, decided to confront communist small wars of aggression (liberation in politically correct vernacular) wherever they surfaced. Definitely if a conflict's locale was in the Western Hemisphere. This meant that we supported the government of El Salvador, despite the fact its adherence to democratic principles weren't up to American standards, by covert means involving the Army's special Forces to suppress communist guerillas willing to fight to the last Salvadorian.

Grenada was invaded in the midst of a communist coup that avoided the spectacle of American medical students, then attending school on the island, from being either murdered or 'prosecuted' for various 'crimes' in totalitarian show trials reminiscent of Cuba's early Castro days. Even though the medical students appeared to be ecstatic upon their return to the states and the Grenadines were pleased, liberal fascists popped their corks screaming that the invasion had been 'illegal' and unsanctioned by the UN. Apparently they believed that the nascent Bishop government reflected the popular will of the people and all that.

From the military perspective, Grenada demonstrated that the US still had a ways to go before recovering its ability to defend itself with ground forces. As a casual observer with some expertise in the subject, I was appalled that all four services needed to dial up 'Ma Bell' in the states in order to communicate with their operational counterparts in the other services. Even Marine commanders had to use Bell South phone exchanges in North Carolina to reach out and touch the Navy's task force commander once the landing force hit the beach. Terrific!

Nicaragua proved a little more difficult. In the late 1970s a proto-communist regime had overthrown Samoza, an unfortunate byproduct of USMC involvement in the country during the 1920s and a regime that richly deserved what it got. However the Sandinista replacement was accompanied by a bevy of 'security specialists' from such democratic models as East German, Bulgaria, and of course Castro's Cuba. The Carter Administration didn't seem to have a problem with this, but to many of the rest of us these outside advisors weren't there to supervise elections—unless it was 'one man, one vote, one time'.

Ergo, the Reagan Administration fostered a nascent resistance movement and for awhile was able to fund it with CIA money. That was until the guardians of liberty lead by one Congressman Bolen stepped in and through a series of 'amendments' buried inside annual appropriations bills, blocked the use of funds to support the 'Contras'. (By this time the Democrats in control of both houses had given up on appropriation bills for each Cabinet Department for fear that RR would veto them so they resorted to one massive bill per year)

This led to one creative Marine Lieutenant Colonel sitting in the basement of the Executive Office Building to dream up more creative ways to finance the Contra war effort that eventually resulted in the 'Iran Contra Scandal. A 'scandal' that had everything to do with overthrowing a proto-communist regime and little to do with the sale of obsolete 'HAWK' air defense missiles to Iran that could at best shoot down a duck, in exchange for Americans being held hostage by Islamic terrorists.

Eventually and much to Vermont Senator Patrick Leahy's, along with others on the Senate Intelligence Committee, unhappiness, the Contras won and Nicaragua has had several free elections more than it would have had the Sandistas stayed in power. Afterwards Leahy moved on to other Senate committees because his Democratic colleague, Sen. Inyoue of Hawaii, got tired of Leahy's office being the best friend any Soviet KGB agent with a camera had, when they could walk around taking pictures of any document that happened to be available.

Finally after George H.W. Bush had replaced the 'Gipper', the Army got it right in an operation even liberal fascists accepted. The 82nd Airborne, with help from the other services, was dropped on Panama City and quickly disarmed the regime while arresting Panama's President Noriega for drug dealing. Then came 'nation building' which in this case appears to have been successful since Panama has since stayed off the front pages with a reasonably freely elected government for the first time since we'd severed the country from Columbia.

The Gulf War

Now came time to deal with the 'numero uno' bad actor in the Middle East—Saddam Hussein. Much has been written about him being the product of our creation and the pundits saying so have a point. The problem is that their comments are usually made without the proper context. America's 'good buddy' originally came to power following internal squabbles within Iraq's ruling Baath Party, something that's hardly been original in the Islamic World. In the process he murdered most of his former cohorts and clamped down a totalitarian regime modeled after that of his idol 'ole Uncle Joe Stalin'.

Next he invaded Iran, succeeding in a modest blitzkrieg before the war settled into World War One type trench warfare that lasted roughly eight years with the thousands of casualties that usually go with the tactics dictated by such a war. To break the resulting strategic impasse, just like his German counterparts in 1915, he developed a chemical weapons capability and used them on his Iranian opponent to no avail—again like the World War One example. Later when the non-Arab Kurds in Iraq's north rebelled, he again used chemical weapons to suppress them.

How much of that the United States is responsible for is debatable. We did provide him with strategic intelligence gleaned from our satellites and funded the acquisition of some of his weaponry, although most of his army was equipped from Soviet sources—except for the Mirage fighters flown by his air force that were made in France. For understandable reasons, the entire world did buy Iraqi oil and that had to have helped considerably in funding his war. Additionally, for good reasons of their own, the Saudis and Arab Sheikdoms 'loaned' him a goodly sum that he doesn't seem to ever have paid back.

The primary reason for the collective support of what hadn't yet appeared to be the repulsive regime it became was Iran and long standing principles of power balance. The 'ayatollahs' had overthrown the Shah of Iran under Jimmy Carter and established their own brand of repressive regime. In the process they'd declared spiritual war on the United States and wouldn't have shed a tear if Persian Gulf oil reserves fell into their lap.

In fact, they were trying to help that process along by attacking any oil tanker departing a Gulf port, especially Kuwait, and had already had a few violent confrontations with the US Navy based out of Bahrain. For all practical purposes then, the United States had spent much of the 1980s conducting a 'quasi war' with Iran. Throw in a few hostage issues, terrorist attacks against passenger planes et al, plus direct support of Hezbulloh in its conflict with the Israelis and there were good reasons to help Saddam short of letting him win. The enemy of my enemy is my friend, a principle Churchill articulated quite well when he had to explain Britain's alliance with Stalin during World War Two.

Unfortunately for those who believe in maintaining the status quo, Saddam sent his tanks into Kuwait in August 1990 under the premise that the Kingdom had originally been part of Iraq and ruined everything. Historically he did have a point, but even the UN couldn't allow a 'hostile takeover' to remain in place that resulted from direct aggression and most of its members weren't going to suffer casualties when most only provided moral support.

Thus resolutions were passed by the Security Council that were promptly ignored by Saddam until finally 'HW' had assembled a multi-national force sufficient in size to eject the Iraqis from Kuwait. This drill took approximately six months and retroactively proved that the US could never have re-enforced NATO in time to stop a Soviet conquest with land forces.

The rest is history except for one major point. Most Americans know that almost a month of pounding from air attacks rendered Iraq impotent and the accuracy of our weaponry was unbelievable, even if later analysis pointed out a few flaws. The patriot missiles positioned to protect Israel even seemed to work, although subsequent sober analysis showed hardly any direct hits on Iraqi 'scuds'. However there is the old principle behind anti-aircraft defense that if enough trash filled the sky, an air attack would at least be impeded.

Finally the air campaign was called off and the troops sent in. In one hundred hours, the obvious end-around through the western desert and direct Marine Corps assault on Kuwait City had defeated what was left of Saddam's army. His vaunted Republican Guard, however, remained intact thank's to his timely surrender with terms. Total allied casualties had approached zilch, suggesting that we could actually fight a 'bloodless war'.

Residual Issues

So the great Saladin of Baghdad had lost the 'mother of all battles' at the expense of the regular Iraqi Army and considerable damage to Iraqi infrastructure—mostly roads and bridges. Fortunately civilian casualties were light due to the improved accuracy of American weapons and targeting methods. The air attacks on Baghdad were akin to the those on Hanoi and far removed from the massive bombing of Hitler's Reich where historians have since learned that Allied pilots were lucky when the found the right city, let alone any spot near their assigned targets.

This did not prevent the press from making major issues out of any near misses that might have killed a few innocent civilians. The press also tended to ignore that some of the 'collateral damage' Bush I's grand coalition caused resulted from Saddam's dual use bomb shelter's et al to house communication centers and other targets of strategic value. In the eyes of the world's politically correct, war's supposed to be a sanitized exercise—sort of like a video game, with America excoriated every time an accident occurred.

Even thought the Gulf War was as 'sanitized' as it could be, watching CNN throughout it led this viewer to wonder at times as to who the enemy really was. I also had my doubts whether reporters really cared enough to conduct cursory research into the subject with CNN's Wolf Blitzer repeatedly confusing companies with battalions and battalions with divisions. At least he could have prepared a simple idiot card showing 3 companies to a battalion, 3 battalions to a brigade, and 3 brigades to a division etc.

Outside of Basra, Saddam's generals surrendered and a truce was agreed to. This was not legally peace since that requires a treaty and one was never negotiated nor agreed to by any party. In return for the right to remain on his throne, Saddam agreed to financial reparations for the harm done to Kuwait, keep his army at home, and destroy any and all forbidden weapons subject to UN verification—a process his regime was supposed to fully cooperate with. Finally he accepted the imposition of sanctions until his government had met all the terms of the truce.

Technically the war hadn't ended as the American—UN Coalition, an ad hoc organization created solely to prosecute the war, retained the right to bounce his butt out of Iraq for noncompliance. Naturally noncompliance, almost from inception, was a given since all the essential components of his totalitarian state were still intact—ie: his second army—the Republican Guard, the secret police and intelligence service, and so on.

There were two reasons why the coalition agreed to let the Saladin of Baghdad off the hook. The first was the CIA's opinion that the Iraqis would depose him in retribution so we didn't need to march on Baghdad. This hypothesis was quickly blown out of the water when the Shia rose in rebellion and Saddam used his republican guard to put it down, exterminating thousands of Shiites in the process using the helicopters we'd agreed to let his forces fly for humanitarian purposes.

The second reason was the nature of the coalition itself. The Gulf War was a military operation based from Saudi Arabia and the other Gulf States to free one Arab country from occupation by another. The forces involved included full divisions from Syria and Egypt, plus units from most of the Sheikdoms, Kuwait, and Saudi Arabia. Then there was a division from France, a country that's been very sensitive to Arab feelings every since the Algerians used terrorism inside Metropolitan France to get their point across during the Algerian War for Independence.

With this force configuration, coupled with the fact that the entire logistic structure was sited in Islamic countries, turning American armored forces and the Marines loose to 'finish the job' would have created immense problems—particularly since the 'UN mandate' was limited to ejecting the Iraqis from Kuwait. Thus the long run strategic option had been left in Saddam's hands, not ours, since he had the option to end military operations any time he wanted to as he finally did to his benefit.

So ended a nice tidy little war, making the politically correct happy because the carnage they just knew would happen didn't and American Armed Forces hadn't impaled themselves in the process as everyone knew they would because of Vietnam. This was not the prevailing expectation prior to the start of the war.

The Iraqi army had spent eight years in combat with the Iranians so it should have developed the expertise that combat veterans acquire if they succeed in staying alive. Additionally, this was an army that had more than enough tanks and heavy artillery etc. to fight it out 'manno on manno' with the allies. As the first wave of Marines crossed the berm into Kuwait, this should have been enough to make them realize that a long day was ahead of them—still it was something that had to be done.

Not so in the minds of 41 Democrats who voted against initiating combat on the floor of the US Senate. In the process of obstructing approval of the war resolution they threw up arguments emphasizing a death toll in the thousands and reiterating that with just a little more diplomacy, possibly sanctions, Saddam would voluntarily withdraw from Kuwait. However since possession is nine-tenths of the law and he wasn't the one sitting in a tank outside of Kuwait City, he had no reason ever to leave.

All these 41 senators succeeding in doing was to point out that when aggression occurred, the US would simply bluster and then quit—nothing was worth fighting for, not even our most important strategic interests. If this isn't fear-based thinking, I don't know what is.

'Nation Building'

With the Iraqi departure from Kuwait, the phrase 'new world order' started being bandied about. Given that the Soviet Empire was no more and recognizing the multi-national flavor that went into Iraq's defeat, the collective American psyche evolving out of 'HW's' successful coalition building drifted towards accepting the idea that somehow peace could reign across the globe under the aegis of the United Nations.

Lost in this fantasy was the fact that the victory came from the exercise of American military power—just like it had in Korea or anywhere else 'combat grunt-work' had been needed to keep the peace. Without an American command structure in charge of the whole shebang, peacekeeping by the UN has had mixed results at best; eg: the continuing of the Arab—Israeli conflict and the rolling equivocation that allowed ethnic cleansing to continue for years inside the former Yugoslavia.

Another cold reality of UN peacekeeping efforts is that those third world nations who frequently provide the 'peacekeepers' are in it for the money. As a rule, Pakistanis, Nigerians, Malays et al don't appear in the world's trouble spots expecting to be shot. Their job has been to put in an appearance in hopes that their presence would dissuade the actual combatants from continuing the conflict. If this doesn't work, the peacekeepers step aside and let the conflict continue as per one of the most egregious examples—Rwanda.

The way the game works is that the UN pays for wages and upkeep of their troops while on duty observing other people's wars, which means that old Uncle Sugar pays the lion's share, thus enabling them to maintain military forces larger than needed for external security. Internal security is another matter as these oversized armies are very handy when it comes time to protect the president for life and keep the hometown kleptocracy in power.

It's upon troops such as these that the 'new world order' has been generally based. When the United States gets involved as an alleged equal, problems ensue as it did in Somalia. Never particularly stable to start with and planted on the coast of the 'Horn of Africa' where there's nothing of value that others are interested in, Somalia is the product of a marriage between former Italian and British colonies. For years it had been ruled by a proto-communist dictator (Barre) who'd brutally kept the various tribal factions in line without anyone caring.

Then he died, leaving a power vacuum in his wake. This quickly turned into a civil war and soon virtually all Somalis in the old Italian half of the country were starving to death. In stepped HW Bush to form a UN humanitarian relief effort designed to funnel food into the countryside, by-passing the myriad militia groupings that had created a series of internal blockades as part of their own intra-mural conflicts. Thus a 'hodge-podge of international forces, US Marines and various US Army units entered the country.

Although successful in their original mission and without great risk to themselves, once President Clinton turned the operation into a nation building exercise, the situation deteriorated. The multiple political factions at war with each other weren't interested in nation building and so the Army's Special Operations units were ordered to enforce national unity amongst the Somalis. The rest of the 'United Nations' just sat around and watched under a dysfunctional command structure that apparently left it up to each independent national entity to decide for themselves if they wanted to help out when the Americans got into trouble.

From the movie and book *Blackhawk Down* we all know they did get in trouble and it finally took the belated and begrudging effort by Pakistani and Malaysian armored vehicles to rescue the US Army Rangers. Of course the American media missed most of the story at the time, focusing on the bodies of the dead rangers and overlooking the 500 to 1,000 Somalis the Rangers had killed during the battle. They also failed to pick up in the presence of Osama bin Laden at the helm of the Somali resistance.

This enabled Arab radicals to portray Mogadishu as a great Islamic victory over the 'crusaders' while leaving individual Muslim heroes to find out the hard way that US ground forces had 'teeth'. Had the American media been a little more forthright in their coverage, it's quite possible that the number of Muslims willing to 'die for Allah would have gotten the message and turned down later chances for glory. Unfortunately the 'message' was that Americans cut and run when any of its troops get hurt, ie: when the going gets tough, the US packs it in.

Next came Yugoslavia, a country everyone familiar with the subject knew was going to be a time bomb once Marshal Tito finally died. Subsequent events proved everyone right as the ethno-religious components of the South Slavic Nation spun apart with those unfortunate enough to be living multi-ethnic communities right in the genocide line of fire. This didn't bother European NATO as Slavs massacred Slav on their front door step. The same was true when the Serbs turned to ethnically cleansing Kosovo of its predominately Albanian population.

It took Bill Clinton to jell everyone into taking action to stop 'ethnic cleansing' throughout the land of South Slavs in a mission that's still going on and tying up US troops needed elsewhere. My problem with this mission wasn't that Clinton acted to stop horrific behavior, particularly after UN Peacekeepers stood by and allowed that massacre of Bosnia's Muslim population that they were obligated to protect. It was that this should have been a European operation from the 'get go' and our NATO allies should have risen to the occasion at the beginning. It is hardly to their credit that it took the President of the United States to plant a 'size nine' to motivate them into action.

My second objection arose when the Clinton Administration declared that the use of ground forces was off-limits during the Kosovo Operation. This was going to be a war fought from the air until the Serbs gave up. Unfortunately it was an operation that excluded the use of forward air controllers etc on the ground with dumb bombs dropped from no lower than 5,000 feet. As any Marine trained in the use of close air support knows, the attacking planes need to get a lot lower to be effective—like about 500 feet. Consequently the air campaign resulted in a lot of missed targets and too many dead civilians before Serbia threw in the towel.

Now how much of this was GOC General Wesley Clark's fault has yet to be determined. It's too soon for definitive accounts of the campaign to be published. However, given the nature of the campaign and the alliance prosecuting it and the Clinton Administration's reluctance to accept casualties, it would seem that General Clark's primary role as the senior NATO commander was in eliciting the continued cooperation of the countries that participated; hardly a viable model for future wars.

Clinton's nation building exercise in Haiti turned out to be a carnival gone bad. Haiti's elected President Aristide had been replaced by a military junta, nothing unusual considering Haiti's history. Desirous of maintaining the rule of law throughout the Caribbean, Clinton talked the UN into sanctioning a inter-national effort to restore the former President Aristide and temporarily maintain a peacekeeping force there to keep him in power.

This wasn't what the junta had in mind so it threatened to oppose the Ameri-can military landing. As the troops were just about to land, average Americans saw pictures of the Navy's landing craft stopping short of shore to await resolu-tion of the impasse. Eventually the junta backed down, Aristide returned and var-ious international contingents, Americans included, began a crash project to disarm Haiti's citizens and train an effective police force. They then left and in 2004 President George W Bush had to repeat the drill with Aristide being the one forced into exile.

One would think that someone would have recognized that Haiti has been ungovernable by Haitians going back to when the really black slaves had risen up and slaughtered their lighter skinned slave owners (yes, under French law black descendents of whites could inherit property and become slaveholders. A reality that had totally shocked Andy Jackson when he arrived in New Orleans just before the battle that provided the late Johnny Horton with a number one song).

Thus government in Haiti has been an issue of race, blacks versus mulattos, and a vehicle to provide those in power with all the graft that its dysfunctional tax system could produce. Representative democracy and the rule of law has never been a Haitian reality and there is nothing on the horizon that suggests that this is going to change soon, not without a complete overhaul of Haitian society. That's why any Haitian with any gumption packs up and leaves for the United States and once here, they tend to do much better economically than native Afri-can—Americans.

The only time Haiti actually had a government that served the interests of the average Haitian was when the US Marine Corps ruled the country. In 1916, under the cover of the Monroe Doctrine and desiring that Haitians to pay their bills, Woodrow Wilson dispatched Brigadier General Russell and two regiments of Marines to take over the country. Accordingly, finance officers from the

Navy's supply corps took over Haiti's finances as General Russell concurrently became the US Ambassador and plenipotentiary.

Additional Marines were assigned to form the Garde d'Haiti, which they did by assigning every Marine one rank higher in the Garde than they held in the Corps. From there, individual Haitians were recruited to fill out the ranks. As the Haitians become competent at their tasks, they were promoted upwards to replace Marines at the next hierarchical level. By 1932 the Haitians had finally replaced all the Marines and FDR closed down the operation as part of his 'good neighbor policy'.

During the intervening years however, this arrangement ensured that taxes were collected as per the law and the funds disbursed where they were supposed to go, like paying teachers, the Garde, and other legitimate governmental functions. Roads were built and school teachers were actually made to show up for work. Those Haitians who resorted to 'banditry' to register their objections and augment their incomes were rounded up and jailed, or killed. For 16 years the average Haitian actually experienced law and order—something relative unheard of before or since.

If one wants to go nation building, this is not a bad model to follow, at least to some extent but it's not one the UN or American 'liberals' approve of. Unfortunately even the General Russell's of the world need to retire and after considerable pressure from Haiti's elites, who clearly missed the economic opportunities offered under normal conditions, the country was returned to their control and 'Papa Doc' emerged as the next president for life.

5

Oil, Terrorism & Iraq

It's All About Oil

In a way it is all about oil, but not in the sense meant when some ditzy Hollywood type makes that comment on a late night talk show to verify 'cool' to a knowing audience. Nor is it about oil the way e-mails from the '2004 Kerry Campaign' and politically correct hucksters would have one believe it. The core premise behind these pronouncements seems to be that the United States invaded Iraq to enrich George W. Bushes 'oil pals'. As Massachusetts Senator Ted Kennedy has put it, the War in Iraq was cooked up in Texas GOP cloakroom.

Splendid thinking and always good for a sound bit on the national networks and totally erroneous. Both President Bushs are 'Texas oilmen' and as such have a lot of friends amongst them and those who did business with them. George W. grew up in the heart of West Texas oil country—Midland, Texas; so naturally many of those he grew up with are also in the oil business.

The same can be said of me and retail stock brokerage or my dad in advertising trade magazine publishing. The demographics of where we were brought up and what our parents, later us, did for a living has a lot to do with whom we associate with. It's only natural that if one grows up in North Hollywood or Beverly Hills, the immediate surrounding world would be the movie industry—no big deal.

What eludes the erudite minds of the politically correct is the part of the oil industry the Bushs participated in, and to a certain extent Vice President Cheney during his tenure as the CEO of Haliburton, is categorized by Standard & Poors as 'exploration & production' or 'oil service' companies. These are companies whose activities are predominately limited to North America, exploring for oil and mostly natural gas. Once discovered or enhanced through developmental work in older fields, these are the companies that organize the physical infrastructure to get that domestic petroleum to market.

Today most of these companies work amongst America's extensively developed fields that the major oil companies have given up on. Or they'd 'wildcat' throughout the 'over-thrust belt' in the Rocky Mountains where potential new fields are too small to justify the interest of what used to be the 'Seven Sisters'; the large vertically integrated international oil companies who'd originally developed Middle Eastern fields.

These latter companies are the one's who benefit the most from any invasion of Iraq that would bring that country's potential four million barrels of daily production onto the world oil market. That's because, given that they're also refining and retailing companies, they're in a 'spread business' with profits derived from the difference between the retail price of refined product and production costs that include the amortization of exploration costs.

A significant portion of the profits internationals acquire is derived from their size and corporate ability to use that to maximize economies of scale. This is why they have little interest in 'bits and pieces' of small fields. They need the big hit that only the investment of billions of dollars into major discoveries can bring. Small old fields throughout the Gulf of Mexico northwards into the 'over-thrust' require too much administrative labor to be of use to them.

That's why there is room for the George Bushs of the petroleum belt who collectively have a large impact on American oil supplies but individually don't count for squat. Theirs is a world where trading well participations amongst themselves to minimize risk and gradually lowering their production costs is key to long term survival. It's also a world where one is definitely affected by the world price of oil, but also one that confines that impact to the value of North American oil and gas.

Not being vertically integrated and in a spread business, the oil world of the 'Bushies' wins when the world price goes up and clearly looses when it drops. They were the ones who saw everything they owned disappear in local Sheriff auctions during the 1980s. The last thing they need to see is a four million barrel increase in daily world crude oil production.

Another thing that politically correct intellectual heavyweights don't grasp is that crude oil is a commodity just like #2 yellow corn that's grown throughout the Middle West and traded in Chicago. Once crude oil is loaded into a tanker, no one can tell the difference between Saudi oil and Iranian oil except by reading the shipping invoice and bill of lading. In fact it's more fungible than #2 yellow corn as are the refined products derived from it. Thus, like #2 yellow corn on the Chicago Board of Trade, various futures markets have developed around the world over the last 20 years to trade the stuff with West Texas crude having its own contract with one distinguishing virtue—it is domestic.

Ergo, regime change in Iraq doesn't really benefit of George W. and his fellow 'exploration and producing' buddies. In fact it tends to hurt them because it brings more oil onto the world market which tends to lower prices, so any claim to the contrary either constitutes malicious slander or points outs some intellectual deficiencies amongst the politically correct.

The Saudi Perspective

For the Saudis, it's a different story. Oil is everything and their strategic position in the world depends upon the ability to function as the 'swing' producer' who has the ability to manipulate oil prices by adjusting production volume on the margin. However, this position is at risk for two reasons—first is the potential emergence of other 'Saudi Arabia's'. The second is the need to preserve the Royal Family's grip on power that is increasing at risk due to economic and social conditions within the Kingdom. These are interlocking problems and both have the potential to blow the House of Saud right off the gravy train.

Because oil is a fungible worldwide commodity and despite erudite analysis by the politically correct, it exists almost everywhere. The issue is only how to 'discover it' and bring it to market. During my early years as a stockbroker in the latter 1970s, there was a 'world oil shortage', one of the many recurring ones the world has seen since Drake punched the first hole in Western Pennsylvania, with forecasts suggesting that $60 oil was just around the corner. To take advantage of this looming largess, oil companies of varying types, including George W's, embarked on crash programs to discover as much as they could before the world ran out.

Then came a magic day when the now defunct Dome Petroleum Corporation announced a major-major find in Canada's McKenzie Delta. Although this oil has yet to really come to market due to environmental issues (its all marshland from the Yukon to Edmonton) and other problems, I started dancing around the 'bull pen' singing about how there was oil in the Beaufort Sea.

What I'd caught onto at the time was that just about every major river delta in the world had oil where it entered into the sea. I then turned to a map and starting counting river deltas and gave up because there were too many of them that hadn't been 'explored' yet. I also started selling oil stocks and by the boom's peak, they were all gone—sold to Merrill Lynch clients because their analysts were still 'true believers'.

Today the main issue isn't whether there's enough potential oil out there to last for a long time, its how to get it to market—particularly oil and gas from Siberia down through the former Islamic Republics of the Soviet Union. This is something the Saudis and everyone else in the world oil industry are well aware of. If these Central Asian fields can be successfully brought to market, Saudi Arabia's ability to maintain price equilibrium at levels that suit its needs are gone.

The good news for the Saudi's is that to accomplish this, massive pipelines need to be constructed throughout the region to bring the crude to either Mediterranean, Black Sea, or Persian Gulf ports for transshipment via oil tankers. No matter how the potential routes for this massive infrastructure are drawn up, they have to pass through regions containing large bodies of disgruntled Islamic Fundamentalists.

Bingo! This suits Saudi interests to a 'T' because it feeds right into Saudi strength—the legitimizing force of Wahhabism. Fundamental Islam with its terrorist derivative, if properly nurtured, can prevent this oil's arrival for a least a generation provided it doesn't destroy Saudi interests in the process. This is the challenge for the Saudis and the problem that has helped change the world for the rest of us. Fortunately the Bush Administration has figured some of this out. Unfortunately the politically correct and their choice for presidential heir apparent seem clueless.

The great risk, as Western Nations work to confine the problem and Saudi Arabia's royal Family tries to avoid ejection, is that it all blows up and the Royal Family has to get out of Dodge. Unfortunately this would leave the country's Wahhabi Ulama in charge of the world's largest oil reserves with possible armed conflict raging across the Central Steppes.

This is where it gets complicated and one needs the requisite historical perspective for understanding—a task quite beyond the scope of this book, which is why various references are provided at the end. Anything written by Princeton's Bernard Lewis would be a good start. Israel's former ambassador to the UN Dore Gold's book *Hatred's Kingdom: How Saudi Arabia Supports the New Global Terrorism* helped coalesce my own thoughts on the subject, although the topic goes back to 'what if' discussions I had with a few of my clients back in 1979.

Foundations of Islamic Terrorism

The core root of the whole linkage between Saudis, Islam, and today's terrorist threat really does go back to Mohammed. He was both the Prophet and the Head of State, juxtaposed to the western tradition where priest and king were separate. The latter is part 'Jewish Theology' preceding the 2nd Century BC and the rest blind luck resulting in how Christianity developed and was later incorporated into the Roman Empire.

Consequently the non Islamic world can understand and live with the 'separation of church' and state with a thriving secular society independent of 'God's Will', for a lack of a better analogy. Not so with Muslims. Because Mohammed was both 'priest AND king', state and church are forever the same in Islamic Societies. In fact, Islam is the submission to God as laid down in the rules contained in the Koran and a Muslim is merely one who does that.

The Nation of Islam is the collective body of all Muslims living together as a world body of brothers obeying the law God handed down through Mohammed as transcribed in the Koran. Thus there can't be a secular state independent of religious authority as we understand it. Any Muslim who thinks otherwise automatically becomes an infidel, subject to punishment by Sharia (Islamic Law) according to the extremists.

We in the West also need to understand that Muslims do not have a priesthood per se. Each Muslim's connection with God is direct—no priests and accompanying episcopal hierarchy acting as intermediaries. The role of clerics in Islamic society is that of teachers and interpreters of the Sharia, 'qualified' lay persons can lead prayers just as well as anyone.

Sharia itself is simply the 'rules and regulations' of life listed throughout the Koran and behavioral examples from Mohammed's life, which excludes the concept of an evolving common law and that created by secular legislation. The big problem is that Mohammed died and the resulting solution was for Islamic legal scholars to add to the body of Sharia what Mohammed would have done had he remained alive to deal with new situations as they came up.

This was both workable and acceptable since Muslims recognized that things changed dramatically from the days when Mohammed was alive and the Nation of Islam was limited to the Arabian Peninsula before the acquisition of the ethnically diverse Arabian Empire in the following centuries. However, by the 13th Century the Islamic World had stabilized to where the Sharia could be closed to modification based on assumptions about Mohammed's hypothetical behavior.

Ever since, Islamic legal scholars have argued over whether they'd done the right thing by closing off Sharia circa 1300. Another issue was whether or not 'true' Islam required Sharia to be cauterized as of the early 7th Century on the day Mohammed died. During the 18th Century one of the more fanatic proponents of the last position, Abdul al Wahhabi, generated a large following amongst the wandering tribes of Arabia that eventually were consolidated under the authority of the House of Saud.

Within this tribal state, Wahhabi provided moral legitimacy while the Saudis produced the necessary military protection. This is the relationship, reinforced by the House of Saud's conquest of the Hejaj from the Hashimite Kings the Brits had installed to rule Mecca, Medina, Jordan, and Iraq with Jordan's King Abdullah the sole survivor, that rules Saudi Arabia to this day. Ergo, the Royal Family stays in power at the sufferance of the Wahhabi clerics with the understanding that state police power can be used to limit the Ulama up to a point.

The ticking time bomb the world faces is that one of them will decide to eliminate the other and smart money is on the Wahhhabis. This is because most of the Royal Family, representing 1,000 or more members who share most of the oil wealth amongst themselves, are in fact Wahhabis. Since Saudi Arabian succession to the throne does not follow the rules of primogeniture typical of European monarchies, each member of the Royal Family is theoretically an heir to the throne, or at least until the Wahhabi Ulama collectively approves the family's choice—hardly a stable situation.

So how does the Royal Family seem to deal with the problem? Because they're Wahhabis to start with, they practice their faith and adhere to Sharia as the clerics believe it was during the time of Mohammed. Meaning anyone who's not a Wahhabi is either an infidel or apostate, both being capital offenses and the bar to the paradise promised by God in his 'talks' with Mohammed.

This creates additional contradictions, leading to many prominent Saudis being simultaneously both the friend and the enemy of the United States, amongst a long list of contradictory behavior throughout Saudi society that totally confuses westerners and fosters derogatory opinions of Arabs in general. Of course this little worm burrows both ways as many of Islam's leading terrorist have been educated in the west and go on to act on the revulsion they developed from first hand exposure to western ways.

The twin solution for the Saudis is to satisfy the Ulama by repressing any sign that the Kingdom is becoming westernized through the religious police, while using the army to secure the country's borders and the 'national guard' of Bedouins to protect the position of the Royal Family. Hopefully this continues to satisfy Wahhabi Clerics, so that when all three entities operate effectively together, the Royal Family can remain safe behind the walls of its palaces doing whatever they please in private.

In public they behave as good Muslims and do what they can as individuals and as a united block to foster the charity required of all Muslims by the Koran. This naturally includes advancing Koranic education as defined by the clerics throughout the Nation of Islam and financing Islamic causes, including aid for

Palestinian families whose sons have blown themselves up in the cause of an Islamic Palestine, that further the advance of Wahhabi extremism. It also means financing the Mujahadeen's war with Godless communism and the replacement of secular apostates in the Middle East and across the Eurasian plain.

On the other hand, if the Royal Family is forced to depart the Peninsula, there is all that get of town money stashed throughout American and European capital markets. This makes whatever happens to the Dow Jones Industrial Average extremely important to them. If one has to leave, given the expensive lifestyle they've grown accustomed to, a bull market in New York becomes the best friend an exiled House of Saud can ever have.

Thus Saudi leadership lives life on top of a very pointed pole and any mistake made in juggling events can easily impale them. Furthermore, it makes them very difficult for US policy makers to deal with since all have a vested interest in having American common stocks appreciate, but lack the same common interest in returning the world to the 7th Century.

Why Suicide Bombing?

Fifteen of the nineteen suicide bombers on board the planes that conducted the terrorist attack on 11 September 2001 were middle to upper middle class Saudi's. They weren't the Arab equivalent of 'trailer trash' coerced into the project, nor were their families bribed like adolescent Palestinians whose sole purpose in life consists of killing as many 'Jews' as possible. Why?

Picture having more than enough money to at least meet better than moderate needs and having nothing to do for the rest of one's life. Hobbies are out because they're frowned on by the mullahs. Inter-gender relations are forbidden because the sexes are totally segregated. On top of that, the education one received consisted solely of learning to 'read the Bible' and listening to its contents explained everyday, eight hours per day, for up to twelve consecutive years. If one's lucky enough to go to college, the only available courses are more lessons in theology.

In America, the expected response would be to say goodbye to religion and embark on a life of desolate behavior. Drugs and alcohol would probably show up, particularly if one's available finances were virtually unlimited. If one's a Saudi, these other options are ruled out and can result in capital punishment if one is caught by the religious police. Thus one must either find a way to fit into the family political structure, become a cleric—often a fanatical one, or 'become a missionary for Allah' as part of the 'Jihad', even better if one gets to be one of the four piloting one of the planes on '911'.

This is the Saudi reality because most Saudis don't work as we understand it. It's beneath their Bedouin dignity. Remember the Saudis are only a couple of generations at best away from the days when they were nomads and herders. In many respects life kind of took care of itself under harsh climatic conditions, ergo the attitude that 'Allah would provide' prevalent in Arab society.

The male role in this society was left to physically defending 'hearth and home' and attacking neighboring clans to seize whatever booty one could carry away. Women and slaves (purchased from East Africa through Zanzibar) took care of 'supporting logistics'. Free time under this regimen ended up being devoted to pleasant conversation over coffee and the study of the Koran under clerical supervision—ie: Wahhabis.

This is still the way it is today. 'Grunt labor' and housekeeping chores for those who can afford it are performed by imported labor—Bangladeshis and Filipinos. The more sophisticated work needed to maintain production levels in the oil fields has been turned over to trained western engineers, mostly Americans, few of whom are Muslims. This has to create a morale problem reminding Saudis that nothing works in their society that results from an individual Saudi's effort. Take away the foreigners and Saudi Society collapses.

The flip side is that such a collapse would punish those who've gone astray and open the door for 'Islamic Purification' by the Wahhabis. In fact this has become an emotional reality throughout the Nation of Islam as the woes of Muslim despair are being attributed to apostates and infidel influences with the United States representing the source of these evils—ergo, the Great Satan. This has to be a given because the failure of Islamic society to meet most of the needs of its members has to be blamed on someone because a macho fundamentalist society like Arabia cannot blame it on itself without starting to deny basic tenets of the Faith.

Another aspect of this can be seen in pictures of the protest parades of Muslim militants where they all carry rifles, fire them into the air, and trot around with that stupid chop-step. Instead of being real soldiers, this exhibitionism is mostly a parody of the real thing and designed to re-enforce self esteem when no other outlet for the development of a sense of personal self worth exists.

Thus there's nothing that the US can do to change this. Only the Arabs can! Even if not Wahhabist, Arab society as it's traditionally configured needs an enemy and we're it from a process of envy, or one corrupting Islamic values leading to the deterioration of the Nation of Islam.

The western mind would suggest that the Nation of Islam should make some drastic changes, which would be like expecting Nazi Germany or Imperial Japan to reform prior to the start of World War Two. Something it can't make without undermining core premises of fundamental Islam. Instead the answer that's been accepted by a large minority of Islam is to return to the Faith in its alleged pure form and attack the perceived creator of the problem.

Thus the emergence of Osama bin Ladin, Al Qaeda, '911' and a bad start to the 21st Century. If it wasn't going to be Osama himself, then just as easily it would have been one of his spiritual kindred and killing him tomorrow won't eliminate the terrorist threat as the politically correct would have us believe. Someone always percolates up and takes the leader's place with the threat remaining just as real.

Detour Through Palestine

Some of the politically correct now seem to be blaming the problem on American support for Israel, making Yaser Arafat hero de jure while relegating Premier Sharon to the vat of the fascist pantheon. To a certain extent they have a point, sans the role reversal assigned to Palestine's key players, and its true that for decades Arab leadership has used the American Israeli relationship to deflect Arab anger away from its proper target—the Arabs themselves.

It's pointless to go back to the root cause of the problem, as a few are inclined to do, because that's the day Jewish Zealots rose up against Emperor Nero, if not earlier. However the hatred of envy, as it relates to today's 'problem', does have roots in the massive influx of Europe's displaced Jews following World War Two. These are the people who hunkered down and built a modern commercial society that creates some of today's leading technology juxtaposed to the 'old Europe' that's fallen behind and the Arabs who've never really tried.

As Palestinians today look over the border into land they once owned, forgetting that in response to demands from Islamic clerics their parents had willingly given it up by leaving, they see a world of material success that by right should have been theirs. Of course they've overlooked the fact such success only comes from innovation and hard work that stems from Israeli determination to turn nothing into something.

It's just still in their face after decades of Palestinian deprivation and failure to make something of the West Bank and Gaza. Only now negative feelings are even worse as Jordan is beginning to emerge as a 'Mecca' for Arab capitalism with one or two Amman based companies now publicly traded on Western bourses. Then there's Lebanon, where after years of less than civil war, other Palestinians and Arabs have restored Beirut to its former role as a Mediterranean resort and banking center.

The real problem is that the original promise made to them by the secular Arab Nations and the Mullahs when Palestine was evacuated in 1947, remains unfulfilled. Not that surrounding 'Arab Nations' haven't tried to exterminate the 'Jews'. They've initiated four wars in that cause with the Israeli Army clobbering Arab manhood every time. As each war was quickly lost, more Palestinians piled into refugee camps that have become cities with substantial buildings and ever more Palestinians needing to have 'Allah provide'.

When 'Allah does provide', often in the form of millions in aid the United States has funneled through the UN to them, it fails to satisfy them or purchase their love for America as resentment still grows. This is to be expected because a society living on 'something for nothing' where only a minority works and more often than not, only because of employment opportunities in Israel and not in other Arab countries except for the bedpans of Saudi Arabia, leaves people devoid of self-esteem.

Additionally, for the average Palestinian, education is basically eight years in a Saudi financed madrasa and mind numbing recitation of the Koran. In a society that invented the 'zero' and the algebra upon which highly technical western capitalism is dependent, this is quite a fall and one that leads a large coterie of willing suicide bombings willing to die for a 'free trip to paradise'.

Again, since to look inward to identify the problem would be an affront to Arab manhood and requiring a revaluation of Islamic tenets dearly believed in, the logical answer is to outwardly express their resentment by killing all the Jews in Palestine. This is the nasty secret that some in the West and many Israelis know and most would just as soon avoid. However Ariel Sharon and other Israeli leaders do understand it and following a last effort to see if a responsible Palestinian state could be formed, they've given up and are now in the process of fencing in the vermin.

Equally likely is the fact that Yassar Arafat also understands this. Probably one of the reasons why he's twice turned down the offer of a Palestinian state and refused to take serious measures as head of the Palestinian Authority to reign in radical Islamic terrorists and test his standing by establishing the rule of law amongst his followers. The great fear for him is the likelihood that the trappings of his power are ephemeral so if he tried, he'd be quickly dead, as would anyone assisting him.

None of this particularly bothers the Saudis, who clearly benefit from deflecting radical Wahhabism from focussing on flaws in Saudi adherence to the 'core tenets of fundamental Islam' and 'freeing' their Palestinian brethren from infidel oppression represented by the Great Satan across the Atlantic. Because many in the Royal Family are likewise Wahhabis, this means that ample funding of madrasas and terrorism is available for Wahhabi allies inside the West Bank.

What's sad is that after years of supporting the right of Israel to exist, many of the politically correct in Europe and in the United States as evidenced by college protests on behalf of the 'Infantada' during the Bush II Administration, are beginning to plead the Palestinian cause. The apparent hope is that this might reduce the potential for further Islamic terrorist attacks.

If nothing else, blaming the 'Hitler Incarnate' currently in the White House for not being more sympathetic to Palestinians despite the fact that he's gone further than any other President than Arkansas Bill to push for a Palestinian state, alleviates them of any responsibility for actions that might inconvenience them.

Afghanistan

Then there is Afghanistan and the CIA's culpability for what it did under the Reagan Administration. Worse yet, the Bush I Administration simply walked away following the Soviet withdrawal and left a power vacuum for Osama. Again there is enough truth here to arguably support this claim, but it is a claim made out of context and one that ignores the situation at the time.

The *Washington Post's* Steve Coll does an able job of presenting in detail the Soviet—Afgani War in his book *Ghost Wars* and one should read it for a comprehensive understanding of how CIA involvement in the expulsion of the Soviets from Afghanistan laid the groundwork for what's followed. The short version starts with Soviet efforts during the late 1960s and 1970s to subvert the Afghans by converting them from traditional Islamic beliefs to divine believers in Marxist-Leninism as a buffer preventing the resurgence of Islamic belief in its Turkic Republics that might have undermined Soviet control.

They were fairly successful in doing this but the response of Afghans desirous of remaining true to their faith caused many to move towards more extreme versions of Islam. This left the middle road vacant. Thinking that this was beginning to create more problems than it solved, Yuri Andropov, then the head of the KGB and later *Time Magazine's* favorite Party Leader because he preferred Scotch to Vodka, helped convince the Politburo to invade Afghanistan and install a 'puppet' regime. So on Christmas 1979, the Red Army marched in and the US pulled out of the 1980 Moscow Olympics in protest.

More importantly, Afghanistan's Muslims rebelled and initiated a guerilla war that lasted until the Soviets finally left the country in 1989. In this effort they were materially helped by the CIA, Pakistan's ISI (Inter Services Intelligence),

Saudi Intelligence and money—all working at cross-purposes with mixed agendas at the behest of their respective national leadership, or least some of it anyway.

The CIA's goal initially was the more dead Soviet soldiers and destroyed equipment the better. Later when Bill Casey became CIA director, the objective was expanded to achieve victory and even harass the Soviets inside the borders of its Turkic Republics—each of whom had ethnic kindred inside Afghanistan. Of course the CIA's role had to be restricted to 'plausible deniability' due to the nature of the American Soviet relationship and potential for someone to push the MAD button.

Saudi objectives were a little more straightforward. First, the Soviet-Afghani War provided an opportunity to advance the cause of Wahhabism and confront the forces of evil represented by Godless Communism by financing Afghani resistance as long as the resistance forces were radical Muslims—no moderate secular types allowed. (Osama bin Ladden was initially one of the Saudi 'bag men', along with other assigned tasks) Secondly, they had a genuine strategic motive, one that also concerned the United States, of preventing the Soviets from extending the conquest to Baluchistan and the Indian Ocean. No one, including obviously Pakistan, was thrilled with that idea.

The Pakistani position was more complicated given its ethnic and political demographics that reached back into the 19th Century. Afghanistan's Pustans and Pakistan's Pathans are one and the same with the division between them the product of British defensive lines established under the Raj. The rest of today's Pakistanis reflect other ethnic and tribal mixes, which is why President Musharif looks like an Indian from Delhi. On top of this, Pakistan's upper classes are the products of Sandhurst and Oxford, juxtaposed to the average man on the streets of Karachi.

As luck would have it, when President Zia overthrew his predecessor, he entered into an alliance with radical Islamic Fundamentalists to retain power and to further this relationship he loaded the Pakistani intelligence services with those spiritually aligned with the Muslim Brotherhood. Basically the Egyptian variant of Wahhabism and eventual co-equal partner with bin Laden in Al Qaeda. Since the Afghan Mujahedin's training camps and all supplies, money, etc were predominately funneled through Pakistan's ISI, President Zia got to pick which of Afghanistan's myriad resistance groups got the goods and which were left to fend for themselves. Needless to say, the more moderate Muslims were excluded.

We now of course, know the final outcome. The Soviets withdrew in 1989 after suffering extensive casualties, along with the accumulated loss of material and the money that represented—something they couldn't afford. Then the whole edifice collapsed and with victory in hand, the United States dropped out of the picture under Bush I, which in retrospect was a mistake but one easily made under the belief that the Afghans were responsible for their own future and that the Cold War was over.

The Saudis and Pakistanis though, stayed involved as the various Afghan factions jockeyed for position using traditional means of assassination and tribal conflict to achieve power. The mutual goal was the establishment of an Islamic state, abeit the Saudis preferred a Wahhabist one and the Pakistanis favored their ethnic kindred—the Pashtun for strategic geographic reasons. However configured, Tajik, Uzebec, and various Shia factions were slated for exclusion, laying the seeds for continual conflict even after the Pakistani sponsored Taliban took over in 1994.

This ensured 'peace' throughout most of Afghanistan although that peace included oppression, murder, and nascent totalitarianism necessary to create a pure Islamic state ala the 7th Century. It also sent several million Afghans across the border into Pakistan, laying the base for more problems and risking Pakistani political stability, such as it is. From the American perspective, these were other people's problem and if it weren't for 911, we probably would have left it at that.

But, after a consolidation of the various 'Muslim Brotherhoods' under the blanket of Al Qaeda, Osama bin Ladden arose as its spiritual and organizational head with Afghanistan becoming the administrative and logistic home of Islamic terrorism under the protection of the Taliban. This wasn't a totally altruistic exercise since the ample financial assistance Osama continued to provide the Taliban required reciprocation and was of mutual benefit.

From this Afghani nexus, Al Qaeda proceeded to conduct sophisticated terrorist attacks against the Great Satan's interests around the world starting with the attack that almost destroyed New York's World Trade Center in 1993—ostensibly motivated by the continued presence of American troops inside Saudi Arabia. An attack that involved the help of Iraqi Intelligence in preparing the false passports used by the key perpetrators.

Although Americans felt that its forces were on the Peninsula to protect Saudi oil from Saddam Hussein in Wahhabi eyes we were 'desecrating Islam's Holy Sites'. In Osama's eyes, enforcing the 'no fly zones' that kept Iraqi Shia and Kurds alive and preventing an Iranian closure of the Persian Gulf to the benefit of the Sheikdoms wasn't a factor because Arabs didn't make war on other Arabs. Furthermore we were rubbing Arab noses in it by proving that its Bedouin Warriors were not up to the task, thus another affront to Arab manhood and shot to their self-esteem.

Of course the United States eventually retaliated to the stream of Al Qeada attacks by firing millions of dollars worth of cruise missiles into bin Ladden's training camps and destroying an 'aspirin factory' in the Sudan that Clinton believed to be manufacturing chemical weapons. The last didn't make the United States any friends in Khartoum, not that we had any to start with, nor improve relations amongst average Arabs, but it did make a point.

Blowing up Afghan desert, a few tents, and maybe a few junior Al Qaeda in an attempt to 'shoot a camel in the ass' was a futile exercise since everything we destroyed could easily be replaced and was. Thus Al Qeda remained virtually intact under the Clinton Administration that preferred to use a legalistic approach when dealing with terrorism rather than root it out tooth and nail. Accordingly the US worked with Interpol and used it judicial system to track down, arrest, and finally prosecute terrorists after the fact. This is why the Clinton Administration turned Sudan down when they offered to hand over Osama bin Ladin. They didn't have enough 'proof' to indite him at the time so they let just him go.

This was very much akin to punishing the family dog for a mistake on the living room floor. After hearing about the 'bad dog', the delinquent animal quickly goes into a penitent mode and the master assumes that the message was received. Al Qeda wasn't much different as Clinton's sporadic and ineffective responses with cruise missiles only served to remind Osama that America could bluster, but there weren't any real consequences in response to Al Qeda's behavior.

After 911 our response was a different story. In conjunction with the adroit deployment of special operations forces on the ground to coordinate the efforts of the non-Taliban opposition and provide forward air control, 911 led to the massive air campaign that quickly brought down the Taliban and freed the Afghanis. So much for the historic rule of thumb about Afghanistan being the death of any army attempting to conquer it. The United States had done it in the blink of an eye with unheard of technology and a small ground force commitment.

Next has come the work of restoring a viable government in Afghanistan that all Afghani factions can live with. Not an easy task when one has warlords like the Pastun Hekmayter, who has marched to his own drummer since 1970, ready to pounce no matter what the constitutional regime. Thus this is still a work in progress, but it looks like the effort will be successful although the historically fractured nature of Afghan society suggests that the outcome will not entirely be the perfect democratic republic the politically correct would like to see.

Already they're raising objections about conflicts with residual Taliban forces as if they expected that the fall of Kandahar would have ipso facto prevented it.

Further objections address the issue of continuing conflicts between factions and some of the country's warlords preventing the extension of national sovereignty into their regions of control. Ergo, George and his key subordinate are incompetent or worse. They're by definition stupid, a thought recently expressed by the real estate mogul Donald of Trump who's currently got enough problems keeping his casino empire out of bankruptcy, because the magic wand hasn't instantly turned Afghanistan into perfection.

Then there's the ultimate sin—bin Laddin is still alive despite the subsequent military effort between the US and the Pakistanis to run him and Al Qaeda down. The fact that over a third of his directorate is either in jail or dead is immaterial. In their simplistic minds, a dead Osama guarantees the instant end of terrorism and nothing else is relevant—like Osama's replacement is already in line to step up and continue the Jihad. All things considered, in the real world Afghanistan is now in the best shape its been in since the King was overthrown almost 40 years ago.

Axis of Evil

In his 2002 'State of the Union Address' after American forces had run the Taliban out of 'Deadwood', President Bush cited three nations as the 'axis of evil'—Iraq, Iran, and North Korea with an inference that Iraq might be next. All three posed significant but distinctly different threats to the United States and thus required different strategies to neutralize. The nuances involved with each didn't seem to register with politically correct chronic complainers who've continually complained that because North Korea has an existing nuclear arsenal, it was accordingly the greatest threat amongst the three; ergo, solve that problem first and then work down the list, leaving Iraq for last.

There's no question that the North Korean regime of Kim Jong Il is one the world can do without. Its economy is virtually non-existent and dependent up on outside aid to keep its people fed enough to avoid immediate death from starvation. North Korea also has one of the world's largest standing armies and there's ample evidence that Kim would starve all his people to death to keep those in its ranks alive long enough to keep him in power. Given the choice between food and the where-with-all to develop long range nuclear missiles, Kim definitely prefers the latter.

However, given North Korea's extensive bunker complexes built to protect what's important to Kim, a pre-emptive strike to take out North Korea's nuclear facilities using the weaponry employed in Afghanistan is not likely to do the job. Additionally, the North Koreans have enough heavy artillery spread along the

38th parallel to destroy Seoul, South Korea in retaliation. Finally the US would need 'boots on the ground' to finish the job. There's nothing in this equation suggesting that this should be the first choice—which might be why the politically correct placed it at the top of their priority list.

Plan B represents measures short of war such as diplomatic efforts to convince Kim that he should really be a nice guy and not build nuclear bombs to start with. Bribes involving greater economic assistance and offers to help North Korea develop a nuclear power industry for further industrialization were tried by the Clinton Administration in its 1994 deal where Kim promised to pretend not to continue developing nuclear weapons in return for American money, or reasonable facsimile.

Conversely, when the Bush Administration caught on to the shell game Kim had been playing under the noses of its predecessor, it blew the whistle and shifted to an alternative—collective pressure from China, Japan, Russia, South Korea, and of course us and the Brits. This is time consuming and a work in progress with Kim still in possession of his 'nucs', which is why President Bush is pushing ahead on the anti-ballistic missile defense program that so infuriates 'liberals'. Without it, San Jose, California and its 'Silicon Valley' technology cluster remains 'ground zero' and therefore a hostage to North Korean demands.

To keep the North Koreans from trading their only internationally viable product (the 'nucs') off the market, the United States and some of its allies have taken to intercepting vessels on the high seas and inspecting them for contraband from North Korea. Essentially this is a quasi blockade and there're reports that the UN has provided its blessing.

Massachusetts Senator John Kerry, now that he's running for the White House, has concocted a new plan, which he feels will produce results. If elected he plans on 'going to Pyong Yang for one-on-one talks' with the North Koreans. Translated, this means that he'd offer the Koreans much more money in return for what they promised to do in 1994. In the meantime he'd postpone deploying the anti-ballistic missile defense until it's totally perfected, leaving California's 'ground zero' wide open to destruction on Kim's whim as soon as his missiles gain the range.

Because this 'Munich approach' doesn't involve the risk of war for the present and provides the appearance of success if Kim agrees, the politically correct have signed on board and praised Kerry for his 'progressive thinking'. However the only way Kim's going to give up his nuclear weapons program that's designed to keep him in power for the rest of his life is if the latter suddenly looks shorter than planned, or he's dead sooner rather than later. Conversely, Libya's Colonel

Kaddafy, following Saddam's emergence from his hole, saw the light and has now agreed to terminate all aspects of Libya's NBC weapons program and subject his country to vigorous international verification.

This wouldn't have happened had not the Bush Administration figuratively pointed a gun at his head and made it very clear that it had no compunction about pulling the trigger. Of course Libya is right on the Mediterranean Coast, easily accessible by the United States Marine Corps and former President Reagan had already once attacked Kaddafy over terrorist activities; proving that not all presidents for life are slow turning on the switch.

Iran, although it shares some similarities with Iraq with its authoritarian theocratic rulers and demonstrated desire to harm all things American while developing nuclear weapons of its own, is potentially subject to successful 'moral suasion'. Remember this is Persia, not Saudi Arabia, and is a country where one can scratch a Muslim deep enough and find a Zorasteran—the grand father of all monotheist religions that still rooted in the country's many mystical Shia sects.

This creates a different dynamic from that of Wahhabi Jihadism, particularly in a country with a democratic-republican political process fighting for power through a constitutional process. Consequently there's a rational expectation that Iran can evolve a government based on the will of its people. But if its ayatollahs continue to be intransigent about Iran's efforts to become a nuclear power, then we might have no choice but to take out their facilities using air power. If we don't, then the Israelis probably will.

Iran is also right on Iraq's border so that any use of ground forces to support an internal revolt by Iran's democrats, or to take out 'state sponsored terrorism' and the nuclear program, can be done using Iraq as a staging base. Something that couldn't be accomplished with Saddam still in power, thus another reason for the 'Iraq first solution'.

6

Saladin al Saddam et Saladin al Chirac

Iraqi Interregnum

Returning now to the situation in Iraq following the Gulf War, where everyone was content except for a few loose ends, mainly those centered on stopping Saddam from killing thousands more in the process of stabilizing his regime. The solution that Bush I came to was the establishment of the 'no-fly zones' covering both the northern and southern thirds of Iraq to protect Kurds and Shiites alike. 'No-fly zone' enforcement, where US and British fighter jets would shoot down any Iraqi war plane caught within them, created its own problems.

This required the continued use of bases within Saudi Arabia because Air Force F-15s and F-16s lacked the range to effectively patrol the southern no fly-zone and operate from Diego Garcia or any other island in the Indian Ocean. Plus the US Navy was extremely reluctant to risk stationing one of its super-sized carriers inside the confines of the Persian Gulf for fear that this would create too easy a target for the Iranians. The northern no-fly zone was patrolled from Turkish bases and so didn't cause a problem provided that we guaranteed that Iraq's Kurds would remain south of the border.

To almost everyone's satisfaction this arrangement worked for over a decade, albeit a constant game of chicken was played with Iraqi air defenses with the need for occasional air strikes to sustain the message. It wasn't until the lead-up to the invasion of Iraq that the no-fly conflict heated up with almost daily Iraqi air defense radar 'lock-ons' to American planes with accelerated retaliation. In effect the United States conducted a quasi air war with Iraq for thirteen years to protect the lives of Kurds and Shiites.

It's the 'almost' that's created the problem that Americans have had to live with because the continued presence of American forces inside Saudi Arabia and at war with another Islamic country infuriated the Wahhabi clerics and of course,

Osama bin Laden with his ilk. Having the infidel's military, no less than those belonging to the Great Satan, parked on the sacred peninsula housing the Holy Cities represented desecration and another excuse to start a terrorist jihad. The United States, for the most part, remained blithely unaware of the 'consequences' of its presence in Saudi Arabia—they were still one of our oldest and staunchest allies however mixed the motives on both sides really were. The largest oil reserves in the world had its strategic value and both know it.

Occasionally Saddam attempted to play 'payback', as he did when he arranged an assassination attempt on the first President Bush after he'd left office. In response, President Clinton resorted to the cruise missile message, one that he again used in an attempt to elicit Saddam's cooperation and to destroy Saddam's chemical weapons in 1998. How successful that was, no one knows and even Bill Clinton has admitted that some, all, or none of the chemical weapons were destroyed in that attack.

The real problem that the world focused upon was the impact of the economic sanctions on Iraq's people. From the end of the Gulf War until Saddam kicked out the UN inspectors in 1998, he played 'catch me if you can' with them. In the process some weapons had been destroyed, many continually remained unaccounted for. Therefore Saddam remained out of compliance with the agreement that allowed him to stay in power and the sanctions designed to prevent the further development of his NBC capability remained in place.

As far as the world oil market was concerned, this was just as well since it kept Iraqi oil from entering the market in force and pulling the rug out from underneath recovering oil prices. This was the only vehicle available for Texas oil and gas producers to see their companies return to generating positive cash flow, while providing some incentive to continue drilling and to buy oil service equipment. As of 1996, America's oil belt had yet to really recover from its post oil boom depression so the sanctions the Clinton Administration fought to maintain were a plus for them.

The Iraqis though, were not happy since the sanctions initially blocked them from access to the international market for the necessities of life—like food and medical products. This led to countless stories of babies starving from malnutrition and other accumulated miseries for the Iraqi people that did not play well on the 'Arab Street' and amongst the politically correct. That Saddam used whatever international resources Iraq still had access to for building his palaces and rewarding his closest intimates didn't seem to be particularly troublesome and rarely made the front page of the daily newspapers; only the suffering did.

In response to the pressure these stories triggered, the UN eventually modified the sanctions and instituted an 'oil for food' program where, under UN supervision the Iraqis could sell oil and use the proceeds for life's essentials. To pay for the overhead the UN incurred administering the various trust funds involved and supervising the flow of goods, it received a 1% commission based on gross purchase and selling prices.

What a golden opportunity and one that apparently many took advantage of. To what extent has yet to be determined, but the *Wall Street Journal* and a few other publications have dug-up enough evidence to suggest that the largest provided by the 'oil for food program' was substantial and dispersed amongst many. Hopefully, how many and how much will be determined by both a Congressional investigation and the one set up by UN Secretary General Kofi Annan under the aegis of former Federal Reserve Board Chairman Paul Volker. Another one and the one most likely to get to the truth, is the one the Iraqi's themselves will conduct now that Saddam is gone.

This is an international political time bomb that many would just as soon avoid, including the ostriches amongst America's politically correct. The extent that corruption within the 'oil for food program' pulled in the French, Germans and Russians easily explains why they didn't want the US in Baghdad reviewing invoices. As American troops discovered as they went into Baghdad in April 2003, 'Made in France' was all over the place, including thousands of freshly made munitions and gallons upon gallons of Rhone Poulc (NYSE: RHP) manufactured insecticide.

Obviously the French were violating the sanctions all along and the bunkers underneath Saddam's palaces were the best German engineering could build as reported *by The History Channel*. Then there was all the money that French oil service concerns and the Russians were making off of various Saddam 'kick-back schemes'. Plus, everyone was aware of the contingent billions they would benefit from once the sanctions were lifted and they could enter the country to rebuild Iraqi oil fields and develop new ones without fear of Anglo-Saxon competition.

Thus, when George W. Bush walked into the UN General Assembly to argue for 'regime change', none of this triumvirate were pleased. In front of the world, he particularly told the French and Russians that the United States was going to blow up the money machine with or without their help.

No wonder they didn't line up to support us and it says much about America's politically correct that they can't figure it out as they rant about how Bush II's foreign policy has cost America the respect of the world. It's almost as they believe the US Marine Corps exists to sustain French corruption and life style.

One that requires everyone to take a seven week vacation during the summer no matter how many Frenchman end up dying of heat stroke, as they did in 2003 when temperatures exceeded 100 degrees for days on end.

WMD & the Al Qaeda Link

September 11, 2001 of course changed everything. Without it there would not have been a compelling reason to change the rules of the world order. When four Arabs fly jet passenger planes into office buildings in hopes of killing thousands in the name of Islamic Jihad and restore a perfect world for their version of an Aryan Nation that never existed, someone needs to pay attention to the wake-up call. However, it's understandable when people prefer to look fondly back on the days before such an event happened and wish there was a gentler and softer way of preventing a recurrence.

On the other hand, as the world found out after Prime Minister Chamberlain returned from Munich in 1938 with the pronouncement that he'd achieved 'peace in our time', the gentler, softer way can become a death sentence for civilization. This is what George W. Bush and Britain's Prime Minister Tony Blair instantly grasped. They were quick to perceive that the deep motivating force that had driven Nazi Germany and Imperial Japan to start World War Two in the name of a mystic past was equally true of Islamic Jihadism as preached by the likes of Osama bin Ladin.

Then there was the matter of coupling this with weapons of mass destruction, noting that the word 'mass' applies to the degree of destruction and not the quantity of weapons. This is a distinction that the 'ranters and ravers' amongst the country's politically correct adult children seem to miss. One would have thought that 'anthrax episode' following 911 where the virus, shipped via the postal service to Senate Minority Leader Tom Daschle's office and others while leaving a few dead in the process, would have made a more permanent impression. With pictures of both Houses of Congress and their staffers out on the street waiting for hazmat teams to finish their clean-up, one would assume that the imagination could make a connection with anthrax possibly appearing on a Hollywood movie set. But apparently not given the rhetoric from the 'looney left'.

Another problem is that even one person infected with smallpox, using an inoculation method prevalent prior to Jenner's discovery of 'cowpox inoculation', walking around let's say a Laker basketball game before a full house can eventually produce the death of thousands before the virus works its way through the matrix. A vial or two of Ricin, the deadliest poison in the world made from the common castor bean, which we've since found, properly dispensed throughout the food in a school cafeteria can eliminate a local school district's need for funding by sundown.

Liquid insecticide is another good one since in its gaseous form, its nerve gas. Just ask your veterinarian what he needs to do if your pet licks off the 'flea and tick' preventative. The answer will be to bring the pet in for a shot of atropine—the same shot that troops on the battlefield have nine seconds to inject following exposure to nerve gas. Following that they're dead after writhing in pain for up to half an hour; done deal.

Of course one doesn't have to use nerve gas, there's always that original World War One product—chlorine, as in swimming pools. It's not as deadly as nerve gas when used in gaseous form, but anyone who's read about its first use inside the Ypres Salient in 1915 knows that exposure for those unprepared at least precludes one from being the 'picture of health' ever again because how its caustic properties work on the lungs.

Then there is the nuclear terrorist option, best employed after stealing a small bomb that can be thrown in the back of a pickup truck and set off with a cell phone (one reason we were afraid of homegrown WASP terrorists in the 1970s). Failing that, one can make one since the methodology can be found in any library. In fact, one doesn't even need to create a nuclear reaction to make a radiation mess because radioactive material imbedded with conventional explosives can apparently render half of New York uninhabitable if the device is powerful enough.

The trick is in making these splendid things in weaponized form. That requires relatively advanced laboratories and trained physical chemists and a biologist or two. The bad news is that the US and its western allies don't have a monopoly on available talent. Under the Soviet Regime hundreds were trained to specifically develop NBC weapons, especially the biological and chemical ones, with a vast number of these folks having been unemployed since the fall of the Soviet Union. More WMD weaponization specialists live in the Middle East after their education was paid for by the regions less than democratic regimes; eg: Saddam's Iraq.

Even Al Qaeda has the qualified talent. From intelligence found throughout Afghanistan's cave system and from prisoner interrogation, we have found ample evidence that Osama and his boys would like to have these weapons. From their perspective, they don't need 55-gallon drums of each, just a few vials and suicide attackers willing to undergo the pain that a successful attack would entail. The good news is that despite how easy it sounds to produce them, weaponization of the BC part of NBC is still very difficult.

Thus Al Qaeda's need for Saddam Hussein. Cooking chemical solids in a cave or an apartment in Spanish Harlem without killing oneself can be rather dicey so its best to use some form of laboratory facility, which Saddam's regime clearly had; even though the mobile labs the US thought were chemical/biological warfare facilities turned out to be for other purposes. Additionally it requires some skill to extract chorine from various salts and then 'boil it' into gas without it chemically combining itself with another element. Then one has to weaponize it by combining the chlorine gas with a dispersement device.

Although everyone figured this out during World War One, the Germans with the world's then most advance chemical processing plants were first on the block because they had the industrial facilities in place to do it. So did Saddam's Iraq with its modest but productive dual-use petro-chemical industry and scientific talent as evidenced by the gassing of Iranians during that war and subsequent gassing of the Kurds.

Thus to be successful in weaponizing hazardous chemicals, it clearly helps if one has access to the necessary industrial infrastructure. In fact having the infrastructure means one doesn't have to have the weapons stockpiled ready to use because it has never taken any country long to 'cook up' enough to meet the need. World War One proved that to be true.

Because post war searches have yet to find Saddam's alleged stock of chemical weapons, his long run strategic plan might have been to retain the infrastructure within a 'dual use' industrial organization and then manufacture all he desired without scrutiny once the sanctions were lifted. He had all the raw materials. The same can be said of the biological weapons every one believed he had, particularly since less than perfect control of existing stocks within the former Soviet Union implies that at least a base stock can be readily purchased.

From Saddam's viewpoint, Al Qaeda had its virtues despite the surface dichotomy between his secular Islamic life and the core Wahhabi goals of Osama bin Laden. The one key point the politically correct inside the United States forget while trying to be cool is that 'the enemy of my enemy is my friend'. Given that the Great Satan in the West was the bitter enemy of both, it made sense for the two to cooperate when the cause of each could be advanced; albeit this was not true of 911.

This meant that in all likelihood at least biological or chemical weapons transportable in small vials would be available to Al Qaeda through the Iraqi Intelligence Service. Along with the necessary training needed to 'cook up' a batch of chemical weapons when the amount Al Qaeda planned to use was to great for clandestine shipment. This was the way the Soviets operated when they discreetly transferred poisons to Bulgarian intelligence to kill dissidents from Eastern Europe and set up the assassination attempt on the Pope.

Additionally there is evidence that Saddam provided terrorists with hospital services, particularly for senior Al Qaeda management including Mr. Zarqawa whose leading their forces in the current Iraqi Insurgency, plus various mock-ups for training purposes that included a large passenger plane found by the Marines during their march to Baghdad. Added to this were a few modest training camps as per the one for Ansar al Islam on the Iranian border and home to several hundred rabid terrorists from all over the world that the Army's Special Forces cleaned out during the invasion.

Besides the Czech Intelligence Service's report of a meeting between an Iraqi agent and one of the key 911 players that's yet to be refuted, there is ample evidence of linkages between Al Qaeda and Saddam's intelligence services. These included the warnings that Russia's President Putin provided President Bush based on intelligence information captured in Chechnya. Even the Co-Chairs of the 911 Commission affirmed the existence of connections between the two despite the mass media's effort to structure their reportage to 'prove' otherwise.

Contained in the trial transcripts of the terrorists convicted of perpetrating the first World Trade Center bombing in 1993 were clear references to doctored passports prepared by Iraqi intelligence. Additionally there's the wrongful death suit filed in New York by attorneys for the estate of John O'Neill against Saddam, et al, because of an alleged connection between Iraq and Al Qaeda that led to his death in the World Trade Center on 911. Apparently because O'Neill had recently retired as head of FBI counter intelligence, the estate's attorneys feel they have enough evidence that they're not wasting time and money in pursuing the matter according to the rules of civil procedure.

However the Bush Administrative has never said that there was a connection between Saddam and Al Qaeda and the 911 attack. That's just something the politically correct have made up so they can turn around and make fun of us 'hillbilly' Bush supporters. President Bush did apparently direct the CIA and others to find out if there was a Saddam—Al Qaeda link with 911, for which he has been greatly pilloried by those who can't grasp that it would have been irresponsible not to have checked out a possible connection.

Finally there's been much ado about the report from Britain's MI-6 regarding Niger's sale of uranium 'yellow cake' to Iraq leading up to the invasion. The Brits still stand by this report, two years later. Additionally, reports are now emerging that Niger had been approached several times in the past several years about the possibility of purchasing of uranium 'yellow cake' from them by five potential terror sponsoring states including Saddam's Iraq.

The fact that the documents confirming the reported sale of uranium 'yellow cake' from Niger to Saddam turned out to have been 'fabricated' does not make the issue moot. The Marines found tons of the stuff just south of Baghdad in 55 gallon drums with the cache shown to the world by the various imbedded reporters on the cable news channels. The big fear at the time, since many of the drums had been broken open and stolen with their contents dumped on the ground, was how many Iraqis were going to die from radiation poisoning.

Left out of the commentary was the ultimate question. What is a country with all the petroleum reserves that Iraq has doing with all that uranium? This is a country that doesn't have a nuclear power plant. Nor does it have a need for one and processed radiation materials for medical purposes can easily and legally be purchased, leaving a future desire to have a bomb as the only logical reason for the uranium's presence. Thus, under the 'if it looks like a duck' theory, Saddam had provided ample evidence of his intentions.

Turning to the UN

So when President Bush went to the UN he had a case. The inspection regime that often was an exercise in 'rope a dope' had summarily ended when Saddam kicked the inspectors in 1998. Something Clinton's subsequent cruise missile attack failed to overturn. The weapon stocks that Saddam had in place that the UN knew of as of the end of the Gulf had never been accounted for—especially the liters of anthrax.

According to UN calculations, Saddam had so much of the stuff at the end of the Gulf War and they could only account for the destruction of part of it. This left a lot unaccounted for and the inspectors had to assume that Iraq still had it stashed somewhere. There was also a question of whether the missiles he'd had that exceeded the authorized range had been completely destroyed, a few of which the inspectors later found and later a few more were found by the US.

Therefore every intelligence agency in the world believed that Saddam's Iraq was still armed with weapons of mass destruction to some extent. That was never in dispute and we even had input from Saddam's son-in-law during his brief mid 1990s defection attesting to Iraq's ongoing weapons program. Nor was the idea that he was eventually going to have a nuclear bomb as witnessed by the discovery of the 'yellow cake' south of Baghdad. Besides, by 2002 Pakistan, India, and by its own admission North Korea, had joined the 'nuclear club' with Iran not far behind. Ergo, in the case of Iraq, the question was more one of when rather than if.

This left only one real question for the UN to decide and President Bush made it perfectly clear that if the UN didn't act, the United States and a 'coalition of the willing' would. So another resolution (number 14 of a sequence) was passed calling on Saddam to disarm, only this time the phrase 'or face serious consequences' was added. In response Saddam re-admitted UN inspectors and continued to play 'rope a dope'. The documentation 'verifying weapons disposal' he submitted was merely xerox copies of the last he'd submitted in 1998 and the game showed every likelihood of going on forever.

That prospect didn't stop the politically correct from demanding more time to let the inspections work. Their point was that a couple of months didn't matter one way or the other, so that inspections should involve going 'above and beyond' in the vain hope they might work. As all knew, this was at best wishful thinking and totally ignored the situational reality.

For months the United States and Britain had been building up force levels inside Kuwait that concurrently involved the extensive training of the troops who were slated to conduct the invasion. After a point, everyone starts getting over trained and the edge is lost. Once everyone has reached the point of optimal preparedness, an operation either has to be executed or canceled. A football team cannot be left in the locker room in full gear overnight to play a game that's suddenly postponed for a day or two.

There was also the issue of weather. No one has succeeded in finding a war to fight with an ideal climate. Every war produces a battlefield where one is either hot and miserable or cold and miserable. Often perpetually 'wet' enters the equation. That's how I felt in Vietnam as I lost over 20% of my body weight in a few months due to climatic conditions.

Yet residence geniuses like California's Senator Feinstein et al, wanted to wait until summer temperatures in Iraq would make it so hot that heat stroke would become a greater enemy than the Republican Guards. My gut feeling at the time was that someone needed to lock her and her California colleagues, Barbara Boxer and House Minority Leader Nancy Pelosi, up in old Chevy and park it in the middle of the Mohave Desert for a day without access to water or air-conditioning. Maybe then they'd catch on as to why the attack had to be launched when it finally was.

In the meantime President Bush and Britain's Prime Minister Tony Blair continued the military build-up to the war that would be staged out of Kuwait—something Saddam could have pre-empted or at least interfered with had he wanted to. The debate continued about what to do as the inspectors found a few missiles that exceeded legal limits until the 'coalition of the willing' forced the issue. For the UN, President Bush had called on it to exercise some moral courage and institutionally it found ways to rationalize expediency instead—just like it had in Yugoslavia.

Both Britain's Parliament and Congress, after much wringing of hands of course over the potential death of troops on the battlefield, passed authorizations enabling both leaders to conduct military operations leading to regime change in Iraq. Some US Senators did declare after the invasion started, now presidential wannabe John Kerry for one, that they never really expected that their votes would lead to war. They just 'wanted to strengthen the President's hand' in dealing with Saddam in hopes that he'd give up if given more time in the face of 'creditable force'.

The problem was that, despite the build-up in Kuwait, our force was not creditable given the prevailing world-wide rhetoric. Mere threats of course weren't going to going to convert Saddam into a global angel, not even when President Bush gave him 48 hours to leave town or else, and the else was parked on his border. He had no reason to budge because his good friend French President Jaques Chirac had told him that the French and Russians would veto any UN resolution authorizing his forcible removal in order to protect the profits from their own investment in his regime.

The second and possibly more critical reason Saddam wasn't going to bow down in the face of a military threat, no matter how creditable, was that cooperation under duress would undermine his position as the 21st Century Saladin defending the gates of Islam against the Great Satan. His spiritual role in the Nation of Islam, or least as he apparently saw it, was to defend the Faith's lands against exploitation by Washington's Plantagenets de jure. Acquiescence would destroy that image and the moral force provided by his role as the modern equivalent of the Great Kurd to sustain his regimes strategic position would crumble.

Thus Saddam neither cooperated nor left and as advertised, the tanks rolled in to start the illegal war of regime change, or at least that's the way the politically correct saw it. Soon the Halls of Congress echoed with the screams of Senator Ted Kennedy and others about how the United States had never in its history engaged in regime change. Apparently his aids forgot to tell ole Ted about that obscure song that begins with 'From the Halls of Montezuma to the shores of Tripoli'.

The history of the USMC is all about regime change starting with Lt O'Bannon and Ambassador Eaton's epic march to remove the then ruler of Derna during Jefferson's anti-terrorist war against Tripoli and the maritime pirates of North Africa. An effort that required his successor to send the US Navy back to reiterate the message with 'shock and awe'. After the fall of Mexico City to General Scott, Santa Ana was replaced as president for life by his people and at one time or another, the Marine Corps engineered the replacement of numerous Central American and Caribbean regimes during the early 20th Century.

The ultimate regime change at the point of American bayonets of course, was the defeat of Adolf Hitler in World War Two and downfall of Japan's militarist government following Nagasaki. So where was ole Ted and his compatriots when it came time to take history in school, or maybe their repeated propaganda was designed to take advantage of the average American's ignorance. If something is repeated loudly and often, those who simply respond to the noise eventually come to believe it as both Lenin and Hitler well knew.

Equally overlooked as American 'peaceniks' traveled to Iraq to provide human shields protecting innocent civilians from becoming collateral damage, was the extent Saddam's regime murdered its citizens. Following the fall of Baghdad we found countless mass graves where thousands had been exterminated. All told the estimate is that roughly 1 million Iraqis died at the hands of Saddam's regime.

With this background, a few more dead Iraqi civilians incidental to eliminating the regime and ending the carnage hardly mattered. Many Iraqi's, as per reports on the cable news channels, had reached the point where they were so demoralized that any military effort on our part offering hope was worth the price. In this context, one must understand that the concerns of the politically correct over potential civilian casualties has a hollow ring to it since none of this ilk ever complained about the Pot Pol's genocide in Cambodia beyond the expediency of blaming Nixon

From other quarters came the 'trash talk' about the invasion's legality because the UN failed to explicitly authorize it, conveniently forgetting that France militarily interferes in West African countries with regularity without any thought of the UN, nor that the UN never gave its blessing to military operations in Bosnia. This position presupposes that the UN is a legal sovereign rather than a cooperative debating society with various tasks assigned to it by mutual agreement. The UN has no legal authority under any country's constitution to do anything. In the case of the United States, sovereignty and legality is solely what the US Constitution say its is, no supra-international authority is recognized in that document.

That requires individual national approval by each nation with some specifically choosing to honor the organization's requests and others opting not to.

Every 'UN military action', starting with the Korean precedent, involving the US has seen America act unilaterally with the UN eventually coming on board after the fact—not the other way around.

So the UN's approval was throughout an academic exercise for internal political reasons aimed at American and British political correctness. Both George W. Bush and Tony Blair had to 'prove' that they'd gone the extra mile to gain international approval to do what both felt was imperative in the national interests of their respective countries.

They clearly believed that Saddam and his contingent ability to arm terrorists of whatever ilk with bio-chemical weapons, along with a host of other reasons of which 'payback' was not one, had to be eliminated. Letting him use them himself in his own free-lance terror operations that had a history going back to the early 1990s, if not earlier, was equally repugnant. The problem for the rest of the United Nations was that both men exhibited the moral courage to act according to their beliefs—a very politically incorrect thing to do.

Finally there is the murky confusion over 'international law'. There is no such thing per se. The whole idea that there must be a rule of law between individual sovereign nations is a theoretical construct going back to Grotius in the 17th Century. Since his death countless of mutually beneficial rules of international conduct have been agreed to between nations for pragmatic reasons.

International 'rules' that have stood the test of time have done so because adherence is mutually beneficial, not because there is some amorphous enforcement body out in 'never-never land' supplanting individual national constitutions that define national jurisprudence. Ergo, the vociferous complaints by the politically correct that such an international body does exist and that if afforded the opportunity, it would rule the invasion of Iraq 'illegal', totally lacks a factual foundation.

However, if the politically correct continually re-iterate the falsehood and enough fuzzy thinkers buy into the rhetoric, then maybe a custom would be established that eventually over-rides national sovereignty. Hopefully that doesn't happen, but given the hue and cry emanating from today's Democratic Party, it's quite possible that a euphemistic version of 'international authority' emerges in its party platform. Given recent demands by some of country's more visible politically correct that the US agree to the provisions of the 'World Court' and turn some of our judicial sovereignty over to the likes of Belgium without amending the Constitution, this is quite possible.

The War in Iraq

This has actually become two wars—the actual invasion, followed by the inevitable insurgency after the successful invasion. Thus the fact that an insurgency followed our victory shouldn't have been a surprise to anyone, but it looks like it was to the Democrats who opposed the war to start with; or at least they've used that for political advantage. The question for them is what do they think General Scott's army was doing in Mexico City after they'd won, or better yet, why was General Lucius Clay still in Germany for a couple of years following VE Day handing out 'purple hearts'. Is it possible that not all Germans had accepted the reality of VE day?

Anyway, forces from the 'coalition of the willing' crossed the frontier and embarked on a blitzkrieg campaign that produced the fall of Baghdad inside of a month. With the number of sources available describing the actual campaign and the film we all saw in real time from the 'embedded' reporters, there's no point in rehashing the details beyond making a few points.—the first being that this campaign has to rank right up there with McArthur at Inchon and Scott's march on Mexico City in American history.

This doesn't mean that everything went smoothly or that there wasn't opposition—far from it. It means that the use of maneuver, coupled with the air support that's become the hallmark of American military operations, thoroughly confused the Iraqi high command so that the opposition never could organize an effective defense.

This point seemed lost on some of the retired Generals who were in command during the Gulf War. They had rightfully depended on massive bombardment and a substantial logistic tail to win. Despite the second invasion's different circumstances however, they complained about the invasion's perceived flaws and that it didn't replicate their 1991 strategy, noting that these 'flaw' were therefore destined to bog down the operation to the Iraqi's benefit.

Far from it, the invasion had to be a blitzkrieg in order to succeed because of the potential Iraqi use of bio-chemical weapons everyone believed Saddam had to use to save his skin. This is why allied forces went into battle wearing extremely uncomfortable hazmat suits and gas masks. Unlike the Gulf War, everyone in the field expected to be gassed somewhere on the road to Baghdad and consequently were prepared for it.

Even the Iraqis expected that they'd use gas as evidenced by all the Soviet era gas protection equipment and vials of atropine that American forces found littering the battlefield and stored in volume amongst Iraqi weapon stores. The question for Iraqi forces then, was not one of if, but who'd been assigned to carry out the gas attacks. Apparently and thankfully those missions had been given to the unit 'next door' to the extent that apparently no one ended up with the assignment.

Still allied forces had to assume that bio-chemical weapons would appear on the battlefield and even though wearing protective gear 24/7 would keep most everyone alive when that eventuality happened, the best defense was to preclude its use. This meant a war of movement so that fixed positions conducive to the tactical use of gas couldn't form. If no one stands still long enough to be gassed, then the attack cannot succeed, especially when the perpetrator's forces are also in a state of flux. The latter particularly makes a gas attack just as dangerous to the user as it would be to the target force.

Ergo, the goal was to get to Baghdad as fast as possible so that an effective gas attack couldn't be set up by the Iraqis and the regime brought down before the chain of command could order one. The fact that subsequent events have established that the gas attack contingency was moot is beside the point, albeit we have found isolated sarin shells. Since the Iraqi's had previously used chemical weapons in combat against the Kurds and the Iranians, they obviously had no compunction about using them against the infidel.

The one problem with a blitzkrieg campaign is that it tends to leave lines of communication vulnerable. This worried Hitler and his generals during World War Two and it clearly worried the talking heads on television. The harangue about not having enough troops was constant, overlooking the fact that Kuwait lacks the room for a massive staging of the 'recommended force structure' with the Army's historically large logistic presence every time it has shown up the battlefield.

This was definitely one of the problems that we'd inflicted upon ourselves in Vietnam as LBJ's defense department tried to make the war as 'comfortable as possible'. The result of that decision was the vastly enlarged base camps that had to be defended at the expense of putting troops in the field to run down the Viet Cong. Unlike the Marine Corps where every man is a rifleman first, the Army has to make sure those in the rear are adequately defended, thereby tying up infantry that should have been taking the fight to the enemy.

By going 'light', the Army avoided this problem and reduced its logistic tail, albeit by USMC standards it was still substantial. It also meant that the extensive convoys still needed to re-supply the 3rd Infantry Division leading the way were vulnerable to guerilla attack based out of the cities bypassed en-route. However as space cleared out to the rear as the attack advanced, the Army slipped in the 101st

Airborne and a brigade of the 82nd Airborne to secure communications lines and the problem was solved. The 1st Marine Expeditionary Force and clearly not the Marine Corps that I served in, assigned a similar mission to the brigade sized 'Task Force Tawara' from the Second Marine Division left behind in North Carolina.

Once Baghdad had fallen, the talking heads finally shut-up about this problem and left others to pick-up on it as the riots and looting ensued. Later the emergence of the insurgency was blamed on the initial lack of manpower tasked to take Baghdad. The overlooked point is that there never could have been enough 'boots on the ground' for perfect security and to prevent the looting and lawlessness that followed the fall of Baghdad. Looting that turned out to be greatly overhyped by the network news and lawlessness not quite up the standards of a good old American race riot.

Forgotten too was the fact that Saddam had released every criminal parked in his jails on his way to 'seclusion'. To place this in context, Saddam's action is the equivalent of the State of California releasing every one incarcerated in its prison system—from Pelican Bay to overnighters in the LA County jail. Remember, there is a reason individuals are stored in Pelican Bay, located in Crescent City, CA and geographically difficult to drive too as many Californians discover when they go there for salmon fishing.

With the end of direct hostilities and the return of the naval forces and the vast air armada that supported the victorious ground forces, President Bush flew onto the USS Abe Lincoln as it approached its homeport in San Diego to the continuing disapproval of the politically correct. That he's a former fighter pilot and naturally wanted to land on a carrier deck once to see what his father had experienced during WW II weren't considered a valid reasons for doing it—the PC just bitched about the alleged cost to the taxpayer. Then he made his 'mission accomplished speech' where he thanked the sailors for their effort and then reminded us all that a tough road still lay ahead, a point deliberately ignored in the vitriolic personal attacks that have followed.

The Occupation

Of course 'Mission Accomplished' didn't mean that the ground forces were going to be rushed home for their parade. Pershing's Army didn't leave Europe right after the Armistice either as they occupied Germany until the Versailles Treaty was signed in 1919. Others ended up in Northern Russia to protect the Arctic ports when civil war between the 'Reds and Whites' broke out. Those troops who landed after Dewey's victory over the Spanish at Manila Bay ended up staying until 1902, fighting an insurrection that ultimately sucked in over 100,000 more troops—National Guardsmen to boot.

It is true that the Iraqi Army simply faded away during the conflict, precluding any viable ability to use it as a security force immediately after the fall of Saddam, but there were and still are more than enough disgruntled unhappy Baathists willing to continue the fight—nothing new here. One can't blame them since any new regime would have little use for them and might even execute them for 'crimes against humanity', of which there were thousands over the years Saddam was in power. So why shouldn't a relatively few of them turn to a guerilla conflict in a last ditch effort to retain what they'd never be able to otherwise reacquire and to possibly avoid execution.

There's even ample past precedent suggesting that they might succeed starting with American proclivity to 'cut and run' when the casualties add up, as per Mogadishu under Clinton and Lebanon during the Reagan Administration. Since Vietnam, prevailing opinion in many parts of the world is that when the going gets tough, Americans pack it in. To some extent this is what Presidential wannabe John Kerry is now suggesting when he states that he'll have most our troops home by July 2005—once they're replaced by the French and Belgium's band.

What America's ample supply of hand wringers forget is that it takes only a few determined guerillas to totally disrupt the functioning of a country. The 20,000 or so armed opponents currently (7/9/04) believed to be operating in the Iraqi 'Sunni Tri-angle' are more than adequate to do the job. Then there is the prevalent Muslim attitude that armed violence in the name of a 'holy cause' is an important component of political leverage. Ergo the recurring effort by a Shia minority to carve-out an enclave within the Holy Cities and part of Baghdad through violence.

Finally there is the Saddam Fedeyeen of 'foreign fighters', Al Qaeda types willing to 'die for Allah' if it results in the defeat of the Great Satan. Some of the politically correct argue that by our presence in Iraq, we are creating thousands more of these terrorists by giving them a visible target that they can attack. However, these guys existed before the invasion of Iraq and their arrival on the scene probably helps us reduce that population; they're going to have to be either killed off or incarcerated forever at some point, might as well be now in Iraq.

This isn't quite the way the post-invasion insurgency has been presented to the American public by the mainstream media and that's one of the problems as American perception of the situation in Iraq has been materially different from Iraq perceptions for quite some time. Having lived through the period and serving a combat tour in Vietnam where the *LA Times* once reported on a battle in my neighborhood that never happened, I'm seeing the press report the same drum beat of pessimism that undermined morale during Vietnam.

The media needs to note that any reasonably trained group of 10 to 20,000 desperate individuals willing to die for their cause, with access to an unlimited supply of munitions is going to create a big security problem. With the resulting mayhem presented daily on the small screen in 5-second sound bites, it's very easy for the public to come away with believing that Iraq had turned into a quagmire ala Vietnam, which presupposes that their fallacious perception of the latter is accurate.

The reality, as usual, is markedly different. Most of the extensive violence is centered around Baghdad and the notorious 'Sunni Tri-angle', leaving only sporadic violence occurring in the Kurdish north and allied occupied south. Thus leaving most of he country relatively peaceful and progressing towards the restoration of a civil society. To a lesser extent, this could be said of the principal region of conflict as American Forces continue to conduct extensive 'civic action' operations resulting in reconstructed schools, re-opened medical facilities, and the establishment of bottom—up local governing bodies for the first time in decades.

This is major progress, albeit slower than many Americans seem to have the patience for and parallel to the evolutionary process that won over the 'hearts and minds' of the South Vietnamese, the key reason that I and others dependent upon their goodwill are still alive. Despite this developing foundation and the 28 June 2004 transfer of power to the transitional Iraqi government that many pundits attributed to fear after declaring that it couldn't be done due to prevailing levels of violence, the politically correct still prefer to emphasize the negatives suggesting inevitable failure.

True most Iraqi's do view the US as occupiers etc, which is to be expected, but they also recognize the necessity of our presence and that life is getting better because of the overthrow of Saddam. Now if they can only get that point across to the politically correct and their agents in the media.

Chapter Footnote: Although the details are currently rather murky, there is considerable suspicion that the bribes and 'kickbacks' involved in the UN's 'oil for food' scandal led to a lot of money being routed to Al Qaeda through shell corporations controlled by Saddam Hussein and Osama bin Ladin. This thesis is highly creditable considering that the *911 Commission Report* stated that it took some $30 million per year to fund Al Qeada's activities. Since Osama's assets in Saudi

Arabia have probably been frozen for some time and that whatever he had in the Sudan was confiscated prior to his departure to Afghanistan, its reasonable to believe that Al Qaeda was having financial problems requiring Saddam's help.

7

Residual Issues: War on 'Terror'

Not Enough 'Boots'

Through out the campaigns in Afghanistan and Iraq the continuing harangue has been and still is about the lack of forces assigned to the mission and the chronic complainers have a point. Barely, and it has nothing to do with the inference that American forces are incapable of 'walking and chewing gum at the same time'. The United States does have a troop shortage that is partially the result of the downsizing of the Army from 18 combat divisions under Bush I to only 10 when Bush II took office.

When the Army/Marine Corps commitments are spread all over the globe like they are today, the strategic reserve of ground forces disappears. Without this strategic reserve, the force needed to respond to other problems doesn't exist and when existing conflicts 'take too long to resolve', the troop strength available to relieve worn out units likewise doesn't exist, putting considerable stress on everyone concerned.

This is particularly true since American force structure is increasingly dependent upon the Organized Reserve and the National Guard that have increasingly become more like full time units due to more frequent and longer deployments. This is the way it was planned during the 1990s when few expected military operations to rise to the level they've reached today.

Additionally, American ground force structure has been organized to concentrate armed combat units within the active forces and skew logistic and administrative support tasks towards the reserves. The problem, considering the Army's historically large logistic tail, is that it takes two or more soldiers filling a support billet for everyone in a combat position. Thus, for every additional brigade committed to Iraq, the Army needs the equivalent of two brigades in the rear to support them and these support units come from the 'weekend warriors'.

Another problem involves the manpower available for specialized jobs ranging from 'special operations' to personnel fluent in Arabic and the various Afghani dialects for various intelligence/counterintelligence missions. Given the demographic structure of the United States the latter skill set is going to be in short supply no matter what, especially when combined with security clearance requirements. It is also necessary to have bilingual personnel around when conducting routine patrols during an insurgency and when undertaking various civic action projects with the locals.

The complainers do have a valid point when declaring that the War in Iraq has 'robbed' the War in Afghanistan of essential people. There aren't many around willing to become special operations types and it takes a unique personality to be able to be successful in the field. Of those who are willing and do have the necessary personality profiles, many do not make it through training. Even Marine Corps Officer Training, based on my experience as a staff platoon commander at Quantico years ago, results, on average, in barely 40% of the incoming candidates making it to commissioning.

Special Operations certification is much tougher. When I was a midshipman at the Navy's Amphibious Base in Little Creek, VA we were just down the street from the UDT School. Everyday we got to see UDT aspirants getting in shape by running after a jeep. By the time we'd left, there was only one or two left out of an initial herd of many running behind that jeep. Whether these two eventually passed 'swimming school' is problematical since the final exam was then a five-mile swim off the coast of Puerto Rico.

When all is said and done, these rigorous requirements don't leave many 'special ops' types available for duty in both Iraq and Afghanistan with an occasional vacation between tours. Otherwise, unless one can adequately explain how tanks running around the rugged Hindu Kush can effectively crush Al Qaeda and Taliban remnants, the War in Iraq has not detracted from our ability to finish off bin Laden.

This job belongs to the 10th Mountain Division home based near the St Lawrence River with augmentation from the 82nd Airborne and various USMC battalions in conjunction with all the special ops units integrated within various Afghan militias. The forces in Iraq, on the other-hand, are desert fighting units heavily dependent upon armored vehicles for mobility and have no place operating in the mountains.

The politically correct argument that one war cannibalizes the other overlooks another strategic issue in that the base structure built to fight the Soviets in Afghanistan was designed to provide the Mujahedin with sanctuary inside Pakistan. Ergo, to pin down bin Laden and his Jihadist defenders the Pakistani Army needs to be the aggressor, or allow American forces conduct operations on both sides of the border with impunity. For a host of reasons, this isn't going to happen so bin Ladin can hide quite comfortably in his mountain redoubt no matter how many Americans are out looking for him.

Nor can one with any knowledge of military operations argue successfully that Coalition troop strength inside Iraq has been inadequate. True, the Americans and to a lessor extent the Brits who do have recent experience in this type of conflict thanks to the Irish Republican Army, aren't specially trained for what they're asked to do today in Iraq. And something can be said for increasing the number of military policemen in country. However, they are trained and are now combat veterans with skills that are transferable to counter-insurgency operations.

This still leaves gaps in existing force levels, ones that can only be filled by Iraqis. Thus when Defense Secretary Rumsfeld states that force levels are increasing as we train Iraqis and once that's completed, the insurgency will become gradually easier to contain, he's stating the truth. This is by definition a ragged process and one that doesn't instantly lead to highly proficient Iraqi military units, just as it didn't with the Koreans and South Vietnamese.

Those that argue that our failure to employ the defeated Iraqi Army has caused the insurgency to spread are equally off target. This was an army that had ceased to exist, along with local police forces, the day the 3rd ID showed up in Baghdad, nor was it an acceptable force for the job from our prospective since it was many an army of Shiite draftees led by Sunni—Baathist officers. Its NCOs might have had stripes, but they weren't non-commissioned officers in the sense that Western forces define it.

Therefore the Provisional Coalition Authority needed to start from scratch in rebuilding Iraqi security forces. This meant re-training several hundred thousand partially experienced troops from the basics up. Officers had to vetted so that only those committed to a free, democratically elected government filled the command structure. Recycling Saddam loyalist merely rearranges the chairs.

The officer corps must also be able to do the job and the only way to identify those who can is to force true leaders to percolate up from the ranks, not by appointing those who'd gotten their 'bars' through political connections under the old regime. All of this takes time and the important point is that the Iraqis appear to be more than willing to assume the burden despite prevailing violence within the Sunni Tri-angle that's now targeting them.

The sudden appearance of either NATO or the UN like Custer's 7th Cavalry rescuing a wagon train isn't going to instantaneously produce peace and tranquility throughout the land as many of the politically correct have maintained. Leaving aside other issues, they basically don't have the troops to start with.

Following the collapse of the Berlin Wall and ensuing economic stagnation, our 'continental allies' have effectively disarmed and spent little in sustaining the viability of the forces they do have. Throw in the troop level they've committed to security operations in Afghanistan and the Balkans, plus unilateral deployments by the French throughout its former African colonial empire, and the cupboard is bare unless one wants to believe that the Belgian band would make a difference.

Then there is the question of whether we even needed them during the invasion or since. Iraq was invaded by forces from three countries with a few small units from several others sprinkled in, using the logistic facilities provided at some risk by the Gulf Sheikdoms. The British had their own area of operations in the Southern third of the country with an Australian task force attached. Besides the common language, both countries have operated together throughout the world for decades as an integrated force sharing common operational procedures. To the north, the Marines, who don't quite have operational procedures in common with the US Army had their own axis of advance. This left the US Army to operate as it saw fit to the west of the Marines and basically spearhead the attack.

Adding a broad mix of battalion sized multilingual units to the mix would have complicated command and control to the detriment of the operation. Therefore Rumsfeld was correct in questioning the utility of having a mish-mash of NATO units tagging along for cosmetic reasons. Their presence wouldn't have helped. This was a blitzkrieg to Baghdad, not the set-piece battle of the Gulf War and even in that war, most of the forces provided by the allies were assigned collateral missions with Anglo-American forces tasked with the primary job of defeating the Iraqi Army.

As far as the post war occupation is concerned, the Administration lined up a number of allies to participate and bundled them up under Polish command as one division of multi-national troops with their own zone of operation. Altogether this international hodge-podge has involved some 31 different countries with several contingents suffering proportionally significant casualties.

The claim that the Bush Administration has turned the War in Iraq into a unilateral American effort is therefore totally without foundation, yet today's presidential wannabe John Kerry has called it the 'coalition of the coerced and bribed'. Considering the casualties incurred by other members of the coalition and the countries involved, his comments and those of his political kindred are reprehensible. And they're hardly appropriate of a man who professes to be able to 'rebuild the image of America in the eyes of the world' however cool it might sound on 'Saturday Night Live'.

Allies or the Lack of Them

The real reason the politically correct attribute to George W. Bush's 'failure' to internationalize the war effort was that he acted like the 'Texas cowboys' they'd watched on the silver screen and that 'W' wanted to go it alone just like John Wayne. This is basically a crock as the above indicates. It also overlooks the French, Russian, and to a limited extent German, 'rice bowls' that broke when the first American crossed the berm into Iraq. A problem that was further aggravated by the billions Saddam owed them going up in flames as a result of what in finance is euphemistically referred to as 'unsuccessfully financing one's customers'.

They mistake 'liking the US' with respecting the US when it stands up for its interests. Expecting full and devoted cooperation from someone that's going to be nailed financially because of what we proposed to do is quite an imaginative stretch. Given the money involved, there was no way the Bush Administration was going to bring these three, particularly the French, on board. Once bought, the French planned to stay bought, plus there was a potential problem of what the Iraqi archives contained regarding the degree of French sanctions violations.

Then there's the 'hee-haw' over Cowboy George deliberately 'ticking off' our continental allies because his childish foreign policy—something only Francophile John Kerry can fix. This too is good for a chuckle amongst the knowing, but once again it's politically correct hubris without foundation based on the fantasy that alliances between nations are forever—which given the American divorce rate is something that cannot even be said about marriage.

The truth is that the western alliance structure built around NATO no longer serves a purpose. The Soviet Union that it was formed to oppose has collapsed, and like every alliance in history created to oppose specific enemies, NATO members are going to go their own way as dictated by their national interests following victory. In the case of the US, that means pursuing both globalization for economic gains and forming ad hoc arrangements suitable to the war on terror. For the Europeans, it means pulling up the walls surrounding a continental bastion.

It's the nostalgia for fonder days that prevents us from seeing this and leads many Americans to assume that we should remain bound at the hip because our values are the same. This isn't true. Though we are a country of immigrants, with many descending from our nominal NATO allies, none of us have been the same since our ancestors stepped off the boat. As Americans we are the product of those who rejected the restrictions of European values and for this reason have often been disparaged by the envious who stayed home—for several hundred years.

Somewhere in all the mythology surrounding French military help during the Revolution and the fact that the French Revolution was inspired by ours with its clarion call for liberty, fraternity, and equality, we overlook many things about the French starting with the supposed similarities between our two revolutions. Our revolution was the result of an evolutionary process of longstanding self-government built upon customary law and the Whig principles that had enmeshed the British Crown in parliamentary rule. Theirs was a horrific 'temper-tantrum' which has led to multiple forms of government and extensive periods where the French have been incapable of governing themselves.

In the mystic mist surrounding Lafayette, we tend to overlook that French military support during our War for Independence was an opportunistic effort to recover some of what had been lost during the Great War for Empire (1755—1763), not because Louis XVI believed in the underlying American republican principles. Then there's the first war we fought as a newly emergent nation—the Quasi War with France where we objected to French privateers seizing American ships on the high seas during its war with an English led coalition. After losing a few frigate battles, the French got the message.

Yes its true we were allied with France during World War One thanks to common interests, but after that war the common interest dissolved quickly at Versailles and both countries operated at cross purposes for most of the next 20 years. World War Two brought us back together again, but the first armed contact faced by the US Army in the European Theater was against the French when we had to shoot it out with them in North Africa. Concurrently, the US Navy was forced to sink a French naval squadron off of Casablanca in the only sea battle it fought in the European Theater.

Finally there's a reason France is not part of the NATO military alliance—it is only a member of the political alliance thanks to Charles de Gaulle's desire for French military independence and emotional need for its own nuclear weapons arsenal. As a result, he threw a tantrum and tossed NATO's Supreme Allied Headquarters out of Paris. That's why it's been in Brussels for over three decades.

Ergo, the French have a long history of periodic opposition to American interests of which today's problems with them are only the latest. One would think that the politically correct and the Francophiles of the Democratic Party would read a history book and bring themselves up to speed before they pontificate from ignorance, but that's not necessarily the 'cool thing to do'.

There's another problem with the French and the rest of 'Old Europe' for that matter. If one looks at economic statistics for these countries since the fall of the Berlin Wall in 1989, it becomes clear that the hopes surrounding the establishment of the European Customs Union haven't materialized. GNP growth in 'Old Europe' has been minimal at best and the 'New Europe' of the former Communist Block has been siphoning jobs and capital from the old for more than a decade.

This has proven to be a frightening prospect, especially for the French since it has never been an entrepreneurial society to start with. And a fear based one ever since French elan meet reality in 1914 and crumbled inside of 60 days in 1940 because the French never really had their hearts in the effort.

Since then nothing has really gone quite right for France to where French policy is now oriented towards preserving a gentile decrepitude where everyone gets 'three hots and a cot'. Remember, France's premier university is the Ecole Nationale whose primary purpose is to provide career bureaucrats for the state, juxtaposed to America's diverse system consisting of the Stanfords, MITs, Harvard Business Schools, et al.

Therefore in a globalized world, France finds it hard to compete and needs markets like Saddam's Iraq where sanctions etc prevent the rest of the world from stepping in and scoffing up business at French expense. Compared to politically correct rants from America's liberal fascists about George W's immature foreign policy, this is a much more plausible reason behind the adamant French opposition to regime change in Iraq—French business needed the money.

It also goes far in explaining French policy inside the European Union. By pushing for a 'federal constitution' so long and convoluted that not even lawyers can read it in one sitting, France seems to be imposing its own bureaucratic structure. with all the inertia that has virtually frozen all French institutions, on the rest of the continent. If the 'New Europe' of former communist countries allow this to happen, they will become like France with their economies frozen in a bureaucratic nightmare to France's competitive advantage. This contingency is not in America's interest because it would turn Europe into an economic fortress barring entry to American goods and services.

It would also preclude commercial alliances like the one between US Steel and various East European steel companies that have benefited all parties at the expense of Old European steel companies, because the economic advantages that these alliances create would disappear into the morass of European bureaucratic procedure. So at this point, French interests and ours are diverging rapidly with or without the issue of Iraq and there's nothing Francophile John Kerry and his ilk can do about it without suborning American interests to those of the French.

No Plan, No Exit Strategy

Once Baghdad fell, the 'talking heads' had to move on to complain about other stuff and the politically correct needed to find something else to blame President Bush for given the resounding victory over the Iraqi Army. It didn't take them long to shift their continuum of whine to the Administration's failure to properly plan for post-war Iraq and develop an exit strategy.

For some reason they've failed, or been unwilling, to recognize that the American exit strategy was obvious. Restore order and basic governmental functions and establish some form of interim government of Iraqis. Concurrently the goal was to get the Iraqi utility and oil infrastructure functioning again while developing a new security force structure that could relieve American forces in the inevitable counter-insurgency. Finally, we wanted to return sovereignty back to the Iraqi people once they'd agreed to a democratic republican constitution—hopefully non-secular and federalist in nature.

The problem is in the details and not something that can be plugged into nodes of a Navy 'Sea Bee' critical path construction plan where everything is mapped out in an exact time sequence. There's the old military axiom that when 'the plan meets the enemy, all bets are off' and eventual withdrawal from Iraq is no different. Anyone who's ever had to plan anything and then see the plan through to completion knows this. However, most of the whiners, being lawyers and commentators, have made their livings finding fault with others so they generally have no concept of what's involved.

Listening to them, it is almost as if they're demanding surrender on the installment plan based on the false assumption that our effort in Iraq will become a quagmire like Vietnam, forgetting that Vietnam turned out the way it did by choice. Even if one expects our presence in Iraq to unfold like Nixon's Vietnamization program, it must be remembered that the gradual replacement of American forces by the ARVN was timed according to the situation. A lot of work went into preparing the South Vietnamese for the day the last American unit would leave.

It also takes the United States six months to turn a new recruit into a functioning Marine and nine months to train a brand new second lieutenant under wartime conditions. Then they're fed into already functioning units. In the case of Iraq, these functioning units, with the requisite cohesiveness needed to accomplish security missions under insurgency conditions didn't exist. Thus the whole edifice had to be constructed basically from scratch and we've only been there 15 months as of this is being written—hardly enough time to even begin the process of rebuilding an Iraqi army.

Another reality that there's been much 'to do' over has been the Provisional Coalition's failure to restore basic utility services throughout the country and restore oil production. Here the United States was surprised considering the relatively advanced nature of Iraqi society and the fact that coalition forces had gone out of their way to avoid damaging Iraqi infrastructure.

When enough order had been restored so survey teams could go out and access reconstruction needs, they found that electric power under Saddam had been provided mainly to Baghdad, leaving much of the country without it, and that Iraqi infrastructure was in worse shape than anyone had thought. Saddam's regime hadn't spent a dime on preventive maintenance in years, if not decades. Some of the country's electrical generators were so old that repair parts for them hadn't been manufactured since Saddam originally assumed power.

What was kind of working had been jury rigged so many times that only the last guy who'd repaired it had a clue as how to fix it. Plan B was to tear everything apart and figure out how to re-assemble the pieces in hopes that a working machine would result. Even the country's water treatment plants, being mostly pipes and valves, hadn't worked in years as evidenced by the many TV pictures broadcast into American homes by the embedded American reporters.

This leads to another rhetorical question for the PCs to answer. Since the water treatment plants had been left to rust away without any apparent concern by the regime over many years, why did Saddam's regime need to buy massive volumes of chlorine from India when the primary civilian use for chlorine is water purification?

Once the Provisional Coalition began to get a handle on the extent of the problem, it could finally commence reconstruction and begin rerouting the electrical grid so that all of Iraq could have some access to electricity. This meant that the amount of power available to Baghdad had to drop way below pre-war levels and this gave commentators considerable ammunition to use in pillaring the Administration.

Since speed was essential, both to appease the Iraqis who expected instant perfection and appease the administration's critics, Haliburton was given the contract for the initial stages of reconstruction and to arrange logistic support for those activities the army no longer provided itself. (eg: mess halls and food service, gasoline and lubricants) This really stoked the rant first crowd because Vice President Cheney had been the company's CEO prior to his election. Ever since we've been subjected to a barrage of claims that the war was fought to make Halibuton and the Vice President richer.

Lost in all the screeching is that fact that there are few companies available that could have stepped in and done the job right from the 'get-go'. Besides Haliburton's Kellogg, Brown & Root division, there's the Bechtel Group and the old Morrison & Knudsen now morphed into Washington Group—who'd made a strategic decision following its second emergence from bankruptcy to avoid low margin projects such as the one KB&R stepped into the day Baghdad fell.

Given that KB&R will do well to net out something between 1% and 3% after taxes, contracts for the reconstruction of Iraq can easily turn out to be a booby prize. This is something that the politically correct, who've never read a financial statement can't grasp in their fixation that a contract's total size represents 'free money'. So why should KB&R step up to assume a misery that it could do without? The answer is simple and involves values. KB&R volunteered to do this during every war the United States has fought beginning with Guadacanal.

As a result of suddenly reallocating corporate resources and jumping into an unknown project with both feet and incurring amorphous costs, Hailburton has been repeatedly hammered over just about anything one could find wrong. From over-billing the government for food services, to excessive prices for gasoline shipped in from Kuwait, KB&R has been attacked for 'profiteering' for the Vice President's benefit, despite the fact that he no longer has a financial interest in the company. He sold his stock before taking office. Overlooked is the fact that the food service issue has forced Haliburton to carry over $160 million in accounts receivable on its books and borrow the funds needed to finance the cost of providing food service to our troops.

Nor are the whiners particularly concerned that there are unique reasons the price of fuel shipped in from Kuwait greatly exceeded that brought in from Turkey in the north and what the average American pays at the pump. Fuel from the north involves a slightly wider range of refineries and safer journeys for the drivers. Fuel from Kuwait, however, has a much riskier trip with tank-truck drivers receiving greater compensation as a result. Then there's a Kuwaiti mandate to use local intermediaries who in turn are drawing fuel from a much smaller local supply source. This creates a situation where the demand for fuel from coalition forces greatly exceeds the available supply with boom prices the result.

The ultimate irony occurred when the Congress authorized $18 billion for the Iraqi reconstruction effort. This was taxpayer money, not French or anyone else's, yet the politically correct surfaced to complain when President Bush restricted access to the related contracts to companies domiciled in countries who'd provided troops during the ground campaign, which of course excluded the French, Germans, and Russians.

Again the Bush Administration was accused of unilateral action and further provoking those allies we'd become estranged from. What chutzpah! Why on God's green earth should the United States hand over $180 to $540 million in after-taxes profits to French companies and an equal amount to Jacques Chirac's government in taxes after all the money they'd made violating the sanctions regime and helping arm Saddam.

This position is especially egregious because two of its most vociferous proponents are now running around the country decrying foreign outsourcing of American jobs in their drive for the White House. What could be more hypocritical when one wants to see American jobs, represented by the Iraqi reconstruction contracts, handed over to 'Old Europe'. Naturally they don't see it that way since one of the hallmarks of political correctness is too focus on the complaint de jure without the need for linkage with other positions—everything in isolation, without context or perspective.

Despite all the complaints, charges and countercharges, Iraqi reconstruction has been progressing about as well as can be expected considering there's an insurgency still going on. As anyone watching the *'Fox News Channel'* over the past year and a half can attest to, thousands of schools have been rehabilitated. Medical care is much more available and of higher quality that under Saddam's regime. Oil production is now exceeding pre-war levels, as is electric power generation that's now available throughout the country. Even the water treatment facilities are working to some extent.

By any standard this is a success story and reflects much better conditions than the Germans and Japanese were living with fifteen months after World War Two. That's not to say that as of today all is perfect between the Tigris and Euphrates. The insurgency involving residual Baathist, foreign terrorists, and related riff-raff is still gong on. Not a day passes without a suicide bomber blowing himself and others to pieces and Americans are still subject to ambushes and their vehicle convoys attacked with 'improvised explosive devices' that are at times quite sophisticated—more so than anything we saw in Vietnam.

Much of this is the result of the insurgents having access to all the explosives they could ever want and the Coalition has been taken to task for this with some justification. Under Saddam, Iraq was turned into one vast ammo dump that proved to be to extensive for coalition forces to properly secure. In many cases these munitions stores were too large to destroy in place since the resulting explosions would have leveled whole cities. In other cases, due to the effects of aging and deterioration, they couldn't be moved safely.

This left disposal to a small group of explosive ordinance disposal experts to methodically work their way through the massive inventory, something impossible to do before the insurgents had gotten their hands on some of it. The good news is that between EOD and the insurgents, they'll eventually blow it all up and then things will quiet down, just like it did in Vietnam.

Although a major problem, this isn't all that bad considering that most of the country is at peace, despite the perceptions created by the national news media, and out of a population of some 22 million, only several thousand are actively opposing the occupation. Had the degree of Iraqi opposition been as universal as some PCs would have us believe, our position inside Iraq would have become impossible months ago.

Yes the Iraqis complain early and often, but this is the first time they're gotten to do that without being murdered in decades and some of their complaints are legitimate. But we need to remember that a lot of the things they complain about, Americans also complains about—especially in our inner cities. What's needed on our part is some perspective.

Abu Graib, 'Gitmo', & POWs

The same is true of the POW issue that flared up when the pictures of the prisoner abuse at the 'POW'/interrogation facility in Baghdad—Abu Graib. Clearly this behavior was beyond the pale as anyone with military experience can explain. It should also be noted that the only reason these abuses came to light was because of the Army's response. There was never any effort to cover-up the 'problem' despite inferences to the contrary.

Based on my own reading of the situation, the Army reacted properly by immediately initiating investigations under the premise that these would lead to criminal actions against the perpetrators and relieved those up the chain of command for failing to exercise proper command supervision to the detriment of their careers. The key point is that it looks like the junior troops involved pretty much acted on their own based on their own perversions and probably boredom from serving on the night shift. The recently completed DOD investigations have confirmed this while broadening the list of perpetrators to include some of the prison's interrogators and their immediate superiors.

Secondly, even though the investigations were conducted at the behest of the American commander in Iraq, everyone in the chain of command had to review the findings and comment appropriately on them as per Judge Advocate General requirements. Not until this has been done could the final report be submitted to the Secretary of Defense and the Joint Chiefs, something that was done by late August 2004

However the politically correct complained early and often. Beginning with the idea that the Army did not act quickly enough and overlooking the fact that the investigations had to be conducted in a way that protected the accused right to due process which slows everything down. Next they accused everyone from President Bush on down of 'ordering' the prisoner abuse as if both the President and the Secretary of Defense personally directed that the POWs be leashed and paraded around naked.

Then there was the old argument that the junior enlisted personnel were merely following orders and thus not culpable. This too is a crock. Everyone in the US military is trained to know the difference between lawful and unlawful treatment of prisoners and that they're required to report any such abuse to their superiors. In fact no one in uniform is required to obey unlawful orders and many have refused to do so through the years. The 'Nuremburg Defense', then, doesn't hold up as the perpetrators are going to learn the hard way in the near future.

Finally the politically correct made a big deal out of the Geneva Conventions with regard to the abuse, overlooking that the prisoners concerned were not for the most part covered by the Geneva Conventions. They were not former Iraqi soldiers operating under the orders of the country's military chain of command since they'd been picked up hither and yon during the course of the insurgency after direct combat had ended and legitimate Iraqi POWs sent home. A number of them weren't even Iraqis, having arrived in country at the request of Al Qaeda and its affiliates and were thus legally terrorists.

This specious thinking is also present in the politically correct's view of the prisoner confinement at 'Gitmo'. As the theory is currently being advanced, those individuals the US has secured behind barbed wire at our base in Cuba are entitled to a judicial review of the rationale behind their continued confinement by American civil courts—not military.

The fact that these individuals represent a select group culled from the multitude of prisoners captured on the battlefields of Afghanistan and, for the most part, have expressed the clear intent to perform terrorists attacks against the United States is apparently immaterial. Additionally, the US is still in the process of running down terrorists around the world and it doesn't make sense to turn these individuals loose once we've finally captured them.

Therefore, the coterie of 'stalwart citizens' confined at 'Gitmo' are there for the duration of the war on terror. As terrorists they are criminals under any country's criminal code and thus properly confined. The relevant point is that despite the circumstances surrounding their capture, sans the isolated abuse issue, all of the odd assortment of people American forces have confined during the course the current conflicts have been treated as if they were subject to the provisions of the Geneva Conventions. Or in the case of the most pathological, they've been treated no worse than Americans who've earned their incarceration in Pelican Bay.

Intelligence Fiasco

With several commissions looking into why 911 wasn't prevented, along with perceived intelligence failures pertaining to Iraq's apparent lack of weapons of mass destruction, this is not the place to pre-empt their eventual findings. However it seems that we've lost sight of the fact that intelligence is not an exercise of producing evidence before a jury as per American rules of evidence. 'Beyond reasonable doubt' can never be produced by intelligence.

Nor is screaming on the Senate floor that they'd been lied to because the intelligence available caused the politically correct to make the 'wrong decision', that's something children do on the playground when they don't like the result. Equally egregious are the pronouncements that President Bush pressured CIA analysts into doctoring their opinions to justify the invasion of Iraq, something that the recently published 911 Commission Report refutes.

Intelligence gathering and processing is more like assembling a puzzle where one has too many pieces and can't look at the picture on the box. In raw form, intelligence is a giant collection of trivia piled high and deep which analysts must sort through to ascertain what the puzzle's picture on the box might look like. If they're a little bit lucky, they might actually get it right—a process akin to solving the 'problem' on 'Wheel of Fortune' after buying a couple of vowels.

There are of course, ways to structure the process to improve chances for success. As I remember from the distant past, the military catalogs source quality from A to F and information quality from 1 to 7. Greater weight is thus placed on all intelligence rated A-1 with F-7 stuff generally ignored. This is still a subjective process and problems arise when working with information that falls within say the B-5 category. It might actually be good stuff, but the odds suggest that it really isn't.

Another challenge is in drawing the correct conclusions even when all the material the analyst is working with is A-1. Given enough analysts in the kitchen and several plausible conclusions can be drawn so that the ultimate decision maker has to chose between column A and column B, maybe even from column C—no guarantee that the end result is going to be correct. Only subsequent events can determine that.

The process can be further refined through the use of probability matrixes, game theory and on a very high level, Monte Carlo simulations. However someone must still assign probability values to each information item going into the 'what if model' before the button is pushed to obtain the scenario's most likely result, which takes us back to guesswork.

There were several nights in Vietnam when my troops spent hours in their fighting holes waiting for the inevitable attack that intelligence types further up the chain of command assured us was a guaranteed deal. Naturally we were always ready, but the VC never showed up for the show. Then there were those nights when out of the blue, they just appeared and the fight was on—ready or not.

Turns out that the most reliable intelligence we had that we could use was either the weather or the moon cycle. When the typhoons showed up and flooded the rice patties, we knew that the VC couldn't swim any better than we could so there'd be no war that night. The VC didn't want to be out in the paddies during a full moon anymore than we did because moonlight is almost as good as daylight. On the other hand, when the moon wasn't going to show up, it was too dark for anyone to see what they were doing—ergo: no battle.

It was the quarter moon that was the most likely to produce violence since there was just enough light to see and not enough to be silhouetted. Thus we needed to be prepared for an attack during these periods of the lunar cycle no matter what any other items of information might suggest. The quarter moon was a VC moon and anyone overlooking that increased the probability of ending up dead.

Looking at the intelligence available prior to the invasion of Iraq, this was pretty close to the situation President Bush and Prime Minister Blair faced. The United Nations through the weapons inspection program 'knew' that as of 1998, when Saddam kicked out the inspectors, that gallons of anthrax and other bio-chemical delights had yet to be destroyed, or at least accounted for. Without verification of their destruction and because Saddam refused to cooperate in accounting for what happened to all this stuff, the UN had to assume that he still had his bio-chemical weapons.

Next, every intelligence agency in the western alliance, including Israel's Massad as evidenced by that country's pre-war civil defense measures designed to prevent casualties from chemical attacks, believed that Saddam had his weapons of mass destruction. The question is how did they collectively come to that conclusion without any verification from human sources, as it now seems to be the case. That shouldn't have been a big surprise. Totalitarian regimes are almost impossible to penetrate given the brutal way they respond to any hint of treason.

Even with the Soviet Union we were never quite successful in creating many agents deep inside the critical parts of the regime to gain useful intelligence. If it wasn't for our satellites and tapping of its underwater telecommunications cables, much of what we learned on an ongoing basis would have been impossible to know. East Germany, where virtually every citizen was an informer, was shut down so tightly that the CIA could never develop one agent in fifty years. With Iraq, the problem was compounded by the shortage of Americans with security clearances fluent in Arabic.

My own guess is that through the circular process of sharing information amongst themselves and collectively using the same original source, quite possibly the Iraqi National Congress that had been opposing Saddam from exile for years, they might have ended up convincing themselves through group thinking. Part of this could have been the result of a shortage of resources within the CIA due to the Clinton Administration's, eight year campaign, with John Kerry and his ilk's support to starve it of money above what should have been cut following the end of the Cold War.

Now that the 911 Commission Report with its recommendations has been released, the current cry of the Democrats presidential wannabe is that President Bush is going too slow in implementing these recommendations. Like he was supposed to instantly issue an executive order without giving any thought to the report's contents and call Congress back into session from its summer recess to immediately establish an intelligence 'czar' with a Cabinet position.

Besides raising questions of judgement, this call to action ignores the fact that the appropriate Congressional Committees were already in session examining the commission's recommendations and that not all the commission's recommendations are axiomatically good ideas. Just rearranging the chairs and creating another bureaucracy doesn't guarantee improved intelligence and there're good reasons not to have a cabinet level intelligence czar. Other recommendations, such as an all-encompassing database with all the anti-terrorist information every agency collects, have been put in place long before the 911 Commission first met.

In the haste to try and fix everything yesterday however, those leaping on the bandwagon have forgotten that there's a reason that our intelligence agencies have evolved as they have. Originally the intelligence agencies of the three services were consolidated under the umbrella of the CIA in 1947. Since then, the National Security Agency was established to specifically handle electronic signal intelligence. Next the Defense Intelligence Agency was created to re-establish a military intelligence capability under the control of the Secretary of Defense and the Joint chiefs. One doesn't undo this evolutionary process on the 'QT' just to create an impression of decisiveness as Presidential Candidate John Kerry seems to want to do.

The real problem for policy makers was what to do about all the intelligence they had. Saddam, based his extensive track record, was clearly a 'psycho' and one enthralled with his hero Joe Stalin. There's also ample evidence of his own sponsorship of terrorist activities, including the phony passports for the 1993 World Trade Center bombers and the massive training camp for Ansar al Islam along the Iranian border, plus working links with Al Qaeda. All had a common interest in seeing what each could do to further their common objectives; ie: killing as many 'Crusaders' as possible and bringing life in the Great Satan to a halt by sowing fear.

Adding this to the probable availability, either now or later, of the bio-chem 'toys' and the decision to invade became almost a 'no brainer'. Given a reasonable probability that the two entities (Saddam & Al Qaeda) were willing and reasonably capable of conducting a bio-chemical attack on the United States, President Bush would have been derelict had he not pursued the military option and put an end to the contingent risk once and for all. This is the point that eludes the politically correct to this day.

They're also working under the assumption that the War in Iraq has diverted funds away from developing the resources needed to enhance homeland security, something not borne out by recent federal spending. Their idea, reinforced by John Kerry's rhetoric on the campaign trail as he pursues the Presidency, that having more cops on the beat and more fireman standing by in the firehouse will adequately protect the United States from another terrorist attack is ludicrous. The only thing this would ensure is that there'd be more people available to clean up after the next '911' and possibly arrest the perpetrators if any remained alive after a suicide attack.

A more cynical reason to propose funneling more money to our cities to finance the hiring of more 'first responders' is that, after a point, the incremental monies would end up paying for those currently being paid from local sources. Thus 'freeing up' money for other civic activities that have nothing to do with homeland security. As any good infantryman knows, the best way to disrupt a potential attack is through and active defense using listening posts, outposts, ambushes and constant patrolling—which is the Bush Administration's strategy for the 'war on terror'. Just sitting around and waiting for the enemy to strike first simply gives them the opportunity to get their plan of attack right.

Strategic Perspective

So what has been accomplished in the 'war on terror' to this point. First al Qaeda has been materially disrupted with the killing or jailing of many of its 'high command'. However bin Laden himself is still alive and presumably living in a Pakistani cave, as is his number two guy. Several hundred other Al Qaeda terrorists are locked up in jails at 'Gitmo' for the duration where they're not in position to do any one harm. A few thousand more are dead on the battlefields of Afghanistan and Iraq.

How many are left who have been trained in one of bin Ladin's Afghan training camps, no one will ever really know. Presumably there're a few thousand left, but given that estimate, there should have been more terrorist activity than we've seen since '911'. Based on that premise, the number scattered around the world in various 'sleeper cells' and actually available for terrorist attacks is probably no more than several hundred—still enough to cause a considerable loss of life.

From the PC perspective and their fixation on bin Laden however, this means that the 'war on terror' has been a failure because he's still alive and troops were diverted from Afghanistan to Iraq so that the effort to 'capture' him fell apart. This isn't true as previously noted, but it's the fiction that drives their opinions.

The truth is that Al Qaeda is a decentralized confederation over which bin Laden has considerable influence because he's the conduit through which other confederates get financing and technical support. It is not however, a hierarchical organization directly commanded and controlled by bin Laden or anyone else for that matter. It has no doubt also mathaesized, something that would have happened with or without the seizure of Al Qaeda's bases in Afghanistan. Therefore it doesn't particularly matter from Al Qaeda's organizational structure whether bin Laden lives or dies, although his death would be nice.

The problem is in ejecting him from of his cave in Pakistan, or removing him from a villa in Iran as some observers believe. This requires the Pakistani Army to go in after him and risk substantial casualties in the process, something they haven't been willing to do so far—particularly since that would mean having to fight it out with Pathan tribesmen in the Northwest Frontier where the Pakistani government writ rarely extends. America can't do it without Pakistan's permission without risking another war.

The good news is that once a permanent federated government akin to the former royalist constitution that more or less maintained stability for 50 years is in place, a viable Afghani security force ought to emerge. This should confine most of that region's terrorist problem within the Hindu Kush with residual Talibans struggling to survive while being run down by the Afghan Army.

This leaves Iraq—the linchpin to solving the Middle East's terrorist problem. A viable secular democratically elected republican government that should be federalist in nature goes a long was towards changing the dynamic for the better. If nothing else, such an Iraq would be an example showing that Islamic fundamentalism is not the only choice Arabs have in restructuring their lives for the better, a point Dr. Noah Feldman makes in his book *After Jihad*. The key is in separating the extremist from those Islamist trying couple their faith with democratic principles.

We tend to forget that after World War Two, neither Germany nor Japan were considered viable candidates for democracy and we ignore that Islam with its emphasis on creating a just society is possibly more conducive to the establishment of democracy that either of them. Another missed point is that the German Judiciary contained members who'd graduated from law school under Kaiser Bill and retired from the bench during the Bundes Republic. In the interim they'd served under the Weimar Republic and the Third Reich, applying the law as it was and changing their interpretation concurrent with the regime changes. There's no reason that Iraq's well-trained secular legal scholars cannot do the same.

Strategically a democratic Iraq, along with Muslim Turkey, would drive a wedge between Wahabbist Saudi Arabia and the Iran of the Shiite Ayatollahs and provide a model the latter can use in moving towards a democratic future—something Iran is attempting to do. It would also be an effective model for Egypt to follow once the now elderly President Mubarek dies. Furthermore it would cut the Gordian Knot baring a resolution of the Israeli-Palestinian conflict by giving moderates opposed to Yaser Arafat's PLO a model they could use to restructure life on the West Bank.

Success in Iraq would provide moral support to moderates in the Arab World that the US is truly on the side of democracy, like when Reagan gave moral support to the dissidents behind the Iron Curtain, to our strategic benefit. Finally it would represent a clear signal to the Syrians that they better shape up, starting with cessation of terrorist sponsorship, or they're next. Something that Libya's Kaddafy figured out when he opened his country to the UN and its weapons disposal teams while settling financial with the victims of the Pan Am flight that his agents blew up over Lockerbie Scotland.

The question remains whether this is a viable scenario and all evidence to date suggests that it is. The politically correct like to believe that Iraq's mix of Shiite, Sunni, and Kurd with a sizeable Assyrian Christian minority makes civil war inevitable, a point that I heard an academic shove down California Senator Boxer's throat during a senate hearing on Iraq on C-Span. Those who make the three Iraq argument need to review Iraqi history. A history that illustrates that the Iraqis do have a national identity as much as the Afghans do.

Under the British Mandate following World War One and then as an independent kingdom under the Hashemites, the Iraqis proved quite capable of living as an ethnically diverse country. It wasn't until the various military regimes, particularly Saddam's totalitarian state, that a tendency to separate began to appear, mainly because the state existed to reward Sunni Saddam Loyalists at the expense of the Kurds and Shiite. Without this one-sided relationship, which a federal constitutional structure should preclude, there isn't a compelling reason for 'three Iraqs'.

Domestic Conflicts

8

Issues Economic

Hamilton's World

When George Washington first sat down with his cabinet in 1789, there were basically two visions of America's future—one romantic based on a utopian concept and the other derived from the reality of the times. This latter view was that of Alexander Hamilton and he built career as the United States' first Treasury Secretary around fostering it.

The world that Hamilton saw was one of international commerce where Americans sold the commodities they produced on farms, plantations, and extracted from the 'back country' to Europe for the consumer goods that most Americans had become dependent upon. By this time the United States had been a consumer society for at least 50 years, with almost a century of righteous complaint regarding the ill effects of 'luxurious desires'.

Correlated with this consumerism was the issue of 'dependency', which took two general forms. The first resulted from problems involved with one 'free man' working for another in return for wages. This represented what has developed into the principle of 'free labor' where one has the right to sell his labor to the highest bidder according to mutually agreed upon terms (juxtaposed to slave labor) that's the hallmark of today's economy. By giving up his freedom in this way, the 'free man' was by definition no longer free.

The second one derived from consumerism. The demand for European manufactured goods exceeded the ability of Americans to produce enough commodity products to balance the account, thereby generating a net indebtedness to European wholesalers—more specifically, English merchants. The solution, as Hamilton and his Federalist colleagues saw it was in the development of American manufactured goods so that local production could replace foreign importation—something today's economic development specialists refer to as 'import substitution'.

The key difference between the early American approach and that adopted by third world countries in the 20th Century was that Americans recognized that locally produced goods would have to measure up qualitatively to their foreign equivalents. Or at least come close enough so that the cost differential justified the purchase of the inferior good. Thus the cost of domestic transport and availability of financial institutions to mobilize capital became paramount issues needing to be solved.

Out of this construct came the Whig policies of national development where the government undertook the development of projects that were either to large for private capital or benefited the whole without any specific benefit to singular individuals. During the earlier years of the republic this philosophy led to the building of the Erie Canal, the Baltimore & Ohio Railroad, etc, using a mixture of public and private capital where all parties were at risk and profited equally.

As the west was increasingly opened up, the government provided financial incentives for entrepreneurial behavior in return for the increased value of the lands retained by 'the people' and enhanced property taxes, et al. Then came the 'New Deal' with its massive public works projects such as the great dams in the West and the Tennessee Valley Authority that provided cheap electricity throughout their respective drainage's, before culminating with Eisenhower's Interstate Highway System and California's massive infrastructure development of the 1950s-60s.

Jefferson's Romantic Economy

The problem with Hamilton's world, even though it reflected the world then emerging whether anyone liked it or not, was that it was 'messy'. Commerce always is and those who spend most of their lives in some form of self-employment know that it comes with 'chutes and ladders' as one has good years and then bad years with an occasional bankruptcy along the way. It is also one reason why over the life of the republic we've evolved the role of 'government as a referee'.

This was not the original 'American ideal' and reflected a life of perpetual instability that worked against 'free men' retaining their independence because of the risk of ending up in economic bondage, which was always a real possibility. Given that Jefferson and most of his fellow planters were perpetually in debt due to their habitual lack of financial restraint, it was a reality that he lived with as vendors and mechanics constantly hounded him for money.

Therefore banks, merchants, and those who didn't earn their living from the land, which Jefferson felt he did even though he was closer to being what economists term the classic 'rentier', were bad. (A rentier in the French economic sense was someone who lived off the rents collected from inherited estates; today we refer to them as 'trust fund babies' as in Teresa Heinz Kerry and Senator Ted Kennedy) Therefore his personal experience went far in explaining his political opposition to the commercial class and its representative—Alexander Hamilton.

The converse for Jefferson and his fellow 'Republicans', as in the First French Republic, was the idealistic world of the yeoman farmer. Self-supporting and living an autarkic existence on his own land, this individual would remain free of the dependencies that accompany working for wages. Thus one ends up with a republic of freemen serving as the mainstay of democracy—somewhat akin to the early days of the Roman Republic or Athenian Democracy as the founding fathers believed they functioned.

In this construct however, was a belief in a hierarchical society where the 'yeoman farmer' deferred to the opinions of his betters. This was the way Virginian society was structured at the time with the 'first families', of which Jefferson was a member and Washington really wasn't, providing leadership through moral suasion resulting from their superior education. Consequently one can make the argument that Jeffersonian Democracy was based on a sense of equality that was hardly egalitarian.

Utopia Perverted

The major problem with the Jeffersonian outlook, beside that it conflicted with the evolving nature of the American economy, was that it was based on Rousseau and not the traditionally accepted values of Locke and Hume that served as the base for American Whig values. This is what gave it its romantic cast since Rousseau's natural law was utopian in nature, positing that there was a natural law governing the affairs of mankind, subjecting them to the will of the masses.

This 'will of the masses' left no room for opposition because that would undermine the ability of the masses to act in concert. The problem with this is that the 'will of the masses' is undeterminable without someone telling the masses what their will is. In the case of the French Revolution it was a sequence of demagogues following their predecessors to the guillotine after getting it wrong. For Jefferson, it was obviously him and his aristocratic associates amongst Virginia's first Families.

For another group, based on the writings of a misanthropic German Jew who spent most of his days embalmed in gin, the determinate of the 'will of the masses' became the 'dictatorship of the proletariat'. With Marx the whole idea of a world governed by a higher power that even Jefferson and his fellow deists believed in, disappeared into the fog of atheism.

This left man as his own higher power, answerable only to what he perceived to be the correct ordering of the world. More specifically, the perfect world was that deduced by Marxist utopians developing their own theology in the attics of St Petersburg, Russia. Out of this came the religion of communism where the 'enlighten few', based on their intellectual posturing, determined right and wrong.

Anyone rising up to oppose them was automatically defined as an enemy of the people and slated for execution since they were obstructing the world's evolution towards the ultimate paradise—the perfect workers world where no one ever worked for anyone else and all owned the means of production. However, before the collapse of the Soviet Union confirmed the fallacy of communist theology, millions around the world had to die in the name of Marxist—Leninist spiritual perfection.

The question has always been why did so many apparently intelligent people 'buy into' this ideological concoction? The answer has to be that, in 12 step theology, not everyone is capable of accepting life on life's terms and the world's passage through the Industrial Revolution left many at the time with a revulsion about how it came about. Given the 'up close and personal' details of industrialization, it's easy to see how many came to believe that their had to be a 'gentler, softer way' of accomplishing it.

Ergo, the attempt to create an utopian world on earth, rather than waiting for God and Paradise in the here-after, either through communism or its more benign equivalent socialism. Of course there was a problem with the latter when it combined with nationalism to morph into the pathology of Nazi Germany.

Bureaucratic Capitalism versus the Austrians

The melding of American Whigism with utopian theology occurred during he Great Depression of the 1930s. For a long list of reasons, some of which had to do with many of FDR's 'New Deal' measures that proved to be counter-productive, the 1930s in America resulted in horrific economic conditions more reflective of a newly developing economy than a fully industrialized one. Here American pragmatism took over and coupled laizze faire capitalism and socialism with the long-standing tradition of Whig principles of national development.

The result was that the government took over many of the functions local communities and various mutual benefit societies had performed since the Pilgrims landed. This meant that it was now the government's responsibility to care for the sick and indigent, while organizing society for optimal economic development as long as various social goals were being met.

Fortunately this did not lead to the economic planning that was central to communism, but it did lead to a form of corporatism where the economy was allowed to evolve within acceptable parameters. Change had to be controlled, although this was never directly stated, but it was inferred by the structure of our tax codes mandating that the more successful were required to support the less successful.

From the perspective of the politically correct, who are constantly accused those wanting to keep more of the fruits of their labor of being cruel and uncaring, the key to economic growth was the maintenance of aggregate demand subject to the caring interference by government. This was Keynesian Economics tied to social policy that reached its apex when JFK took office and began to preach that the micro-management of the economy by his Harvard brain trust would eliminate the business cycle once and for-all.

Once his successor, Lyndon Johnson, added the Great Society and the cost of the Vietnam War to this mix, the whole edifice began to collapse. This was partly due to exogenous events and the rest was due to the removal of flexibility from the economic system and failure to acknowledge the importance of supply-side economic incentives in fostering economic growth.

Today 'Old Europe', which hasn't caught on to the problems this policy configuration creates, has continued to enmesh itself with the economic inertia that this structurally produces. At one time referred to as the 'English Disease', it has now evolved into bureaucratic capitalism that prevents Frenchmen from working more than 35 hours per week and keeps almost 10% of the German labor force perpetually retraining for new jobs that will never materialize.

Fortunately for the United States, the incentive side of the economic development equation was 'rediscovered' under Ronald Reagan, as it was earlier when JFK got his famous and successful tax cut passed. Despite being termed 'voodoo economics', 'trickle down economics' that only benefit the rich, and whatever else economically illiterate pundits of the left called it, supply-side economics centered around the re-adjustment of the tax code and de-regulation to provide investment incentives had a firm grounding in economic theory; specifically that of the 'Austrian/Chicago School' and Joseph Schumpeter.

When one takes a course in economic development, one learns that there are two vehicles that drive growth—population increases and technology improvements that result in productivity increases. As more people are added to the labor force, assuming that each is equally productive, the total amount of goods and services increases accordingly. Eventually this one for one relationship breaks down as the supply of people starts exceeding available resources and total production tapers off with deleterious results for each individual worker since his share of the pie begins to shrink as it is divided amongst more and more people. This was what Malthus had in mind when he stated that agricultural production grows linearly, while population grows geometrically until there's finally a demographic collapse.

What precludes this inevitable demographic collapse is technological change leading to productivity increases. Leaving aside a 'Cobb—Douglas' analysis, it is through the continual creation and use of better tools that enables one individual to produce ever increasing amounts of goods, thus enabling society to stay ahead of the Malthusian power curve. The challenge is in getting people to perpetually invent the 'better mouse-trap' and the answer has always been to let them get rich by doing it.

America's early farmers took advantage of this as the surpluses they produced generated the capital that they put into local ironworks etc and then newly invented agricultural equipment, freeing up the labor needed by the country's factories to manufacture that same equipment and other goods. As the process fed on itself, eventually agriculture reached the point where it now takes only 2% of America's population to feed the country and often the world. A far cry from the Jeffersonian vision that would have had me and my brother pulling a plow in Upstate New York with my sister pushing it on a small patch of land.

This was Schumpeter's point as he added factors for entrepreneurialship and the social structure conducive to fostering it to the basic Keynesian Model of production equaling consumption plus investment plus government spending minus net imports. Embodied in his model is the concept of 'profit', something that the preponderance of economic theory ignores in favor of French principle of 'rent': as in someone who collects money without producing anything.

'Rent' in this context is not going to motivate someone to exchange near-term privation in the pursuit of an idea that might work for the prospect of enormous profits later. There has to be a connection between the risk of failure and the reward for success, something most of us define in terms of money and the 'toys' that it can buy. If the rewards aren't there, there is no point in taking the risk. Of course not everyone is even remotely interested in taking the risk, which is why there's always a line when government jobs open up.

The most direct way to create economic incentives fostering entrepreneurialship of course, is through the tax code. When the maximum marginal tax rate was 99%, as Ronald Reagan faced during his acting career, there wasn't any point in getting out of bed to make another movie. With marginal tax rates on earned income exceeding 100%, there shouldn't be any question as to why Sweden's most successful and creative people have chosen to leave the country, leaving behind the living dead sitting around and waiting for God to make it official.

For the self-employed where one month or quarter might be excellent and the next abysmal, high marginal tax rates coupled with withholding and quarterly estimated tax payments often means that one's income beyond subsistence is in the hands of the government until the refund check finally shows up. This too, from my own experience of working 60 to 70 hours per week only to see a successful production month disappear in withholding payments, leads to an attitude of why bother.

Then there's the whole issue of taxes on capital gains that skew the whole risk reward relationship against making anything but riskless investments. Because technology change and the invention that produces it requires capital, the higher the tax on the profits produced by capital increasingly negates the benefit of putting it at risk to fund invention—particularly since those who have the ideas usually don't have the capital. The capital has to come from those who are rich because, with the average American's savings rate, the rich are the ones who have it. No rich people, no venture capital.

Finally there's corporate taxes, many of which represent the cost of doing business ie: property and inventory taxes, et al. The corporate income tax is a horse of a different color as it's split after all expenses are paid between those who own the company and the government that has no money at risk in the venture. The share of a company's pre-tax profit kept by the shareholders being a fabulous 'pot of gold', as the politically correct assume, is not true since most companies do well to net out 5% of revenue after the split.

Many economists simply assume that the corporate income tax becomes embedded in the price of goods and services so that it is merely passed along to the ultimate consumer to the extent that price elasticity allows. However, despite many public misconceptions, every company operates in a competitive environment and the presence of competition limits its available gross profit margins, particularly as industries mature.

This means that there is only so much pre-tax profit and available cash flow (free cash flow as financial types call it) for companies and government to split. The greater the portion that goes to government, the less there is for the company to spend on research and development and more employees. Most companies do not spend their profits on the shareholders, mainly because of the 'double taxation' of dividends. The only way a shareholder can cash out with a profit is to sell his interest to another party, hopefully at a price greater than was originally paid for it—but not always.

Another fact of life is that most large corporations finally reach a point where they tend to shed jobs. It's the new companies that produce the jobs as they grow into bigger ones. And the principle way they grow is through the re-investment of their share of the profits, or at least the positive cash flow resulting from operations, back into the company; ie: increased spending on research and development and hiring more people to do the additional work that growth requires. Ergo, if one wants more jobs without a massive government hiring binge or a war, along with a cure for cancer, it behooves the government to allow companies to hold on to their profits.

All this is what Schumpeter's model suggested and what the Reagan administration understood when it adopted supply side economics and pushed for tax cuts and de-regulation. The goal was to cut the Gordian Knot that was strangling the American economy with 'stagflation' by re-introducing incentives for creative people to assume risks and do what they do best—invent. Despite the hue and cry of the politically correct, who rarely pass courses in economics, that it was rewarding the rich at the expense of the poor, it worked.

One of the biggest examples of PC being ignorant and proud of it was in the way they disparaged the 'Laffer Curve' because it had been drawn on a napkin in a restaurant. This naturally made the 'Laffer Curve' intellectually suspect despite the fact that Art Laffer was then an economist on the faculty at the University of Chicago and that all economic theories can either be drawn graphically on napkins or spelled out in simple mathematical shorthand using algebraic formulas. All Laffer did in fact, was draw a standard concave curve with two points on the 'X axis' where Y equaled zero.

The first point represented the amount of taxes that could be collected if there wasn't any income tax. The second would be the amount collected if the tax rate was set at 100%. Somewhere in the positive quadrant of the graph there was a point where an optimal tax rate would produce the maximum amount of tax revenue given total GDP. This is something every 8th grader is supposed to learn, but to determine the actual point, one must take the first derivative of the slope of the curve and set the change in Y equal to zero—basic Isaac Newton.

The need for deregulation was equally obvious and fell within Schumpeter's conditions for an economic environment conducive to business. No one then or now disputes the importance of regulation in ensuring the health of our citizens and environmental quality. Clean water wasn't really the issue, although that is something the PC harp on to this day. The purpose of deregulation was never to allow companies to poison us and maximize profits through rampant pollution.

The question was whether to regulate through coercion, something the PC tend to favor, or through the creation of incentives that would achieve the same result. The former, leaving aside philosophical concerns, always results in a series of rigid rules and interpretations that ultimately require the courts to sort out. This adds both to the cost of doing business and to that of government while clogging the court system. When the smoke clears, often the only winners are those who profit from the litigation process and aim to achieve extremely narrow goals.

Another problem is that the state of the art in the environmental and related sciences overtakes the rules with those least knowledgeable ending up becoming the regulators. This compounds the problem and adds to total costs—often at the expense of shutting down entire industries such as timber in the Pacific Northwest and Northern California. Despite today's hue and cry about the loss of high paying American jobs, those who've done most of the complaining seem to be those who've been responsible for the several thousand lost jobs to protect the spotted owl. A bird who's really quite adaptable until it's eaten by his big cousin—the California owl.

The alternative involving structured incentives, reduces the costs involved while letting companies meet the goal as they see fit with the proviso that the goal will be met. This is the principle behind fuel mileage and emission standards successfully prevailing in the automobile industry. It also avoids the rigidity problem by letting technological evolution dictate changes in regulatory standards and compliance, while requiring only 'prodding' from the government. The result is that out of any company's available revenue, the amount consumed by unproductive regulation is reduced so that prices don't have to be raised to pay for it and more money becomes available for salaries and R&D.

'Bubba' & The Budget Deficit

During the 1992 presidential election, Bill Clinton ran using the campaign slogan: 'It's the economy, stupid'. Once in the White House, according to the *Washington Post's* Bob Woodward, the new President and his cabinet found themselves wondering what do we do now. They didn't have a plan, just the slogan so they cobbled a plan together raising taxes and went merrily on their way.

They were lucky in that the economy had already started recovering from the Gulf War triggered recession, rather mild as it turned out, with real GDP growth exceeding 4% over 1992's last quarter. From there, counter to their pronouncements ever since, the Clinton Administration got a free ride from there thanks to the foundation laid by Reagan and help from Alan Greenspan's Federal Reserve.

The core of the Clinton argument behind his claim to be the 'author' of the subsequent boom, was the generation of a balanced budget and then a budget surplus because of his fiscal measures. The underlying theory was that by balancing the budget, Federal demand for credit would no longer pre-empt private credit demand, thus lowering interest rates and reducing American dependence upon foreign capital.

All of this provides the Democrat's current presidential hopeful with creditable rhetoric, but the reality is a little different starting with the fact that during the Reagan years the connection between interest rates and budget deficits had been cut. When Reagan arrived on the scene, prevailing interest rates had hit a generational if not historic peak. Then came the tax cuts and relatively 'massive' budget deficits resulting from two factors.

First, the Democratically controlled Congress never agreed to spending restraint and passed only one massive appropriations bill funding all governmental activities each year. This put Reagan in a box since he couldn't veto the entire thing because it was 'all or none', so he had no choice but sign off on the entire package. Secondly, Reagan had decided that the US could win the Cold War by outspending the Soviet Union on technologically advanced weapons knowing that the USSR couldn't keep up and if they tried, it would bankrupt their economy—which eventually happened.

Additionally, there are a few other points that are conveniently overlooked. Throughout the Reagan—Bush I years, following the tax cuts, federal spending grew consistently at a rate less than the rate Federal revenues grew. This meant that the smaller number, federal receipts, were compounding at a faster rate than federal spending so that eventually the two would come together. That is until the federal bailout of the savings and loan industry that actually only bailed out the depositors. The S&Ls themselves, counter to popular opinion, disappeared leaving their shareholders with expensive wallpaper.

The problem that was created for the US Treasury was that the depositors had to be paid first and this required some $300 plus million in borrowings under the first Bush Administration. Once this was done, the Resolution Trust Corporation, formed to administer liquidation of the savings and loan industry, was slowly able to convert all the assets it had accumulated into cash. As stuff became cash during the latter Bush I years and the first two years of the Clinton Administration, the extra-ordinary deficit that had been created to finance the depositor bailout was paid down. Thus making it appear that Clinton had accelerated the decline of the annual budget deficit when in fact his success was a function of happenstance.

Then there is the question of whether federal budget deficits really matter. For years I kept telling clients that the key issue was not the actual size of the budget deficit, it was its proportionate size relative to the overall economy and whether the Treasury could adequately finance it. As the United States found out during World War Two, when the national debt rose to a multiple factor exceeding the then size of the economy, a debt of that magnitude could be financed at extremely low interest rates and avoid hurting the economy.

Since that war, the annual federal deficit has tended to range around 2% of the total size of the American economy, albeit rising in nominal size—partially due to the continuing impact of inflation. Probably the biggest problem caused by our national debt is that a significant segment of it is owned by foreign creditors because of the dollar's role as the world's reserve currency and its role in the vast international underground economy, again without a deleterious effect.

The United States has also habitually run a sizeable international trade deficit that likewise tends to grow as the economy gets bigger, thus requiring foreigners to reinvest that trade deficit inside the US, partially by buying Treasury bonds. The problem with this is not one of other countries opting to invest the surplus elsewhere due to a lack of confidence in the 'full faith and credit of the US Government.

It's that someday they might need the cash themselves and be forced to liquidate their Treasury bond holdings for reasons that have nothing to do with the United States. However, if they do, the initial impact will be in a negative adjustment of the dollar's value relative to other currencies. Once that happens, then the Treasury's ability to finance the national debt from international sources could be a problem regardless of the size of the annual budget deficit.

Just as important for the size of the annual budget deficit is the impact of marginal tax rates and the availability of funds to purchase newly issued Treasury bonds and corporate debt compared to the monies that flow into funding 'tax free' debt. When interest rates on long-term taxable bonds were at 10% with the top marginal tax rate sitting around 70%, the after-tax return to the investor was only 3%. Once the top marginal rate was cut to 38%, that after-tax return jumped to 6.8%—almost double. It also re-arranged investor allocations between 'tax-free' municipal debt (bonds issued by states) and taxable debt (federal and corporate debt)—particularly for those in the lesser tax brackets.

Because American capital markets are highly competitive and efficient, the net effect of the tax cut thus was to cut prevailing interest rates well below 10%. In turn the cost of money (debt capital) for both corporations and the US Government got lowered and this lowered cost filtered its way through the economy into lower interest rates on mortgages etc. Once coupled with reduced tax rates on corporations, this same process worked to lower the cost of short-term working capital borrowings and provided companies with slightly higher cash flows to finance inventories and increased employment.

Ergo, one cannot completely credit the Clinton Administration's fiscal policies for the lowered structure of interest rates that helped feed the boom of the 1990s; especially since much of his budgetary restraint came after the Republicans gained control of the House of Representatives following the 1994 election. It was the two working in concert that capped federal spending growth that was further eased by severe cuts in spending on defense and the various intelligence agencies because of the 'peace dividend' derived from the collapse of the Soviet Union.

The Roaring 1990s

We've all heard the repetitive claims by former Clintonites about all the jobs that they created and how their policies created the prosperity of the 1990s. This is a lot like Calvin Coolidge claiming credit for the 1920s boom. Basically the 1990s boom was a direct product of the Reagan years where his economic incentive and deregulation policies triggered advances in computer engineering that finally led to the burst of creative economic activity that crescendoed during the Clinton years. Just like when the development of electricity and the combustible engine culminated in the 1920s boom with Cal Coolidge going along for the ride one as did Bill Clinton seventy years later.

The initial stages of this cycle started in the 1980s following the first Reagan tax cuts, which included a reduction in the capital gains tax. This freed up frozen assets because investors no longer needed to hold on to stocks for a lifetime out of fear that the tax bill would devour years of appreciation. Now they could sell what were once 'blue chip' growth companies but had since slipped into 'middle age' paying salaries and taxes without much further benefit for their shareholders. Investors could also now invest in more speculative but promising stocks, knowing that they could sell them for a profit without paying predatory taxes.

Collectively this freed up a lot of 'dead capital' and released investment funds for high tech start-up ventures that ultimately changed the world of commerce. Furthermore, it opened the door for 'high priced talent' to exchange cash based salaries for stock options or a percentage ownership in the venture. If the venture succeeded, they stood to make more money than they ever could in a salaried status. On the other hand, the use of 'incentive based compensation' allowed newly emerging companies to retain the cash they needed for research and development, prototypes, and marketing—a 'win-win' situation all around and the driving force behind Silicon Valley.

Eventually, as enough of these start-ups became successful and went public, more start-ups followed with enough of them going public at gradually more inflated prices as the whole process gained a momentum that didn't appear to be stoppable. Technological advances, especially in computer science and telecommunications that fed an ever increasing number of technological advances until the world finally choked on it all and the boom collapsed.

As the mantra of new business paradigms marched onward, those with the ideas and affiliates whose pay was based on incentives kept making more money. With each new public offering, those in on the ground floor, plus many others, cashed out some of their profits and used the proceeds to 'buy' bigger toys. Because no one can accurately gage the financial impact of a technological revolution, just like the 1920s and the late 1960s—early 1970s, imaginations ran wild with assumptions of bigger markets than there were going to be for each new 'high tech' product.

The inability to forecast cash flows with any kind of reliability extended to both state and the federal government. The net effect was that budget projections with their accompanying planned expenditures, began to exceed reality as tax revenue piled up. This, coupled with the structural changes in social security in the 1980s that planned for surpluses until the baby boomers started retiring, is what finally produced the budget surpluses—massive projected surpluses that would last into the foreseeable future.

'George W's Recession'

It was all smoke and mirrors, but not the product of a deliberate effort to deceive the American people as a few have claimed. Once the boom collapsed, all the incentive based compensation, including stock options and capital gains from the over exuberant stock market, collapsed with it. Of course the tax revenues projected to come from this house of cards likewise evaporated, leaving budget deficits 'as far as the eye could see' in its wake.

This is what the politically correct cannot grasp as they harangue the Bush Administration for causing the problem. When George W. walked into the White House in January 2001, the party had been over for several months and the country was already in a recession. Even former Vice President Al Gore has stated that he believes the recession started in March 2000. Next came the destruction of New York's World Trade Center in the '911' attack that was followed by a severe dislocation in the air transport and hospitality industries.

Finally we had the inevitable emergence of corporate scandals whose number fell way short of perception, just like the 1930s, with their subsequent negative impact on stock prices. While its true that the collapse of Enron, MCI World Com, Global Crossing, et al hurt a lot of people and destroyed retirement accounts, the real economic damage was the multi-trillion dollar loss in stock values across the board.

Suddenly everyone had less money. The fact that more investors should have sold out long before the bubble burst was immaterial because it wasn't going to happen since that's the essence of a speculative bubble. Instead they blamed their losses, just like after 1929, on the corporate accounting frauds that occurred under Clinton and, despite the fact that these have been vigorously prosecuted under President Bush, the latter's the one 'blamed' for their occurrence.

As nascent 'dot.coms' and their ilk collapsed all over the place, many respectable companies like Lucent Technologies (the old Bell Laboratories unit of AT&T) had to downsize in a hurry because the customers they'd rapidly expanded to serve suddenly evaporated. That left them with billions in excess inventories that quickly became obsolete. Jobs were shed with a vengeance. The world had suddenly became a sad place in a hurry.

So why didn't the economy tank as it had after similar episodes of this nature? The first reason probably is that America has learned to live on consumer debt, which is quite possibly the most worrisome long term economic problem we face as it continues to pile up at very unhealthy rates. Between an endless number of credit cards and taking out the equity in their homes via second mortgages made cheaper by the lowest interest rates in 50 years, the average American has been able to keep spending—job or no job.

The Federal Reserve under Alan Greenspan has also helped out by maintaining more than adequate liquidity in the economy to offset any deflationary pressure that might have materialized. The final reason, unlike the Hoover Administration's reaction when faced with similar conditions, George W. Bush took the bull by the horns and got Congress to cut taxes. Unfortunately, like the Reagan tax cuts, the Bush tax cuts were structured to phase in over several years; thus causing a deferral of income recognition and mitigating their impact while extending the recovery process.

The end result was that the American economy went through a rather mild recession where the economy barely grew in 2001 after producing the obligatory two quarters of negative growth to count as a recession. The unemployment rate eventually reached 6% of the labor force—versus something under a historically abnormal 4%. Of course the federal budget deficit grew too, rising to roughly

4.5% of American GDP greatly due to the surge of spending for homeland security, the twin wars, and expansion of the medicare benefit to partially cover the cost of prescription drugs for senior citizens.

These are hardly earth-shattering events, particularly since continued economy recovery will start bringing the budget deficit back to its normal 1% to 2% of GDP. However this is not the way the politically correct are portraying the situation. From their ranting and raving, assuming one took it at face value, under George Bush the economy has suffered its worse debacle since Herbert Hoover was in the White House.

This claim blatantly ignores a lot of negative downturns in the business cycle over the past 70 years, including several during my career in the securities industry that I could have done without. As recessions go, the 2000—2001 recession was amongst the mildest. A far cry from the days when FDR sat in the White House when unemployment rates topped out at 25% of the labor force with women not even part of it, to the 10% to 14% rate prevailing towards Pearl Harbor.

We haven't had a real down year in real GDP growth since the 'rust belt crisis' and collapse of the oil industry in the early 1980s and nothing like the more than 25% drop in economic activity that occurred from April 1930 through 1932. However the steel industry did pirouette again as a result of continuing structural problems within that industry. A problem the Bush Administration attempted to 'solve' by imposing tariffs on imported steel. Unfortunately, though he did buy the steel industry some time to 'restructure', the tariffs effectively raised steels prices to the detriment of steel users' global competitive position.

Even their cry that the tax cuts only benefited the rich is bogus. The real rich have adequate tax planning so they can avoid the higher marginal brackets, just like John Kerry's trust fund wife did in 2003 when her effective tax rate came in around 17% despite being the heir to the Heinz Foods fortune of close to one billion dollars. No, the high income beneficiaries of Bush's tax cuts are those who have a chance to become rich because their income comes from performance incentives or periodically productive years of self employment, provided the tax code doesn't chop them off at the knees.

These are the taxpayers who the Democrats want to make pay higher taxes despite the fact they already provide the preponderance of income tax revenue the federal government collects. Most of the rest of us, almost 50% of American families, have effective been removed from the income tax roles with many in the lower income levels receiving the earned income tax credit. (in reality a negative income tax) This still doesn't stop their 2004 presidential nominee from promoting his election by promising to tax the 'wealthy' and using the money to provide a tax cut for those who no longer pay federal income taxes, a rhetoric that implies a socialist agenda.

Another reason this is a fallacy is that the top 1% of American incomes paid over 32% of the total federal income tax for the 2003 tax year compared to 31% during the 2000 tax year. For the top 20% of all American incomes, the overall income tax load for 2003 came to just over 82% versus the 81% for tax year 2000. Even when the Congressional Budget Office's inclusion of the social security/medicare levy is considered, the top 20% pay a disproportionate amount, 64% for tax year 2003 versus 65% for tax year 2000.

The reason for the modest swing once FICA is considered is that this levy is and has always been regressive in nature; something the Democrats don't want to bring up in their 2004 platform calling for 'class warfare', a term describing socialist political strategies for over a century.

The Job Market

The only complaint the politically correct have pertains to job growth, but even there they ignore reality and that reality is greatly a structural problem created by technological change. This is hardly a new problem as the whole process of industrialization has been one of inventing machines allowing semi-skilled workers to offset shortages in skilled workers and then replace them. In fact, the conflict has been raging ever since the high middle-ages when medieval guilds began to lose their monopoly over industrial practices.

The difference this time was that the computer science revolution has replaced management and knowledge workers with machines and they never expected it. Up until the appearance of Apple's first microcomputer, the 'big irons' had been used to sort data and crunch numbers under the closely guarded watch of corporate data-processing departments. Data storage space and processing time was still 'expensive' so that the layers of management that had been built up over the years were still needed to collect information, consolidate it and then funnel it up the chain of command. Management, under this regime was a hierarchical monitoring process.

Once the ubiquitous universe of PCs, workstations et al reached a critical level throughout the business world, the productivity they brought to the office eliminated the need for several layers of 'monitoring' and middle management became redundant. This was the 1980s and corporations, needing every competitive advantage they could squeeze out of their operations to avoid annihilation by Japanese firms, dismissed thousands of them.

There were some hard feelings generated by this, particularly when some financier would see a brain dead company that rarely did anything more than pay taxes and salaries—one that was ripe for 'restructuring. After assembling the financing, the 'corporate raider' would then buy up the outstanding shares, reorganize the acquisition's entire operation—selling off components, that were often the product of the conglomerate craze of the 1960s boom, that didn't fit. Finally, once completed, the restructured entity would be resold back to the public for a substantial profit.

These were highly leveraged activities because they could only be done with borrowed money given the size of some of the corporations that were restructured. Additionally, it was the high degree of leverage and the potentially significant profits that could be made that justified the risk involved—a risk that could only be justified in light of the much lower marginal and capital gains tax rates represented by the Reagan tax cuts.

Naturally there was a lot of pain involved, that left bad feelings in its wake. But the restructuring had to be done if American business wanted to remain competitive. The alternative would have been to emulate the French with the resulting economic stagnation that old Europe suffers from today. Without Reagan's changes to the tax code, American enterprise probably wouldn't have undergone the necessary change.

One resulting irony is that the Japanese, whom many at the time felt would replace the United States as the world's premier economy, are now only beginning to 'restructure' as their historically inflexible corporate structures have proven incapable of pulling Japan out of its decade long slump. Unlike the Japanese and the fact that jobs have been lost forever, the emergence of new businesses induced by the Reagan incentives eventually brought most of middle management back into the labor force.

We're seeing this again with the disparity between the household survey that counts the self-employed and the employment statistics that doesn't. This results in more people acknowledging that they're employed and implies a higher rate of job creation that than latter suggests because people who go out and start their own businesses do not show up on payroll reports until they've begun to file personal income tax returns. Unfortunately for the political process, the politically correct don't get this as their rhetoric focuses on the false premise that only existing companies create jobs.

As noted, the cycle that emerged during the Reagan years continued to compound leading to the technology structure in place today throughout the commercial world. A structure that's clearly decentralized, automated to a level that no one twenty years ago could have fully expected, and functions through 'cheap telecommunications' with the internet as its hub. This has made globalization of knowledge a reality and geographic location inconsequential.

Today engineers working in India can collaborate with their colleagues in Detroit without leaving their desks. Stock analysts can do their research in Idaho and e-mail the results around the world. Through e-commerce, companies can link their entire supply and distribution chains with business partners without ever having one piece of paper change hands. Tele-marketers in Cape Town or Dublin now cold call prospects for an insurance company based in Des Moines, and so on.

The big shock is what this is now doing to 'Silicon Valley' and its kindred cluster centers. It was one thing when robots replaced factory workers, creating massive productivity and quality gains that's held down prices and increased profits that have been shared with employees. But now it's leading to the replacement of computer science engineers within the United States by equally competent ones in India, etc.

However outsourcing and the use of foreign labor has always been a source of complaint as businesses use technology as a tool facilitating the employment of cheaper labor. The primary difference today is that, thanks to the internet, is that 'cheaper labor' doesn't have to be imported like it was 100 years ago. The 'work' can now be shipped electronically to the source, which is becoming just as competent in some fields as American labor thanks to the extent we've educated third world nationals in our universities. Of course the United States under a President Kerry could put a stop to this by refusing to grant student visas to foreign students and thus eliminate the potential labor pool for jobs to be outsourced overseas to.

This problem's especially acute given the massive employment build-up within computer related technology during the 'dot.com' bubble. However unfortunate this is for 'Silicon Valley' it's inevitable and represents the price to be paid as many parts of their world grow into mature industries. Furthermore, the information technology revolution has now morphed into an evolutionary process as the marginal benefit of upgrading one's IT infrastructure has continued to shrink. And this isn't going to stop as further dislocation is on the horizon, particularly in developed nations like the US.

As Schumpeter put it—creative destruction is the hallmark of free enterprise. It can't work any other way as new technology and improved goods and services provide consumers with an incentive to replace the stuff they already have. The process seems to work a little better when the clothes we wear are new and not the ones we inherited from our great-grandparents as was the case several centuries ago.

Nor can policy makers expect industries to stay put like they did decades ago, allowing them to 'milk the golden goose' for all it's worth while constructing the perfect regulatory world in the name of 'social goals'. As many cities and states inside the US have learned the hard way, companies can just pick up and move. Wall Street is hardly confined today to New York City. It's now in New Jersey and Connecticut. Part of 'Silicon Valley' is now in southwestern Idaho. Even Germany is seeing its companies shed jobs to more receptive economic climates in its Eastern European neighbors.

There comes a point where public policy drives business away and the solution isn't to build bigger walls making it stay as the politically correct behind the 2004 John Kerry Campaign for the White House propose. Raising taxes on businesses, especially punitive ones for companies who outsource jobs overseas, increasing the regulatory burden, and then sealing off our borders to imports from every country not meeting our environmental and labor standards would only accelerate the departure.

It's also been tried before. Under President Hoover and his immediate predecessors, labor force growth was choked off by stringent immigration quotas. Both business and personal income taxes were raised in a vain attempt to balance the federal budget. Then there was the Smoot—Hawley Tariff that effectively closed the American economy to imports and accelerated a disastrous international trade war, driving the proverbial spike into the world economy. Collectively these measures, coupled with the FRB restricting financial liquidity, produced the perfect storm that culminated in the Great Depression of the 1930s.

One of these measures was the minimum wage, which when coupled with the Davis Bacon Act requiring government contractors to pay laborers prevailing union wages closed off employment opportunities to African Americans and other minorities. As many economic studies have repeatedly discovered, minimum wage laws tend to preclude the hiring of unskilled individuals when their productivity value is below that of the minimum wage.

Ergo, anytime the minimum wage is raised above what the market can afford for minimally skilled individuals, their employment opportunities are reduced and businesses end up with a greater incentive to replace those jobs with technology. In my case as a brokerage office manager, every time the minimum wage rose and the State of California increased the administrative cost of hiring people, I went out and up-graded my computer software to reduce the need for employees.

The problem faced today then, as Democrats fan the flames of class warfare while being cheered on by the politically correct, is that the policies their leadership now propose replicates the perfect storm of 1930. They're simply a rehash of what turned a traditional business downturn into the worst economic debacle since Andy Jackson walked out the door and left everyone with a depression that lasted almost 20 years.

Instead, the solution is to let Americans do what they've always done well. Do the value added activities of invention and let the rest of the world fall in behind to refine production processes that lower the cost of what we've created. Granted this seems to be an exercise of staying one step ahead of the wolf, but it's worked for almost two hundred years. The key is to continue to emphasize the incentive and business climate components of Schumpeter's model.

Therefore we need to listen to the 'Austrians' and not the politically correct statists. President Bush did this and the result since mid-2003 haws been the strongest period of economic growth in 20 years; roughly 4% per annum, plus or minus a couple of basis points. (1/100th of a percent per basis point).

9

Other Issues of Public Policy

Education

Probably the one issue that has the greatest impact on the long-run viability of the American economy is education—more specifically, the lack of it and how to correct the problem. The prevailing assumption is that there is a direct correlation between a good education and the amount of money spent on it. If this were true, then how does one explain the educational accomplishments of many third world students, particularly from India, compared to the rather abysmal performance of their American counterparts.

Another rather interesting discrepancy exists between some western states like North Dakota that spend proportionately little on education per student compared the vast sums spent per student in many northeastern cities. If money per student was the primary determinate of educational success, then the graduates of Washington DC's high schools would be statistically the 'best' in the world, while the products of North Dakota's schools would being little more than morons.

Since the reverse is true, money cannot be the sole answer. However the educational establishment and many parents miss this key point. The liberal politically correct candidates offered up by the Democrats who pander to them preach to anyone within hearing distance that George W. Bush's 'No Child Left Behind Act' has been inadequately funded. This is quite a claim since federal spending on education has risen over 30% during the Bush Administration compared to the spending levels of his predecessor.

The reality is that there can never be enough money made available for education in their minds because education is not the primary issue amongst them. The important issue for them is in maintaining the status quo that has served them well, with more money available for salaries, perks, and accruements. Remember, the role of the teacher's unions is to make sure every teacher keeps his or her job, no matter how minimal their performance, and to rake in ever higher salaries for administrators when the opportunity arises.

Over the years, as educational standards have deteriorated since their 1960s apex and the formation of teacher's unions, the education industry has built an administrative edifice to financially support just about every doctoral thesis that's come down the pike with ever increasing numbers of administrators hired to put them into action. Because their salaries are a mark-up from prevailing salaries paid to the 'average teacher', the more the underpaid teacher gets, the more the senior staff gets.

As pay for the administrative staff rises, so do the perks and number of administrative assistants assigned to them, just like any other monopolistic bureaucratic organization. Along with the proclivity for an ever-increasing administrative burden, comes more 'functions' the schools feel they need to perform that ultimately come at the expense of the classroom. Eventually, if left unchecked, all these ancillary activities cannibalize the core mission of educating kids.

The schools of education domiciled in most of our universities aren't much better. When one breaks it down, a degree in education is little more that an junior collage education with two semesters of 'teaching classes' and a one year apprenticeship added to it. Take one almost a full semester for 'social adjustment course' such as 'gender or ethnic studies', and one's down to just over one and a half semesters of a college education before the nascent teacher is thrown into the classroom.

The net effect is that the teacher barely knows more than what one expects their students to have learned by the end of he 12th grade. Given this process, it's little wonder than almost 26% of those teaching in California can't pass the basic skills exams require to maintain their certificates and that too many teachers can barely pass the tests they give their students. The question becomes how can one teach a subject one barely understands?

They can't, which Hillary Clinton discovered when she pushed for education reform in Arkansas while her husband was governor. Based on teacher testing following passage of the reforms, Bill Clinton's state administration discovered that 50% of Arkansas's teachers had failed the general subject tests. By the then recently enacted rules, this meant that half of Arkansas's teachers were supposed to be fired.

But recognizing the political ramifications of this, Clinton's political strategist Dick Morris polled the voters, asking them what percentage of teachers they expected to fail. When the sample came back with a figure of 10%, the state finally fired one out of every ten teachers. This still left close to half the teachers lacking the knowledge necessary to adequately teach Arkansas students so the state remained the national home of the uneducated.

Thus the country has math teachers who've never gone past Algebra II in high school, or science teachers with only two college courses in general science teaching high school physics. Worse, we get gym teachers teaching history and economics. Of course most teachers go on to graduate study since the more credit hours they build up, the higher their salary. Unfortunately, in many cases, these graduate hours are in education—not the subjects they teach so that eventually they do have a master's degree, occasionally their doctorates, but not necessarily in the subjects they teach. The cure as required by 'NCLB' and poorly received by the education establishment is that teachers major in two subjects—education and what they're going to teach.

This is the military system and it works. Every military school, from recruit depot to a command & staff college, uses instructors who have demonstrated knowledge and competence in their field. Once military personnel are assigned to be instructors, they're taught how to teach and design course curriculums before they're allowed in the classroom. In my own case, having been the Academics Officer for the Marine Corps' Staff NCO Academy at Quantico and other instructor assignments, the accompanying cram courses in education taught by EdDs worked out to the equivalent of six to eight courses in anybody's school of education.

A corollary issue is where does the money go once the school system gets it and too often its not into the classroom. One of the more embarrassing moments in the history of the Los Angeles Unified School District was when the *Los Angeles Times* published a report exposing the problems behind the $500 million the district had spent on its new Belmont High School near downtown LA. Turns out that the partially finished campus couldn't be used because it was sited on top of an old oil field where natural gas with its methane and benzene components was still leaking.

At the same time the *Los Angeles Times* reported that kids attending school within the district were lucky if they had textbooks and in a great number of cases they didn't, none at all. Some of the more fortunate did have access to textbooks, but only if their teachers handed them out and let them do their homework during class. They weren't allowed to take them home since the same books were needed for the next period and so on until the school day was finished.

Despite this, the LA USD couldn't find a way to shift resources from its downtown headquarters to solve the problem. Their solution was to complain to the state legislature about the need for more money. What's more frightening is that the problem was much worse in several other school districts within LA County—particularly Compton and Inglewood.

Then there is the issue of standards. One of the requirements of 'NCLB' is that schools graduate students that have met minimum standards. Secondly, as kids progress from K through 12, they must be tested to ascertain whether they're actually learning anything along the way with consequences for those schools that fail to demonstrate progress in meeting these standards.

So far so good, except that the education establishment has fought this every step of the way, demanding more money because meeting the 'NCLB' goals is 'impossible without it'. This shouldn't however be that great a challenge since the standard for high school graduates is little more than an 8th grade education because not every kid goes beyond algebra I and, at least in Idaho, they start taking the 'graduation test' in the 10th grade. Additionally, history and civics don't seem to be part of the equation.

Thus all we're really asking the schools to do is ensure that their product knows how to read and write, add and subtract at the junior high school level. It shouldn't be that difficult considering that the United States collectively spends over $500 billion per year on education.

This gets to another issue—expectations. When I went through Instructor Training School at Quantico in 1972, there were two concepts that had floated into educational thinking since I'd graduated from High School. The first and accepted one was that the Commandant of the Marine Corps sends 30 privates to cooking school and he doesn't expect only 10 of them to walk out the door knowing how to cook. All 30 need to master the curriculum and function as competent cooks or there'd be a moral problem in whichever unit they were eventually assigned to.

It's the second one that causes the problem. Every student needs to be treated in such a way that his self-esteem is enhanced. This is fine up to a point, but there is something to be said for reading the riot act to those unwilling to put in the effort to meet the standard. As a student I too appreciated the accolades. However there were times when having my heels locked before a teacher while being admonished about how I wasn't working up to my potential was sorely needed.

During the first semester of my freshman year at Rochester I went into my final exams with a solid GPA of 0.5 and it was perfectly clear that I had to do something to avoid the sudden termination of my collegiate career. Facing the abyss, since the U of R wasn't into providing a free ride when it came to academic standards, I had two choices—mail it in or suck it up. Fortunately for me I chose the latter and survived that semester with a 1.75 GPA.

The problem today is that kids don't have to face that stark reality. In the interests of preserving their sense of self-esteem, teachers hand out 'Cs' and maybe 'Ds' to failing students and bump everyone else's grades upwards so that nobody ever fails. As one of my professors in graduate school said, 'no one ever flunks out of a California State University campus anymore, they just fade away'. 'F' is the forgotten grade in school, in real life it isn't.

This is actually unfair to the student starting with those kids who do get straight 'As' in lets say one of Washington DC's high schools. Despite the apparent success, they end up scoring poorly on college admissions tests—a test where everyone gets 400 points for simply signing one's name, spelling it correctly is not required. Based on this, they either can't gain admission to one of the country's better colleges or they're admitted under a special dispensation and spend the next several years trying to hold their head above water.

Another variant is what several of us saw when we pushed a company of candidates through the Marine Corps's 10 week summer commissioning program in 1972. Assignment to platoons and companies depended solely on when a candidate checked in to OCS. Those arriving first went to Company A and the last arrivals ended up in Company D, so the population distribution was as random as one is going to get.

Amongst the 240 candidates we ended up with in Company A, four were from the historic black colleges and that evening, we sat all the candidates down on their footlockers and had them write their autobiography as per years of standard procedure. The ones that were turned in by the four from the black colleges were unreadable due to major punctuation problems, the lack of complete sentences and just about every other grammatical crime one can commit.

Other than that, for the most part, they turned out to be successful candidates including one that was outstanding except for problems with academics. This really wasn't their fault. They'd graduated from high school with a least a better than average performance, then graduated from colleges that promised them an education, and ended up with a terminal rank in the Marine Corps of first lieutenant because of their general illiteracy. They couldn't perform the duties of a captain because they couldn't prepare and generate the reports sent up the chain of command that captains assigned to staff jobs, or as company commanders, need to prepare.

Additionally, as I emphasized at the time, if they ever had to deal with educated Africans, they'd have a problem because the latter are taught Oxford English and wouldn't understand why their English was so dysfunctional, effectively writing the African Americans off as 'dummies'. In essence, due to what I still believe is a desire to credential as many African Americans as possible, the schools they went to screwed them for life by not requiring that they meet certain minimum standards.

This is reflective of the soft bigotry that President Bush referred to when he pushed for passage of NCLB. Because of race, expectations are set low and when even these aren't met, everyone still gets a free pass. The result is a credential without meaning because the education it's supposed to represent was never provided.

This is equally true of Hispanics, a rather blanket term encompassing a multitude of ethnicity, and the insistence on bilingual education because its unfair to require them to learn English. The result is neither an education nor proficiency in America's language of law and a need refuted by the experience of the Chicanos within my age group.

We also screw the white kids; it's just done a little differently. When my brother was in high school during the 1960s, his Pre SAT score in English was markedly short of the mark his straight As implied. Taking this score down to the school, mother demanded an explanation behind the discrepancy only to be told that most kids aren't going to Stanford anyway, so why sweat it. Her response was that if her kid did want to go to Stanford, the La Canada High School had guaranteed it wouldn't happen.

Therefore due to soft educational standards and inflated grades, too many of all races end up in college without the skills necessary to do the work—even in what *US News & World Report* refers to as 'category three' schools. This puts universities like Boise State and the California State University system in the position where they have to teach newly admitted freshman high school. The lack of a real high school education has also turned many junior colleges into nothing more than post high school prep schools and neutralized their role as funnels channeling kids to four year colleges with the first two years on the books.

For the kids, this means that four years of college is actually going to require five or six with all the accompanying expenses that's entailed. Expenses that have been escalating at a rate much greater than the rate of inflation for years for reasons that John Kerry needs to ask universities about rather than blaming George Bush for. Whoever's responsible, this isn't fair to anybody, but it does sustain enrollment and thus an accompanying level of tenured faculty and administrators.

One way to enable students to break free of the bonds educators have entrapped them in is to give them and their parents choices, thus injecting that the fearful word 'competition' into the lives of educators secure in their current sinecures. Creating creditable educational choices for parents whose kids are now caught in 'under performing' schools would reverse the educational dynamic from one of process to one producing results.

This is the core principle behind the charter school movement, school vouchers, and 'NCLB'. When a school habitually fails to produce graduates meeting an acceptable educational standard, its students become free to transfer to other schools and if the alternative is a private school, then they're to be given vouchers to cover the cost of tuition. Wherever this regime is in place, existing schools with substandard results lose students and with that loss, they lose funding along with the 'perks' and tenured positions that come with them.

This means that if these schools want to retain students and economic viability, they must rise to the occasion and actually educate someone. Ergo, educators are going to have to change procedures, curriculum, and accept the fact that their students are going to have to learn or they'll lose their jobs. Additionally, they're going to have to redirect resources from all those 'nice to have' programs that contribute little to educating kids in essential core subjects to what works.

Out goes 'the new math' where kids don't need to come up with the correct answer and back in comes recitation of multiplication tables. History teachers are going to have to teach history instead of devoting the daily hour to 'understanding the Beatles' as one Boise ID teacher does (*Idaho Statesman* Apr 04). Hopefully, as a result, we'll have high school graduates who know something about the Normandy Landings instead of Idaho's World War Two internment camps.

Incorporated in all this is the idea of 'merit pay' for those teachers who actually accomplish their mission or provide necessary mentoring to those who can't quite seem to get it. The theory is that this would provide teachers with the incentive to go 'above and beyond' the minimum necessary to retain their jobs, not that any of them really ever get fired for incompetence. The challenge is in finding a way to make this work because when it has been used on the state college level, the faculty tends to find a way to undermine the process as any good bureaucracy does.

Naturally the teacher's unions are fighting these measures every step of the way starting with the old canard about the 'separation of church and state' since many of the voucher choices in inter-city schools mean a student body shift into Catholic schools. It also means that money goes elsewhere since school districts are compensated by the size of their total enrollment and a lessor enrollment means fewer administrative jobs within any one school district.

The problem the old guard faces however, is that 'choice' works whenever it has been given a chance and where it hasn't, like within the Washington DC school district, the hue and cry to implement it over the dead bodies of school administrators has been deafening. Unfortunately inter-city politicians have too much at stake in their alliances with the existing education establishment to allow 'choice' and they're supported by their politically correct allies in the Democratic Party parked in Congress and state legislatures across the country.

Foreign Trade & Competitive Advantage

If the United States does not solve the education problem, its competitive advantage that's historically been based on invention, entrepreneurialship, and other value added activities, is at risk—particularly since other nations have now caught up and surpassed us in the basic skills of mathematics and science. Today, we're the 'dummies' and if this remains the reality, the American economy will slide towards emulating today's 'old Europe' and take our ability to fund social security and other benefit programs for both the aged and poor with it.

This is a big problem because the demographics behind the 'baby boom generation' mean that the structure supporting social security benefits is untenable. The number of workers officially available to pay into the system isn't enough to generate the cash flow necessary to pay out the current level of benefits starting in 2011. Ergo, the social security system is insolvent on an actuarial basis—has been for years.

No amount of rhetoric pertaining to 'lock boxes' or separating the social security trust fund from the federal government's general fund can alter that reality. First, there is no trust fund beyond what was originally established to remove the payment of social security benefits from the annual congressional appropriations process. Secondly, the only asset available for 'surplus social security funds' to 'invest' in is the debt of the federal government.

Ergo, all social security surpluses are used to finance the 'national debt' and fund other governmental activities. Thus future social security benefits are only as good as the 'full faith and credit of the federal government' produced by the federal government's taxing authority. Thus the payment of benefits is totally dependent upon the strength of the American economy and anything that can be done to foster economic growth, particularly tax cuts creating investment capital despite their perceived impact on the budget deficit, is the only way future benefits can be 'guaranteed'.

There's also a looming problem with the current political issue of 'job outsourcing' where many traditional employment opportunities are shifted to overseas concerns because their retention within the 'lower 48' is no longer economical due to the loss of competitive advantage. When a Motorola has to run 'cram courses' for its new hires with high school diplomas to get them up to a minimal general education level, which Motorola has had to do since the mid-1980s, before they can actually use them in real jobs, America has a problem.

If Motorola or New York Life can find prospective employees in Ireland or India, where high school graduates are conversant in Oxford English, juxtaposed to 'ghetto English' spoken by too many of our high school graduates, they're going to fire the 'gringos' and move that part of their business overseas. The same holds true for much of the computer engineering work within Silicon Valley. During the 'high tech bubble' that sucked up all the available talent, there was a shortage of people having the requisite education to meet the demand for engineers, physicists, etc.

The solution was a temporary visa program that enabled those companies to import educated labor from overseas. Following the collapse of the bubble, the tight job market reversed itself, throwing many in the Valley out of work for the first time in over 20 years. However, as the Valley has come back with its return to profitability and increased R&D budgets over the past few years, the employees they've chosen to rehire are those who'd returned to India, China, etc.

This, thanks to the internet and e-commerce, has led to the emergence of 'high tech' centers in places like Bangladore on India's Deccan Plateau that can potentially displace American centers like the Valley and Boston's Highway 28. The same has been true of many of the country's manufacturing jobs with China and the former communist block as the beneficiaries. Part of this is again the result of advances in technology over the past decade and a need to have a presence in the fastest growing markets in the world. But a lot of it is due to the collapse of the productivity differential around the world emanating from the longstanding deterioration of our educational system.

This does not mean that the United States is doomed, but that the relative dynamic of economic relationships around the world is changing and that Ricardo's 'law of comparative advantage' still applies. This rule of international trade goes back to the 1820s and simply states that if everyone specializes in what they do best and then exchanges the products produced, everyone is better off. It also implies that the flow of goods and services will travel between nations as relative comparative advantages shift and that there is nothing that can be done about it unless everyone is willing to accept a lower standard of living by attempting to block the inevitable.

Ricardo's Law was the motivation behind NAFTA and all the recent free trade agreements that have ensued. The theory is that the economic emergence of developing countries will create larger markets for American goods, as the emergence of our economy did for the demand for British goods starting around 1740, but they need export markets to generate the 'cash' necessary to pay for them. This should be a win-win situation for all concerned and to a great extent statistics over the last decade support that despite the dislocation that has and always will occur between various economic segments within any one country.

This has not a one-way street though. German and French bureaucracy have done a lot to shift the productive flow to the United States because our business climate is superior to theirs—including our educational infrastructure. This is why the BMWs one sees around town are made in South Carolina. What once were imported cars from Japan are manufactured in North America because that's where the market is and whatever competitive advantage there is to making them in Asia is offset by transportation costs.

The sad fact, however, is that the current Democratic candidate for the White House doesn't seem to grasp this despite supporting every trade agreement the US has entered into since his initial election to the Senate almost 20 years ago. Now in an effort to buy votes, he's pandering to every one whose lost ground in the dynamic process, except for stockbrokers put out of business by the internet and earlier Congressional action, by proposing what amounts to trade restrictions aimed to preserve various 'rice bowls'.

What's missing in John Kerry's platform are the measures that help Americans retain their competitive advantage like telling educators to shut up about money and start changing the way they operate. Another point he could address is the regulatory interference that adds to overall corporate costs without leading to productivity improvements. Then there are all the escalating costs built into medical benefits, workers compensation, etc that used to add 30% to the cost of wages but now probably approach 50%.

Reining in the voracious appetites of America's trial lawyers and the toll they take from the judicial system would not be a bad place to start. Particularly since recent figures are showing that the price we pay for litigation costs have been rising some 3% to 4% per year since 2000. This is one reason the cost of employee benefits are continuing to rise at the rate they are, acting as a tax increase on everyone and negating some of the benefit of the Bush tax cuts.

Until these problems are mitigated, the United States can expect to see its competitive edge deteriorate. For the present, American workers are still the most productive in the world, but there are ominous signs on the horizon. Many of these are self-inflected starting with the problems in education where those who drop out of school short of a diploma face a life time of minimum wage employment. Those with a high school diploma aren't much better off because they lack the skills necessary for technology jobs that their schools have deprived them of.

Conversely, the best products of our university system remain the envy of the world, the problem here is that many majoring in the hard sciences and populate our graduate schools are born outside the US. The problem is in mustering the will to rearrange these equations and that's not politically correct. It's not even cool to bring these points up when victimization is being discussed because it's always someone else's fault.

Medical Costs & Pharmaceuticals

Pharmaceuticals represent one of America's premier industries and it's here that all the problems cited above come together—especially in the arena of biotechnology. Most government sponsored medical research, be it within the confines of institutions like the National Institute of Health or the broad realm of university scientific laboratories and medical schools, is basic research. Counter to prevailing perceptions of many of the politically correct, these facilities do not produce the specific drugs used to treat disease.

That role is taken on by our privately owned drug companies, be they ethical drug companies or bio-technology firms, who build on the discoveries of pure scientists pursuing their own intellectual interests and convert them into unique medications that target specific medical conditions. In the process these companies spend billions on research and development and years of detailed targeted research to come up with one blockbuster drug that can make the difference between life and death.

It also takes many dry runs to get it right according to FDA standards and often every successful drug that reaches the market is accompanied by many that don't; which makes the business a high risk one. Because it takes somewhere between $800 million to $1 billion to convert an idea into a drug and then push it through the FDA approval process before it can actually be used on patients, every ethical drug company needs to have several blockbusters continually in the pipeline.

With these costs, too many failures and not enough in the pipeline, even those pharmaceutical companies with historically excellent track records are slated to disappear—creative destruction in action. The same holds true for generic manufacturers where the competition can be fierce and the pipeline is dry.

Biotechnology concerns face even higher hurdles because they are often dependent upon the success of one drug out of the many they attempt to develop. As a rule, most of them lack the capital to see the process through to conclusion so that they're often forced to sell production rights to well heeled competitors in order to have enough funding to 'discover' another bio-engineered drug. This often takes years before that next discovery reaches fruition; which is why I've avoided recommending these companies over the years.

A final nasty fact of life for the drug industry is that although patents extend for a number of years, the clock starts at the beginning when the theoretical concept is presented to the patent office. Next comes several years of additional research before a drug assumes its ultimate form and the FDA approval process can begin. By the time this last step is completed, there isn't much time left on the clock to recover the billion dollars already spent on research and development, plus a few extra bucks to pay for all the failures.

This is what eludes the politically correct when they complain about 'high drug costs' for seniors and they ignore the fact that as medical research advances, every drug that evolves out of it is going to be that much more sophisticated. The days of simply mixing concoctions in petri dishes to produce a new anti-biotic are long gone. Another conveniently overlooked fact in the current debate about imported drugs from Canada is that every country has the right to revoke a patent.

In the case of ethical drugs, this has become a tool wielded by national health care authorities, where socialized medicine is the norm, to force American drug companies to sell drugs to their nationalized medical system at something close to the marginal cost of producing them. This expunges the cost of research and development from nationalized healthcare and why drugs from Canada are always going to be cheaper than drugs sold inside the US.

Because there still remains a positive difference between marginal revenue and marginal cost for each drug sold, America's drug companies have been willing to cooperate with the extortion—as long as American's pick up the tab for the research and the FDA approval process. This is also why, along with public relations objectives, the major drug companies are providing Africa with AIDS drugs for virtually zilch. At this point the marginal cost of producing them is almost nil, but their sale does little to replenish the kitty for future R&D.

Then there is the cost of litigation, another wedge item adding to the cost of medical care in the US and, on the margin, working against widening the productivity gap between Americans and third world labor. Every drug has 'side effects' and for every million or so people who consume a specific drug, a miniscule few will suffer a negative consequence that might include death.

These few represent big bucks to the trial lawyers like the Democrat's 2004 Vice Presidential nominee, Senator John Edwards. By finding a nominal plaintiff that a defined class of injured parties can be built around, a trail lawyer making it to the court house first (hopefully one that's plaintiff friendly) can become an instant millionaire once punitive damages are awarded. This is the great lottery to instant wealth for trial lawyers and every drug company is going to have its day in court whether 'guilty' or not, particularly when juries buy into the 'junk science' trial lawyers often resort to.

Also this is why the cost of malpractice insurance now represents almost half of a patient's anesthesiology bill and where judicial districts have proven to be the most friendly to the country's trial lawyers, whole fields of medicine like obstetrics and gynecology and neurology have left for safer jurisdictions. Ergo, if one has the wrong medical problem in Mississippi or West Virginia, a patient needs to travel to Tennessee for treatment. Furthermore, even where the judicial climate is 'doctor friendly', patients have to pay for unnecessary tests so that physicians can prove the negative in court.

The bottom line is that this ratchets up the cost of health care by adding millions to the cost of drugs and other medical expenses that someone else has to pay for. In some cases, particularly vaccines where litigation costs are notoriously high, this has resulted in companies dropping out of the business altogether. The price paid by the rest of us for this is an uninoculated population, making disease contagion that much more likely and the reason there's a shortage of anthrax vaccines for our troops in Iraq and why drug companies need special exemptions from litigation when it comes to 'orphan drugs'. Drugs for which there isn't a mass market due to the rarity of the conditions they treat.

One choice society has of course, is to nationalize the entire pharmaceutical industry. Doing this presupposes that the government is capable of operating it better than the private sector has to date, which given the track record of government enterprises is asking a lot. On the other hand, government is quite capable of burying any inefficiencies like it habitually has with government run nuclear power plants with their accompanying massive cost overruns and major environmental problems.

Nothing however, can prevent a nationalized pharmaceutical industry from being skewed to finding drugs to cure politically correct diseases like AIDS. With all the money committed so far, we have succeeded in keeping those with AIDs alive for long periods of time and converted it from an automatic death sentence to a condition one can live with.

There still isn't a vaccine for it and because it is a viral infection, there probably isn't a cure for it on the horizon, just like there isn't a cure for any other viral disease such as yellow fever, smallpox, or the ubiquitous flu. Regardless of the truth that we've never found a cure for vial infections, this wouldn't stop the politically correct from clamoring for ever increasing funding for AIDS research at the expense of funding for the medical problems we actually can do something for.

So the question before us, using drug costs as the surrogate for equivalent problems, is what's to be done to keep an important American industry viable, one that to some extent is already at risk due to the lack of potential biologists in the pipeline thanks to the country's educators. Plus, for a number of reasons, the cost of medical care driven by escalating pharmacy costs is working against strengthening American productivity and acting as a increasing tax on the country's consumers.

One step would be to reduce the impact on litigation costs on the industry but the trail lawyers and the Democrats in Congress they've bought, including their vice presidential wannabe, with campaign contributions prevent that. Another measure would be to reform the FDA approval process to reduce the costs involved and have those costs backed out of drug prices. Extending patent life might help so R&D expenses can be amortized over longer periods. This would annually reduce the amount the ethical drug companies need to add to drug prices to recover those R&D expenses, but at the same time it would delay the arrival of generic drugs that come to market without the need to recover that load.

Unfortunately, for the present, it seems that the choice favored by the politically correct is to legalize the importation of ethical drugs from Canada and thus eliminating the cost of R&D et al from American pharmacy bills altogether. This is essentially a shell game because the drugs concerned are manufactured in American plants, then exported to Canada under a price structure determined by Canadian bureaucrats before re-export back to the lower 48.

Now this might be politically expedient, given the media's coverage of seniors gathering together for bus rides to Canada to fill their prescriptions so that they won't have to choose between pills and food, but it precludes the recovery of research and development expenses. So far, on the margin, this isn't that big a threat, but if re-importation from Canada and elsewhere becomes long term policy, there won't be enough money available for pharmaceutical research.

Thus the politically correct in their search for expediency are asking us to forsake a cure for cancer or Alzheimer's in return for lower drug prices today. This is akin to peeing in one's pants to stay warm on a cold day.

The Environment and Energy

These two go together and are coupled with the availability of high paying jobs since the availability of energy is dependent upon the ability to look for additional sources that, thanks to the environmental movement, is often precluded. The truth is that despite the current rhetoric coming from the politically correct, the United States can never be truly energy independent. Petroleum is produced worldwide so that the relative cost of petroleum based energy will remain significantly below that of commonly discussed alternatives. Alternatives that also have their own environmental problems.

However there are things that can be done to reduce the cost of energy and detach some of our energy expenses from the impact of a periodically weak dollar, which was part of the problem in 2004. This goes back to the concept of purchasing power parity that is virtually useless in trading currency futures but is germane when dealing with the price of basic international commodities.

The essence of 'triple P' is that all commodities should carry the same price everywhere in terms of the purchasing power of various currencies. Therefore when the value of the dollar declines relative to other currencies, the price of these international commodities (including oil) must rise to balance. Thus the 2003-04 dollar, compared to the euro and Japanese yen, automatically raised the price of oil and its derivative refined products.

Neither George Bush nor John Kerry has anything to do with it, but the tremendous economic growth we've seen in recent years in mainland China and India does. This aggravates the problem. The equilibrium that's prevailed in the world oil market for years has been destroyed by the explosive emergence of these economies and the accompanying increased demand for petroleum based energy needed to sustain them. Today's world is not our father's Oldsmobile.

Because domestic oil production is priced in terms of the dollar, as are American refining costs and limitations on the ability of American oil companies to export oil, any incremental increase should marginally reduce oils North American price. The problem is that we've eliminated many of our potential new production sources for environmental reasons.

Thanks to various governmental fiats, offshore drilling in new areas is out. The same holds true for exploration in much of the Rocky Mountain's 'over thrust belt'. The most contentious exclusion has been the Alaskan Nature Reserve that experts believe could equal Prudhoe Bay's reserves. President Bush, as part of his long range energy plan the Democrats accuse him of not having despite its submission to Congress in 2001, and the Republicans have fought to open the preserve up to drilling under the premise that no long-term environmental harm would result.

Democrats oppose it because they believe drilling is axiomatically harmful to the environment irrespective of the fact that modern drilling techniques have proven to be environmentally neutral—no more fields of derricks since multiple wells can be drilled from one spot using angled drilling methods. If done properly, there are no leaks and above ground structures are barely noticeable. Once oil is found, all that's left is the central gathering facilities of which most are underground and research in other Arctic production areas have yet to verify environmental damage.

We've also greatly complicated the gasoline market for both environmental reasons, some of them necessary, and the proverbial NIMBY problem. Over the past quarter century not one new refinery has been built in the United States. What incremental increases to refinery capacity that have been built are located in the Caribbean—Trinidad, the Caymans, Venezuela, etc. Given the current political instability in the last listed country, this isn't exactly in our best interests, but that's our only politically acceptable option.

Then there are the 18 separate gasoline markets in the lower 48 created by all the environmentally required special blends required to deal with summer air pollution problems. Having lived in Los Angeles for much of my life, I can appreciate the benefits this has wrought, but the market impact has been to crank up the price of gasoline when these summer blends replace winter blends. This creates disparate markets with accompanying widely different pricing structures and leaves many regions, specifically California, subject to severe price spikes every time a refinery breaks down.

Aggravating the problem is that our pipeline capacity is max'd out so that increases in either the overall demand for gasoline or a need to shift product from one market to another must be transported by truck. Besides the added cost this generates, plus the incremental demand from the trucks used to haul it, transport by tanker truck is the riskiest way to move gasoline due to the increased potential for accidents and now the added risk of terrorism.

The solution obviously would be to build more pipelines, but doing so is expensive and pipelines must run through environmentally sensitive areas. Even though once built, natural vegetation takes over and eventually covers their route so that one hardly knows they're there, building them involves digging with accompanying heavy equipment, trucks and of course roads in wilderness areas. Under today's rules, this is collectively an environmental 'no no'.

Next there is the question of where is the United States going to get more electricity to meet future demand. Conservation is no longer the ipso-facto solution because we've probably reached the point where, on the margin, there isn't much improvement per unit of production left to squeeze out of the equation. Since the last energy crisis in the 1970s, energy use per unit of production has declined 50%. The problem is that the total number of production units has grown considerably so that total energy use continually grows at roughly 2% per year. Thus we're left with either building more power plants or rationing, which might be politically correct today but sometime in the near future the average politically incorrect American is going to rebel.

California woke up to this fact of life when it had its late 1990s energy crisis, one that was brought on as much by legislative acts as it was by the shortage of production facilities. After numerous NIMBY and environmental battles, the state finally broke down and let power companies build smaller gas fired power plants that have so far eased the problem. However, this has created another problem and one that probably the construction of larger more efficient plants couldn't solve in the long run had California's incentive structure been different. Worse, this is not unique to California.

The United States now faces a natural gas shortage made worse by all its new gas fired power plants. This is obvious when one looks at the sharp increase in natural gas prices over the past couple of years and the trend ought to continue until something happens to alleviate the supply/demand imbalance. The first event that could break the shortage would be an economic collapse. Because this isn't the desirable option, the second would be to find more natural gas and this isn't going to happen to any appreciable extent without changing the environmental rules pertaining to exploration.

Of course we could import natural gas and efforts are under way to revive this after a hiatus of many years. Importation however is not the best solution because one must first freeze the gas down to a point where it liquefies. Next it must be shipped in vessels equipped to store it safely and finally it must be offloaded at liquid natural gas facilities before being shoved through already crowded pipelines.

Good luck because the infrastructure to do this beyond today's inconsequential capacity must be built and that requires a lot of money. Another problem is that liquefied natural gas can explode if not handled properly, something that in today's terrorist ridden world makes importation less than optimal. A variant on this would be to use liquefied coal, but that too is expensive. The effort to produce liquefied coal using multiple methods in the late 1970s required oil prices to climb to $60 per barrel before it become cost competitive and today we're not even close to that price—particularly on an inflation adjusted basis.

Another option is the nuclear one. Nuclear power plants operate with the lowest marginal cost per kilowatt of power and have proven to be safe if operated prudently, something the Soviets failed to do as typified by Chernobl and periodic disasters amongst its nuclear powered submarines. Conversely, the US Navy has been operating nuclear powered vessels, both under and on top of the water, for decades without an accident. The only accident of note amongst all the western nuclear powered electrical plants was the fiasco at Three Mile Island that ruined the power plant but failed to emit any radiation.

Despite this record, any time the subject has been brought up the 'greens' and their allies have had a hemorrhage. On top of that, opposition by environmentalist and other politically correct individuals in Germany and Japan have forced their native lands to begin shutting down nuclear power plants and shift to other energy sources; ie: natural gas and other petroleum based fuels. Considering the availability of alternative sources of fuel, this smacks of economic suicide—something 'old Europe' has been getting used to for some time.

The real residual problem with nuclear power plants in today's world though, is the risk of a terrorist attack and the horrendous capital cost involved in building them. This leaves coal as plan B for a power source and explains why President Bush has pushed for more research into new high tech ways of using it while mitigating the pollution problem.

Assuming that advanced chemistry can find a way to economically remove the impurities that cause air pollution, acid rain etc., the country actually has enough coal to be energy self sufficient for a long time when it comes to electric power. We've proven this to a certain extent with the use of low sulfur coal from the Great Plains. The only problem is that President Clinton locked up much of the West's low sulfur coal reserves when he placed millions of acres in nature preserves as he walked out the door.

The politics of environmentalism hasn't been kind to the use of hydro-power either. Once the saving grace for power needs in the far-western states and the Tennessee and Missouri Valleys, the thought of building more dams for water storage and electrical power needs can't even be placed on the table. In fact the current focus is on which existing dams need to be demolished so that the annual Pacific salmon runs can best make it to the sea and back. The premise is that water held in storage and released at a steady rate precludes healthy salmon populations. Of course no one bothers to ask what the salmon did before the dams were built and severe droughts dried up the water flows.

Therefore to expand the available supply of energy, we've left with the politically correct 'wish list'. At one time it was thought that bio-mass power plants would be the solution and many were built in timber country, powered by the scrap and brush that accompanied logging. Now that it is almost impossible to log with the American timber industry almost dead and buried, along with the loss of thousands of its high paying union jobs, this option has been foreclosed and the plants mothballed for a lack of fuel.

Wind energy works but as someone forgot to explain to the average Democrat that the windmills themselves are fragile, something every one who's been dumb enough to invest in them for the tax credits knows. There're also unsightly strung out across Idaho's southern desert and San Francisco's Altamont Pass so they accordingly raise the NIMBY issue again. That's why both John Kerry and Ted Kennedy, politically correct icons to the max, both oppose placing windmills off the coast of Cape Cod.

Solar energy is nice for individual locations, but that too has flaws and so far it has been a nonstarter as far as the investment world is concerned except for the tax credits investors get—no tax credits, no interest. With the lower marginal tax brackets, even that appeal has disappeared. The bigger problem when solar is considered for massive electricity production, is that the number of solar panels needed for maximum efficiency are big and collectively take up acres of land in California's Mohave Desert. There is also a reliability issue caused by the sophisticated wiring necessary to collect and transmit the power, coupled with variance in sun exposure—something also faced by reliance upon wind energy.

Finally we're down to the politically correct dream of hydrogen power and hybrid vehicles. The difficulty with the former is that hydrogen must be separated from other elements and kept isolated. That's tough, requiring the use of other forms of energy to accomplish and as I vaguely remember from my physics, the ratio of energy created to the amount of energy used is close to one to one. Plus hydrogen in its raw state is highly flammable; eg: the dirigible Hindenburg that went up in flames in the 1930s.

Hybrid engines seem to be a different story as they operate in the same way that diesel electric submarines did in World War Two, as do diesel electric train engines. The principle involved is that the gasoline engine charges the batteries for its electric brother and once recharged, the electric motor takes over as in the case of the submerged submarine. (the diesel electric train engine is different because the diesel engine produces the electricity needed to drive the traction motors that actually power the train) Here the issue is one of size. To be a viable alternative to the gasoline engine, hybrids must be small and light enough to fit in a car—something that should be doable.

Kyoto & Hidden Costs of Environmental Policy

There are also hidden costs involved with American environmental policies that inhibit or even materially detract from the competitive position of American companies. In many cases, these have resulted in the virtual shutdown of many old-line industries like the timber industry in the Pacific Northwest, along with all the union jobs they once provided—to the Canadians great benefit. This was particularly acute during the 1970s and early 80s, when capital that could have gone towards investment into improving worker productivity manufacturing concerns needed to remain competitive with East Asian concerns, went towards environmental protection projects instead.

One example was the $100 million that Shell Oil had to pay to install chemical 'scrubbers' years after the fact to eliminate emissions from its Long Beach, California refinery without any incremental addition to California's gasoline supply. When spread across countless industrial plants throughout the land, this illustration strongly suggests that billions were spent on unproductive investments. Investments that ultimately forced industrial companies out of business because of the loss of the competitive advantage they could have maintained had the money been funneled into other aspects of their operation.

There was thus a reason that core industrial areas throughout the Midwest turned into the rust belt by the early 1980s. As the 'rust belt' developed and union jobs disappeared, yet today those responsible now complain about the loss of traditional American jobs when years past they helped destroy them. Today environmental lawyers and agency bureaucrats are still using the court system to enforce the letter of the environmental laws without any consideration of the total picture.

This was clearly true in the way the Clinton Administration made them more stringent. As a result, any maintenance performed on an industrial plant is now considered to be a 'major improvement' requiring the complete installation of state of the art environmental equipment. Because companies don't want to be put in a position to completely overall older plants, they chose not to maintain them. Instead they opt to close them once their competitive value is finished and shed the jobs these plants represent. Needless to say this does not enhance productivity and tends to benefit the Chinas and Indias of the world.

The solution currently proposed by the Bush Administration is to structure a set of positive incentives that would allow companies to trade 'emission credits' from new plants as an offset to shortfalls from old plants. This in theory, would allow companies to upgrade older facilities without triggering punitive environmental requirements. This has been vehemently opposed by the politically correct, irrespective of all the high paying American jobs that will be lost without the Bush incentive program.

The most egregious example of politically correct thinking at the expense of the American economy has been the hue and cry over President Bush's withdrawal from the Kyoto Protocol. First of all, Kyoto is not a treaty since it was never submitted to the Senate for approval by President Clinton and therefore never had the chance to become law. Thus Kyoto is nothing more than an agreement in principle between former Vice President Al Gore and the rest of the world—a agreement 95 US Senators told him not to enter into before he left on his negotiating mission.

Gore though, has thoroughly accepted the premise that the world is warming up at an alarming rate and human industrial activity is the primary cause hook, line and sinker. Now there is creditable evidence that the former premise is true, but the latter portion is based on some tenuous scientific conclusions dependent upon statistical methodology problems and assumptions that place competent geophysicists on both sides.

What the environmental zealots with their limited knowledge of history, Al Gore included, can't seem to grasp is that planet earth has undergone warming and cooling cycles with regularity since the dawn of time. Some of the cycles are longer term such as the 'little ice age' from roughly 1300 to about 1850 when the New York Harbor froze over every year and the 'Brits' could go ice skating on the Thames.

This period was preceded by several centuries of general warming on the European Continent, producing the growth in agriculture that gave rise to the High Middle Ages that ended when it suddenly got cold, causing the famine decades of 1310 to 1330. Even during the 20th Century crop sizes in North America and the accompanying broad swings in grain prices tracked closely with the 22 year sun spot cycle as every commodity futures trader worth his salt understands.

So the question is whether the current warming cycle is a function of human behavior, part of a normal cyclical process or merely the result of recent changes in the sun's activity. Another question is to what degree does this involve the scope of economic activity with its generation of air pollutants—specifically carbon dioxide, which is the current cause celeb. Remember that the process of breathing converts oxygen into CO_2 and Europe has had problems with air pollution going all the way back to the Roman Empire. Back then the City of rome was probably just as smoggy as Los Angeles when I was in high school.

The big problem with Kyoto is that it would force the US to cut back its industrial emissions to pre-1990 levels, which would hammer our economy and preclude future economic growth. Conversely, anything that shackles our economy, relatively benefits the French since it serves to close the competitive gap between Europe and the US without anyone in 'old Europe' required to make any changes in their economic structure. Thus the real reason old Europe got upset when President Bush officially buried what had never been alive.

The true beneficiary of Kyoto would be China since it and other developing nations were exempted from its provisions, while the Russians were given a quota that when matched with its economy, would allow it to sell 'the surplus' to countries exceeding Kyoto standards. Therefore, if Kyoto ever becomes embedded in American law, American business that can will definitely choose to leave for 'Kyoto friendly' destinations, taking jobs along with them. So much for politically correct concern for the jobs of the average American.

10

Liberal Fascism

Neither Left nor Right

The political terms left or right do not really exist in an American context. They're derived from the fact that those desiring the death of France's Louis XVI assembled on the left side of the room as one walked into the hall, while those voting to let the king live assembled on the right. Thus those who went to the left represented the republican principles of the French Revolution based on the tenets of Rousseau and those turning to the right favored retention of France's traditional hierarchical aristocratic government with maybe some constitutional restrictions.

The United States has never really had a traditional hierarchical aristocratic government, even under colonial proprietorships where colonial legislatures could effectively veto 'his lordships' dictates by failing to fund them and the salaries of his agents. This was the basis for 'Whig liberalism' where control of government finances enmeshed the will of the ruler with the sovereignty of the governed.

The question was only whether the Jeffersonian view of society based on free yeoman or the Hamiltonian vision of a commercial society would prevail and in what form. Consequently the United States has never had a 'political rightwing' in the European context. What is falsely construed as a 'political rightwing' is frequently classical Whig liberalism and today's conservatives represent the views of those who seek to preserve that core American political philosophy as the country's governing principle.

Historical Liberal Support of Stalinism

At this point we need to take a detour because one of the unanswered questions in 20th Century history is why have many of America's alleged liberals habitually supported Stalinism despite all the evidence exposing its extreme brutality. A brutality that statistically makes Hitler and his holocaust look like a rather modest affair.

This isn't something that just appeared on the scene. Some of the roots of liberal fascism's enthusiasism with totalitarianism, when the utopia is packaged in the right theology, go back to the progressive era in American history. It was during this time that numerous measures were instituted to improve 'social justice'. Some of which were clearly needed, others like prohibition failed miserably, and a few such as 'eugenics' can be construed as precursors of social policies undertaken by Germany's Third Reich.

'Eugenics' had roots in Darwin's theory of evolution and its accompanying hypothesis of 'natural selection'. In the course of Darwinian behavior, not all the matches made within the human gene pool came out right, leading to various deviant behavior and conditions such as 'down's syndrome'. The fear was that these 'problems' were self-perpetuating and so something needed to be done about them. One solution amongst several was legalized sterilization, albeit on the less than grand scale practiced by the Nazi Germany.

Then there was the post World War One 'red scare' in response to the Russian Revolution and its idealization as the preventative for repetitive wars and path to a just society. America's response to 'red agitation' and the nascent Soviet Union's vitriolic cry for a world wide revolution by the proletariat was excessive with 'Palmer Raids', named after President Wilson's Attorney General, et al. There was however some foundation for this given the country's experience with the International Workers of the World, or 'Wobblys' as they were called, and various anarchistic behavior going back to the late 1800s.

With the post war boom of the 1920s, this problem cleared up by itself. But with the start of the Great Depression in 1930, many began to lose faith in the American system and started looking at Mussolini's Fascist Italy as more effective model for emulation—if only the excesses of the 'black shirts' could be kept out of it. When this line of reasoning became matched up with early 20th Century utopian socialism, the country saw the emergence of policy makers aiming to totally revamp the structure of American society.

This was the 'brain trust' of FDR's New Deal and in many cases like social security, the result was beneficial. In other cases, such as the ultimately unconstitutional National Recovery Act, or 'Negro' removal act as it was termed in the old confederacy since the NRA had incentives built into it's farm production quotas providing a financial incentive for Southern land owners to kick Black sharecroppers off their farms. This in turn led to the vast immigration of Southern Blacks to Northern industrial areas when the existing supply of labor was more than ample.

More deleterious were the New Deal's social welfare programs that converted what was historically a community responsibility left in the hands of volunteers who knew the recipients, into a governmental bureaucratic responsibility. Given that the extent of the problem created by the depression had totally overwhelmed local charitable resources, it's understandable why this happened.

However, over the long run, these measures undercut a core tenet of American society that each of us had a personal responsibility to look after our neighbors. Now all one had to do was pay one's taxes and the government would take care of the problem. If new measures or agencies were needed, then Congress should create them and not bother 'individual liberals' with the details. Concurrently, with the government taking charge of fixing the lives of others, the others soon drifted into becoming wards of the state and no longer responsible for their own choices in life. Thus the seeds of 'victimization' requiring a governmental solution were laid.

For some Americans this wasn't enough. The goal was still the utopian society and the model provided by the illusion of what the Soviet Union was in the process of becoming enthralled them. This was total fiction because at the time Stalin was starving the Ukrainians to death by the millions to force them onto collectivized farms and shake loose the food needed to feed workers forced to labor in Russia's burgeoning industrialization. Unfortunately the reality of the Soviet Union was kept out of sight and therefore out of mind as the *New York Times* assiduously reported Stalin's propaganda as fact, earning a Pulitzer Prize that it's not giving back in the process.

Helping the *New York Times* was a then relatively active American Communist Party, which has always been under the thumb of the Soviet Union despite protestations to the contrary by the politically correct. As Yale University researchers have discovered in their systematic examination of old Soviet archives, the American Communist Party mission was to overthrow the Constitutional Government of the United States. First through the propaganda efforts of the overt party to undermine respect for our government and then through the covert actions of communist agents controlled by Moscow through the visible party.

Later, when Stalin dissolved Comintern in 1937, the roles were switched with the visible party being the agent of Soviet agents through which they controlled America's covert communist party—pretty much the way the Irish Republican Army has controlled its political wing, Sein Finn, during the 'troubles' in Northern Ireland. It was through the former structure that Stalin and Comintern recruited 'useful fools' to go fight for the Republican cause during the Spanish Civil War 1936—39 and muster moral support for the establishment of a socialist democracy in Madrid. To a certain extent Stalin was successful in his public relations as America's intelligentsia bought into it at the time with many joining the Abraham Lincoln Brigade to fight in Sapin.

The truth though, was that the Spanish Civil War was a conflict between two totalitarian visions and we should all be thankful that Franco's Falange Movement finally won it. Imagine what World War Two and the subsequent Cold War would have been like had a Stalinist regime been in place in Spain and Portugal. Given the choices, Franco was clearly the lessor of two evils, despite the backing he received from Mussolini and Hitler, and once in power he turned out to be nothing more than another authoritarian Hispanic dictator whose regime changed for the better when he finally died.

Despite the fact that Stalin eventually gave up on using force to install communism in Spain, he continued to undermine the democracies through the control of active communist parties in Western Europe and the US. When Hitler finally attacked Russia in 1941, Stalin ordered all these parties to actively come to his aid so that French Communists surfaced to become the backbone of the resistance movement, often spending as much of their time killing off de Gaulle's 'Free French' as they did fighting Germans.

In the US, Stalin's dictate sent many American Communists to join the ranks of the OSS, predecessor of the CIA. Additionally his agents actively recruited agents including some in the most senior ranks of government. At one time the Vice President, Henry Wallace, Ted White the Assistant Secretary of the Treasury, and Alger Hiss, who was FDR's equivalent to today's National Security Advisor, were all actively working for Stalin. Fortunately FDR managed to postpone his looming death until after his 1945 inauguration so that Harry Truman became President instead of Henry Wallace, otherwise the country could have been in real trouble.

Then there was the way the Russians developed their first atomic bomb, something Stalin knew we had long before anyone bothered to tell Truman. According to the memoirs of the senior Soviet intelligence officers who ran the espionage mission, deals were cut with Robert Oppenheimer and other key scientists directing the bomb's development in New Mexico. Instead of the key scientists passing secrets directly to Soviet agents, they hired junior scientists who were Soviet agents and by passing information down to them, they effectively shipped our atom bomb secrets off to Moscow.

Now all this is adamantly denied by the politically correct to this day and Alger Hiss protested his innocence until he died. There is also the matter of Julius and Ethel Rosenberg, who some still maintain were judicially murdered for being alleged Soviet spies during the 'McCarthy Era'. Once again old Soviet records and the memoirs of senior Soviet espionage officials come to the 'right's' rescue, along with the archival work by Yale. These sources make it perfectly clear that all of he above were in fact Soviet agents who had actively worked to betray the US.

Consequently 'Tailgunner Joe' McCarthy had it right, but I'll leave it to Ann Coulter's book *Treason* to provide the details since she methodically went through them and assiduously cited her sources obtained through 'Nexus-Lexus'. The big problem with 'Tailgunner Joe', in retrospect, was that he was a few years too late. By the time he finally got his Senate hearings going, much of the problem had disappeared since the emergence of the Cold War had finally scared off many inclined to become American Bolsheviks and thus Soviet agents.

Still the whole episode left its mark on America's 'intelligensia' and Hollywood types who firmly believed in communist utopianism. They become the lionized 'persecuted ones' in some circles when Congress and the Screen Actor's Guild under Ronald Reagan fought back to neutralize communist influence in America's entertainment industry.

These were the days when the West Coast Long Shoreman's Union under Harry Bridges and the Hollywood unions were controlled by Communist Party members. And Reagan's effort to eject them from the Screen Actor's Guild was not well received and forced him to sleep with a '38' under his pillow for protection. The experience, no doubt, taught him a lot about how 'the marketplace of ideas' actually worked when filtered through communist orthodoxy. His response, after recognizing that communism was a tyranny that destroyed the soul and subjected everyone to the interests of the state as defined by a few, was to spend almost 20 years thinking about how it could be defeated.

We're all well aware that he concluded that out investing the Soviets in military technology would bankrupt them into collapse. What we don't often recognize is that he understood that the very moral and spiritual bankruptcy and dependency upon man being the higher power of its citizenry, was the source of its failure to develop technologically. Only a free people aware of their own individuality and not merely cogs serving the interests of the state could do that. In Reagan's mind, that was the strength of the United States and one that could leverage the inherent weakness of the Soviet Union into collapse.

Thus Reagan's continuing efforts to meet the Soviet Union's proxies in the much bally-hoo'd third world wars of liberation with equal force, particularly in the strategically important regions of the American Hemisphere. Thereby giving those fighting to prevent the imposition of 'one man, one vote, one time' on their countries the ability to retain their freedom. This is what led to his invasion of Grenada, the active support of the Contras in Nicaragua that the politically correct opposed, and continuing assistance to the government of El Salvador during its fight with communist guerillas.

It was also the genesis behind the moral and financial support the United States provided Poland's Solidarity and other East European movements working to throw off the yoke of totalitarian Soviet domination. Here he had us fund the printing presses, paper, and underground communications that mobilized the opposition. His speeches served to give these people hope that their cause was not forgotten and thus lifted the spirits of those continuing the fight that finally led to the collapse of the Berlin Wall.

His was also a vision and strategy that was much disparaged during his presidency by the 'hip slicking cool' amongst America's politically correct. Despite many of Reagan's strategic decisions that were frequently counter to the opinion of his cabinet, he was accused of being a puppet in their hands. Nothing could be further from the truth, but the perception promulgated by America's liberal fascists gave credence to their attacks on his foreign policy.

By making his beliefs seem absurd, they could get away with declaring initiatives like his support for the Contras as being 'imperialistic' and designed to deprive the people of Nicaragua of their 'right to self determination', something communists had never exhibited an interest in doing. There was nothing new in this since the same argument became accepted belief when it came to Vietnam and Cambodia, or even Allende's Chile.

The last example incites the American internationale to this day under the mistaken belief that the CIA overthrew Chile's duly elected government all by itself in the name of 'anti-communism and installed a 'friendly military dictator' against the 'will of the people'. Of course the politically correct accepted this view since Allende was a 'populist' man of the people. This ignores the fact that the CIA by itself lacks this kind of power and must have considerable indigenous support to pull something such as this off.

Conveniently overlooked too is the fact that the CIA really didn't have that much to do with Allende's overthrow because the Chileans recognized his regime for what it was—a communist front organization. From the day Allende was sworn in he began to govern extra-constitutionally after installing many known communist in his cabinet. When Chile's Supreme Court overturned many of Allende's executive orders, order that could never pass Chile's legislative process, or were in fact counter to an expressed vote, Allende ignored it. Having had enough of what was beginning to appear to be a nascent totalitarian government, Chileans and their army took matters into their own hands to retain their freedom.

The long-standing question then, is why do the politically correct have such an affinity for totalitarian leftist regimes that so brutalize their people, leaving millions dead in the process. Why do they apologize for Cambodia after Pol Pot exterminated over a third of its people including everyone who had an education, particularly teachers, former government officials and everyone wearing glasses under the assumption that their eyes were bad because they'd spent too much time reading.

At the time this occurred, those on the left who weren't silent blamed the Kmer Rouge on the fact that the United States had bombed Cambodia when in fact all that was bombed where North Vietnamese supply bases in the uninhabited regions of the country bordering Vietnam. Another excuse offered was that becasue we'd invaded Cambodia by finally going after North Vietnamese sanctuaries that were a few miles inside the Cambodian border in 1970, Pol Pot's emergence was inevitable. Intellectually none of this holds water, leaving only the cynical thought that the politically correct felt that the murder of so many of Cambodia's citizens represented essential social engineering that would lead to a more perfect society.

Totalitarian Liberalism

This produces what I've termed totalitarian liberalism as the other thread of current American political philosophy. One that is more akin to fascism, albeit without the nationalistic impulse that's the hallmark of 'pure' fascism and the factor causing 'true fascist' regimes to spin out of control into an international feeding frenzy. It's pathological, none the less, and has the objective of changing the world to reflect an artificial utopian construct.

Fortunately for the United States, this hasn't entailed the violence typical of a Rousseauan revolution, although we came close in the 1960s and as the battle is still being fought out within our Constitutional process. However the goal of totalitarian liberalism is to still create a heaven on earth with 'social justice' for all, particularly in the form of 'three hots and a cot' for everyone, based on the way 'liberal elites' define it. In practice though, the result is to create a dependency of entitlement juxtaposed to government being an agent for opportunity.

The ongoing problem for starters, is that social justice can never be obtained for one group of people because that requires an injustice to be committed against those who must give up something to 'balance the scales' in favor of those who here-to-fore have been deprived of it. Ergo, one cannot have socialism with a human face because of the bureaucratic process required to make it work in practice, eg: the IRS.

Samuel Gompers, when he founded the American Federation of Labor in the 1880s understood this when he removed the American labor movement out from underneath the political party process. He recognized that obtaining 'justice in the labor force' was an adversarial process that could best accomplish its goals for the benefit of its members through direct negotiation with industry. This is why the United States didn't develop a labor party or one where unions have been co-opted by socialist parties as it happened in Europe.

When taken to extremes, government as the arbitrator of social justice leads to a sense of entitlement amongst those benefiting from the reallocation of 'social justice' and only serves to foster further conflict between groups—something the politically correct conveniently overlook. The sad fact is that social justice must be 'earned' and some inequity will always exist in the world. A good example being how the military accomplishments of the Army's 442nd Nisei Regiment bought respect for American—Japanese citizens. Additionally the excellent performance of various all African—American independent combat battalions lead to the acceptance of blacks as combat soldiers and Truman's decision to integrate the armed forces.

In a Catholic context then, this is 'God's Will' and why we all must wait for our reward in heaven after 'earning it through both works and faith' while on earth. For liberal totalitarians this is unacceptable because belief in a God of Faith recognizes that there're limits on what man can accomplish, including the re-ordering of the world as a god of reason would have it.

This is hardly a new issue and its roots go back at least to the enlightenment of the 18th Century when many intellects drifted away from the church of their fathers to become Deists, rejecting any form of 'predestination' or its spiritual kindred while searching for a God of reason. However, almost to a man our Founding Fathers rejected the elimination of the Divine, starting with the use of the word 'Creator' by Jefferson in the Declaration of Independence. But the enlightenment did represent a shift towards a spiritual philosophy where man himself essentially becomes the arbitrator of the world.

Thus we end up having to 'kill' God in order to have a more perfect world and eliminate the need to answer to an authority greater than our own intellects. Ergo, once God is dead, a man viewing himself in the mirror while shaving is in effect looking at the 'universal ruler of the world' who, in the name of his utopian concepts, can justify any measure to bring them to fruition.

This is a frightening concept given the psychological makeup of some of the men throughout history who've replaced God with their own image. The list includes those who dreamt up communism in their Russian attics divorced from any other human contact to Herr Hitler, Joe Stalin, and their many 20th Century emulators. For the utopian totalitarianist, firing God has its virtues beginning with elimination of the idea of having a conscience. If one is the god who writes the rules, how can one ever develop a sense of guilt, which is something that only a belief in the God of Faith can inculcate.

Consequently, if the goal is to create the ultimate utopian state according to the vision of those leading the dictatorship of the proletariat or der Furher in the case of Nazi Germany, the God of Faith and His accompanying accruements must be expunged from society. This includes the belief that the rights of all Americans come from God, not the king or any other human source because if they come from God, then the god of the state cannot replace them with its own values and people retain ownership of their own individuality. Under a God of Faith they cannot be converted into an asset of the state as if they were a lump of coal or a piece of equipment.

This pertains equally to the Ten Commandments. According to the Old Testament, God gave these Laws to the Hebrews and told them to obey them in His Name. Now whether one believes in Judaic—Christian theology, and I lean towards Deism, is immaterial. Through the melding of Greek philosophy, Roman Law, Germanic custom and Judaic Christianity as they evolved as the Common Law of Western Europe, the Ten Commandments provide the foundation for American Law.

Removing the Ten Commandments from American public life, therefore, represents the removal of the God of Faith as the source of individual rights; leaving man himself as the one who bequeaths rights to his fellow man. The problem with this is that what one man gives, another can take away as mankind has discovered throughout several millennium. But if one wants to create an utopian world designed according to the intellect of a few, then the removal of God from all human endeavors is essential.

Thus today's culture wars over religion and the use of the Federal Court System to re-interpret the First Amendment. The First Amendment, extended to individual states by the 14th Amendment, in its literal sense as written by Madison, declares that the federal government's role in the matter of religion is one of strict neutrality. The old practice of using the tax code to pay for clergy and facilities of a specific protestant faith was forbidden. (eg: Virginia's Episcopalians) Under the Constitution, the various protestant sects had to find a way to support themselves without financial support from the government.

Conversely the government is barred from inhibiting the 'free practice of religion' in any way shape or form. In effect the Founding Fathers and those citizens who approved the Constitution, felt that practicing a religion was part of public life, but that one could practice any faith one wanted too without the requirement to financially support beliefs that he didn't support.

This isn't quite the way the Supreme Court in its broad interpretation of the First Amendment views it today. By restating the First Amendment to strictly mean that any religious representation in public life violates the principle of 'church and state' separation, the Court has effectively mandated the removal of religion from public life. By their will, God, however one wants to believe in Him, is consigned to the privacy of one's closet.

An incidental issue, since we're on the subject of the First Amendment, is the way the politically correct 'interpret' another of its provision—free speech. The government, except under circumstances defined by the Supreme Court, cannot restrict what any individual wants to say. This is fortunate for liberal fascists since they've habitually drowned out many a 'conservative speaker' and have resorted to riot to prevent them from being heard in public forums.

Putting the shoe on the other foot generates an entirely different response. When one of the *New York Times* senior reporters gave the commencement address at a small Midwest private college attacking the Bush Administration for the War in Iraq, the graduating students booed him and walked out. In response, the 'gray lady' acted like a dog about to get its paw stepped on—it bitched early and often.

When the 'Dixie Chicks's', a country and western trio, lead singer declared before an English audience that she was ashamed of George W. Bush too, many radio stations ceased playing their tunes and erstwhile fans stopped buying their CDs. Listening to liberal fascists complain about how 'conservatives' were violating the Dixie Chicks right of free speech and suppressing their artistic rights was like watching a flash back to Germany's Weimar Republic.

The same was true when the singer Linda Rhonstadt dedicated her encore to the great American propagandist Michael Moore during a performance at a Las Vegas hotel. The crowd booed and many walked out. The hotel's response was to remove her from the stage and cancel the rest of her gig, again causing the politically correct to have an incontinence problem. The logical assumption being that the First Amendment is written to prevent Whig liberals from objecting to what the politically correct have to say, no matter how ridiculous the later sound.

Now with the presidential election in full swing, the 'liberal media', political cartoonists and all, are going all out to disparage the '*Fox News Channel*' for its 'fair and balanced reporting under the false premise that it's the mouthpiece for the Republican Party. The only point they've proved so far is how far to the left the average American journalist has moved, but the fact that this campaign is underway suggests that liberal fascists are desperate to silence anyone attracting an audience for Whig liberalism.

This implies a fear that average Americans will tune out their leftist propaganda, something the 'Neilsen Ratings' has been confirming for some time, and is reminiscent of the last days of the Weimar Republic. When one adds Michael Moore's propaganda flick, '*Fahrenheit 911*', to the mix and similar products produced by radical Hollywood's more inventive minds, a rather grim picture is beginning to unfold. Couple this with former First Lady and now New York Senator Hilary Clinton's stated objective of working for human reconstruction, whatever that means but sounding ominously similar to developing the 'Soviet Hero' and the 'Aryan Master Race', and one has grounds for uneasiness.

Additionally there is President Clinton's former Labor Secretary Robert Reich advocating that the country select a dominant company in each key industry and provide it with government aid to gain a pre-eminent position in the global market sounds just like what the Nazis did for A.G. Farben. Even today, after all the years of Cuban tyranny under Castro with judicial murders by the thousands and countless Cuban intellectuals being jailed under horrific conditions for even peacefully opposing the regime, Hollywood luminaries flock to worship at the feet of Cuba's 'great man'—Fiedel Castro.

Hopefully their vision is for a more gentle and kinder equivalent authoritarian regime than we've seen so far on the world stage if politically correct wishes do ever come true. The point many of the politically correct don't want to recognize when massaging their own egos is that under a totalitarian regime, most of them would be the first to go since, once in power, the regime would have no further use of them.

The Effect of 'Intellectual Isolation'

Former Congressman Dick Army, now a professor of economics at Texas A&M, once stated that in his experience, 'conservatives' were more concerned with facts than his 'liberal' colleagues. In the world of the latter, fantasy and assumption seemed to work for them with an occasional use of a 'statistic' for appearances.

Armed with this thought, I started paying more attention to the contrast between 'liberals' and 'conservatives' while listening to the talking heads on the cable news channels.

What stood out after some time of close scrutiny was that 'conservatives' do try to answer questions and bring context and perspective to what they have to say. Although they do frequently fail in the short time allotted to adequately make their point, at least an attempt is made to bring fact into the discussion using the time honored rules of rhetoric of 'thesis, substantiation, and then conclusion' based on the facts at hand.

Not so with 'liberal' talking heads. With them, one is subjected to a barrage of 'talking points' that might, or more not, have anything to do with the question. More often than not, the whole liberal discourse is designed not to answer the question because the answer might be embarrassing to their cause. So the moderator who asks the question constantly needs to bring them back to the subject. An effort just as often ignored until the 'spin' is finished and time has expired.

Another trick the politically correct resort to is to retort with questions pertaining to an entirely different subject, or they make two statements and go on as if those 'points' were morally equivalent and related to the point they're rebutting. If that doesn't work, they misapply analogies as *'Fox News's'* Alan Combs did recently when he pointed out that John Kerry served two tours in Vietnam, seven months aboard a destroyer and four months commanding a swiftboat, as if this made him that much more virtuous. He deliberately ignored the fact that each tour in Vietnam represented the 12 or 13 months that I served in country and thus two tours constituted two full years of combat—not the 11 months Kerry served.

Thus the two sides end up talking past each other with the liberals spewing propaganda under the assumption that if the lie is repeated often enough, the average bear will begin to believe it, while the 'conservative' sells an argument through the process of debate. Since I'm prone to the analytical, my response after hearing a 'liberal' declaration is to ask the question: based on what, knowing that 'the what' isn't going to be forthcoming. As I've listened to the Kerry/Edwards 2004 Presidential Campaign, I've been subjected to voluminous claims without any substantiation or causal linkage.

This starts getting us to the heart of the matter because developing an argument based on facts in evidence is hard work, but it is necessary if one aims to solve problems pragmatically without violating the tenets of 'classic whig liberalism'. Conversely, if the goal is to elicit support for a utopian idea that would be rejected if subjected to close scrutiny, propaganda based on an emotional appeal designed to obscure the facts works best. Thus the technique of diverting discussion by resorting to emotional appeals.

I finally began to grasp this after listening to my aunt discuss the power of FDR's speeches during the depression and Churchill's during World War Two. Despite graduating from UCLA and earning her masters in education from USC, most of what she got from listening to them was the eloquence of the presentation—almost like listening to Beethoven's 'Fifth'. The guts of what they had to say never quite registered.

This isn't the way I listen to political speeches. I go for the details, pad and pencil in hand, the importance of which I could never get her to grasp. She also had an affinity for Adlai Stevenson because his debating style was so brilliant compared to Eisenhower's and the fact that Clinton was a 'policy wonk' clinched her vote. I could never get her to acknowledge that the presidency shouldn't be a debating society because as chief executive of the United States, the President's job is to make decisions—often with only imperfect information available. Needless to say she was not a fan of either Bush, nor Reagan for that matter, particularly due to the formers lack of eloquence as much as any other reason.

The latter is also less work and reflects the Rousseauan process of mobilizing the 'sans coulettes' during the French Revolution. So why do America's politically correct elites and the lightweights in Hollywood tend to approach political discourse as if they're Robespierre inspiring the mob to drive the enemies of the state to the guillotine? And the answer is two-fold. First, they are the 'elite', self anointed or not, and thus are superior and need not trouble themselves with details since they already know the answer. Thus they can 'make it up on the run' and need not explain it to the rest of us WOGS (worthy oriental gentlemen) because we lack the capacity to understand it anyway.

I got a belly full of this one night in a bar in Redding, California several years ago when an English professor from Southern Oregon University tried to explain to me why those of us who volunteered to serve in Vietnam were merely ignorant pawns. We weren't swift enough to understand what the war was all about when in contrast, most of those I served with, including the enlisted men, had more knowledge of the issues pertaining to that war than he'd ever possess. All he understood was a 'mish-mash' of assumptions based on a modicum of fact that he turned into a thesis that everyone had to accept because he had a PhD.

That's the problem with academics. They specialize and then often sub-specialize in their fields to such an extent that they become divorced from contact with the real world. Additionally, their extensive academic achievements are not financially rewarding compared to the incomes generated by many lowly sales-men and pizza parlor proprietors.

This has to breed resentment and since they're tenured to the extent that there's little economic risk in their lives, they can pontificate about what's wrong with the world without the need to understand it. This is especially true of the liberal arts where the burning issue is how excited Mary Shelly got when listening to her husband's poems, or the nuances of William Blake in his discourses on 'Buellah Land'. Whatever the opinion, there's never a reality check like there is when I opine on the future course of IBM's stock price

Even finance professors tend to fall in this trap as I found out when I got my MBA. After listening to lectures extolling the virtues of 'modern portfolio theory' that didn't match the 20 years of practical experience I'd acquired from integral participation in the financial markets, I'd mention the dichotomy between the two. The response was at best a convoluted explanation about how my experience did fit within their theoretical confines. Following that, I just moved on to learn what I needed to get my 'key' and went back to investing against the consensus, something that continues to work quite nicely.

A variant to this can be found in the world of 'Silicon Valley' or the Upper Westside of New York. Here one deals with people who are part of the real world in that they have to compete to make the good livings they're accustomed to. However they are still divorced from the world the great unwashed live in because they've never had to deal with it up close and personal, starting with the fact that very few of them have ever been shot at while leading troops from the country's 'lower classes'.

An example of this in action again comes from my own family. While I went to fully integrated schools, my siblings did not because we were living in 'lily white' La Canada, California when they started elementary school. Soon thereaf-ter the city voted to split from the Pasadena School District and set up its own high school as they reached the ninth grade. Instead of going to a University of Rochester with its 'rich' ethnicity, they both went to the University of California at Santa Barbara where most everyone had reasonably similar backgrounds. Upon graduation my brother ended up as a computer engineer in Silicon Valley where the only 'people of color' were those sharing his background.

No living in house trailers while stationed in North Carolina where one's neighbors were moonshiners for him. My brother never had any African Ameri-can troops under his command from South 'Philly' whose conversations were heavily loaded with phrases pertaining to what daddy did to mommy, nor any from rural Georgia who'd grown up with that 'ole time religion'. Neither did any of my cousins with their very upper middle class upbringings and Ivy League educations for that matter. As for my sister, her contact with the 'hoi-polloi' came later in life so that she could embark on the mission of saving them from themselves. Naturally none of them have ever joined the VFW or even the Moose (one way to get a drink in a dry county).

This puts them all in a position where they mentally have to construct a vision of what life is like outside their environment. Not ever having to meet the bulk of the population in the process of working to achieve common goals, like winning a football game, surviving a firefight, or keeping the local veteran's post solvent, the only option they have is to assume what the rest of the country is like. Since they're also reasonably well off and are professionally required to be workaholics, they lack the time to participant in traditional community activities that benefit the common welfare.

At the same time they're aware of the problems of the world around them and like most of us, feel some obligation to assist less well off Americans. But the world of volunteer America isn't really part of their lives, as I once tried to explain to my aunt when she complained about the 'Christian right'. The point I was making was that when I needed volunteers for a Republican Party project, I didn't have the time appeal to her and her ilk so I'd simply go to the North Valley Baptist Church and round up everyone I needed.

For them the solution is to turn the whole process over to the government by supporting various social welfare schemes and then help fund them by paying the relatively high taxes that they feel they can afford. Not being self-employed with incomes all over the map during the year with significant variance from one year to the next, they don't have to worry about living off of credit cards and squirreling away enough cash flow to meet payroll and keep the doors open.

They can afford to be 'liberals' and assuage whatever guilt they might have by letting Hillary Clinton embark on human reconstruction to solve the ills of society without bothering with the details. Under these conditions, 'out of sight—out of mind' works and is often the preferable condition.

If those of us who are 'Whig liberals' object and bring up nasty contradictions to their worldview, we're accused of being greedy and selfishness while impeding the establishment of social justice. Even worse, we're accused of being fascist when most of the politically correct haven't a clue as to what that means. Neither do most academics who've spent years studying the subject, but that doesn't bother the unenlightened when they rant about George W. Bush or Ronald Reagan.

Illustrative Example

Possibly the most egregious example of this thinking at work is affirmative action. The premise is that African Americans are not quite up to the job because they're descended from slaves and have been discriminated against for decades. All of which everyone acknowledges was an historic injustice, but to assume that skin color precludes academic achievement and success in professional fields is fallacious and a grave injustice to African Americans whose history is replete with examples of successful entrepreneurialism, even under slavery.

The key to the problem of black underachievement in America is to make integration work, which means good schools for all that's addressed by NCLB and equal opportunity of which the military experience following President Truman's integration of the armed forces is an appropriate example. I've never met an African American who couldn't meet the standard expected of white Americans if given an honest chance to succeed. That's what the Marine Corps mantra of everyone being treated 'green' meant.

The problem that emerges is when affirmative action and equal opportunity is defined in terms of percentages—a methodology that inevitably leads to quotas and lower standards for African Americans in order to achieve the proper percentage distribution of 'color' within an organization. This leaves out any room for a 'middle ground' and results in diversity by skin color, often at the expense of other forms of diversity—something others have noted is typical of America's mass media.

This isn't 'fair' to those with other ethnic backgrounds, nor is it 'fair' to African Americans who rise because of their own talents—just like most everyone else. Because of the quota process built into the application of affirmative action programs, these Blacks end up carrying the stigma of 'quota fillers' for the rest of their professional lives.

Furthermore, this has created a whole industry that some have termed 'civil rights entrepreneurship'. This is a world built around political influence that Dr. Jack Cashill in his book *Ron Brown's Body* explains much better than I can in this text. The gist of the argument though, is that Congressionally mandated programs requiring federal contracts to have a portion set aside for designated minorities has been pre-empted by the professional civil rights movement.

The way these set-aside contracts work is that one of the business owners receiving a contract must be an African American. The problem is that there is no means test so that wealthy African Americans have an equal chance of participating. In its most abusive form, a group of white businessmen 'hire' a token Black as a partner by giving him a piece of the action. They then run the business to fulfill the federal contract as they normally would while passing a portion of the profits on to their nominal African American.

Given their position in the civil rights organizations and their roles as Washington lobbyists, professional African American civil rights activists frequently have the best access to minority set aside contracts. Just as often they're in the more favorable position to be 'found' by those whites using the system to take advantage of these programs.

This creates a rather incestuous relationship between African American political insiders and those who exist to take advantage of the opportunities offered. Eventually this generates a sense of entitlement amongst those Blacks profiting from the process since they only need to use their influence and skin color to collect the check—the recurring thesis in Cashill's book.

Entering this world of profiting from 'liberal white guilt' over historic black victimization after the election of 2000 was the now 'classical whigism' exemplified by George W. Bush. Unlike his predecessors, particularly Bill Clinton who tended to appoint African Americans to secondary cabinet positions based on the political influence they could bring to the table, George w. Bush went out and appointed some heavy weights.

Colin Powell, the first African American Chairman of the Joint Chiefs of Staff and one of those greatly responsible for victory during the Gulf War, was appointed Secretary of State. Condeleeza Rice, former provost of Stanford University, became his National Security Advisor. These are not token positions and both owe their positions to who they are and what they've accomplished. It just so happens that they're African Americans, which is the way it should be.

Another key player and African American in the Bush Administration is Rod Paige, the Secretary of Education. He and the then Governor of Texas, George W. Bush, met while Paige was the Superintendent of Houston's schools. Based on their common experience working together to improve Texas schools, Bush picked him to spearhead NCLB because George W. felt that Paige was the best man for the job. A job that has seen Paige lock horns with all segments of the country's moribund education establishment in jump starting the emerging improvement of America's schools.

The fact that these three and other African Americans have reached the pinnacle in the Bush Administration based on merit with race secondary, creates a problem for the advocates of victimhood and the professional civil rights establishment. These high profile African Americans, plus many in the private sector like the current CEO of Merrill Lynch John O'Neil, prove that Blacks can make it on their own without the need for 'hiring quotas'.

They don't need the 'passes' that have been the recent hallmark of professional civil rights activist who make their living lobbying Congress for special favors. This threatens the old guard's reason for existence and the perks that come with it. Their 'war' is basically over as a different kind of African American leadership is taking over.

Now we have African Americans like the new owner of the NBA Charlotte Bobcats representing African American progress. It also opens the door for a new direction in social policy and one that African Americans like basketball's Magic Johnson are taking advantage of when they invest their own capital in Black Capitalism, while working with local governments to bring Black owned commercial enterprise back to the inner cities. Something, by the way, that was initially fostered by Ronald Reagan with his inner city enterprise zone program.

However the 'old guard' of the civil rights movement is not willing to go quietly into the night. They're fighting their replacement tooth and nail. Which is why they reminded African Americans that Bush vetoed the Texas hate crimes bill when they ran the TV ad re-enacting where African American Charles Byrd was drug to death by a pair of local 'rednecks' pulling him down the highway attached to the rear of their pick-up truck. Left out was the fact the then Governor Bush vetoed the bill because Texas can only execute a man once.

Recently the old Black Elite have become even more vitriolic in their attacks on the President as he's pursued initiatives like school choice and NCLB that benefit African Americans more than whites. These initiatives, if successful, are a major threat because they point to alternative policies favored by Republicans and the party's classical liberal whig base at the expense of Democrats and civil rights liberal fascists whose power is based on pandering to African American victimization.

Of course African Americans aren't the only beneficiaries of entitlement programs designed to repair the damages of past bigotry. Hispanics too gain from 'victimization' and likewise have their own 'gatekeepers' who profit from acting as intermediaries between the 'dominant Anglos' and downtrodden inhabitants of western barrios.

In performing this role, the 'liberal's' have tended to lump all Hispanics together as one discriminated group regardless of the fact that a Hispanic in America could be anyone from a direct descendent of Spanish royalty living in Idaho's Sun Valley to an illegal hiding out in California's Central Valley. 'Tex-Mex' is confused with LA's barrio culture and New York's Puerto Ricans are dumped into the equation as an afterthought. Left out are Dominicans, et al and the descendents of New England's African American whalers who originally came from the Azores and never were slaves.

The important point is to have as large a population as possible to justify an industry of intermediaries linking Hispanics with the government programs designed to alleviate their lot. Concurrently, since this industry of profession Hispanics would otherwise cease to exist, its important to maintain Spanish as the primary language amongst the country's Hispanics.

This not only creates a need for bilingual speakers that serves the interests of the intermediaries so well, it also guarantees the existence of a client population that will continually need their services. Thus the battle over bilingual education in our schools and the demand that Spanish speaking students be educated in their primary language despite all the evidence that bilingual education leads to academic failure with disastrous consequences for those enmeshed in the system.

However, operating under the assumptions of 'soft bigotry', the politically correct still rise to the bait whenever 'conservatives' demand language immersion because English is the language of law in the United States. There was a reason that the Founding Fathers settled the debate over bilingualism when they rejected the use of German as the second language of law. Additionally there're the ample problems Canada has had with its bilingual society.

Despite this evidence, 'liberals' reject monolingualism as being 'unfair' because it places too great a burden on Hispanics. Monolingualism would also 'break the rice bowl' of the intermediary class, just like successful Black Capitalism is doing to the civil rights entrepreneurs. More debilitating for American society as a whole though, bilingualism as it is currently practiced establishes a permanent under-class of Spanish only speakers or eventually leads to a bilingual society that today few should want.

11

The Political—Cultural Divide

License vs Responsible Freedom

When the Founders sat down to write the American Constitution they had ample examples of how not to do it before them and they had the institutional experience of over 150 years of colonial self-government to draw upon. They didn't want to run the risk of government by the mob that Greek Democracy had turned into. They knew that once the Athenian Polis had voted to execute 8 of its admirals for leaving their sailors behind in the face of a hurricane, only to change its mind the next day and find the now deceased admirals innocent. They also knew that one of the hallmarks of Greek politics was to use 'faction' to incite the mob to strip the minority 'de jure' of their property rights.

Being good amateur scholars, they wanted to emulate the best practices of the Roman Republic centered around its concept of citizenship where one was neither a slave nor subject. To make this work, the people had to be willing to assume certain responsibilities, starting with a willingness to personally assume the obligations of national defense. It also required people to become citizens by keeping themselves informed and to participate in the electoral process while exercising the self-restraint that comes with freedom.

These were amongst the hallmarks of a good Roman citizen, but there was a downside to the Rome's republican constitution. It had no legal restraints built into it to ensure that if faction and competitive ambition were not controlled by self-discipline, the whole structure would spin out of control as it did when Caesar crossed the Rubicon. Given this historical example, our Founding Fathers didn't want to depend upon the individual's desire to be a 'good Roman' by putting the interests of the republic before their own.

Our Founding Fathers were also aware of problems special interests could cause and they understood that every individual was a special interest with their own self-serving motives. Ergo, they wrote the Constitution as they did with its system of checks and balances so that it took a clear consensus to get anything accomplished. To further force the creation of consensus before 'great projects' could be undertaken by the federal government, they added the bill of rights to protect minority interests.

The problem with the Constitution for today's politically correct is that because it was deliberately designed to be inconvenient, those factions desirous of establishing a utopian society would probably fail; a failure that would drive their frustration factor right through the roof. A corollary problem is the idea of self-restraint and citizenship as interpreted by the Founding Fathers—a moral society based on Judaic—Christian principles.

Not everyone appreciates these concepts and all of us, at one time or another, practice neither. The problem comes when people say the hell with both and opt for license, as America's nascent adult children decided to do in the 1960s starting with the 'Free Speech Movement' at the University of California at Berkeley in 1964.

Originally the 'Free Speech Movement' started with students demanding the right to say 'f%$#' on campus in public and quickly degenerated in a rejection of all concepts of citizenship as understood by the Founding Fathers. With the Vietnam War as a backdrop, the whole idea of stepping up to the plate and undergoing the inconvenience of military service with its accompanying risks, along with other implied obligations of citizenship, went right out the window sans protests against the injustices of the world.

Soon the tantrum expanded to into the drug culture where being high on anything except booze was considered to be the ultimate in spirituality. Throw in 'free love' and then dropping out of society altogether to the extent that no one assumed responsibility for anything and license began to reign. Aggravating the situation was the fact that the 'Greatest Generation Ever' knuckled under and mostly let their children run amok, proving in the process that the values of that generation really weren't worth fighting for.

In this scenario there was no room for the God of Faith because that would have meant a conflict between God's Will, represented by one's conscience and an accompanying sense of guilt, and the exercise of license that comes with answering to no higher authority except one's most immediate desires. Thus if one had any higher power at all, it was revealed by hallucinations caused by the most recent LSD trip. Furthermore, to justify their behavior, it became 'cool' to trip out and those that didn't were viewed as Neanderthals or worse.

Of course a few practical problems emerged from this scene, starting with the fact that drug use and its distribution was illegal. The solution was to declare that our country's drug laws were absurd and therefore null and void. This opened the door to the idea that anyone had the right to pick and choose which of our nation's laws he wished to obey and attempts by the authorities to the contrary should rightfully be opposed by force if necessary.

Another problem was unwanted pregnancy. If license reigns supreme and 'free love' becomes the norm, babies will appear at awkward times. Once they appear, they need to be nourished and financially supported; something those who'd dropped out and had no visible means of support could not do. Because the old Roman practice of infanticide couldn't be accepted, even by America's adult children at the time, the only way to avoid the inconvenience of parenthood was abortion.

Fortunately for them the Supreme Court stepped into the picture and made it legal in the infamous Roe v. Wade decision. Somewhere in the Constitution, by a 5 to 4 vote, the Justices found that a woman had the right to choose whether or not she would have the kid once conceived. The problem with this, since few pregnancies involve an imminent threat to a woman's life, is that infanticide inside the womb was now legal. Women could kill something that if left along would grow into a baby and exhibiting obvious human qualities early in pregnancy, as a matter of convenience.

This takes the matter of life and death of the potentially new born out of the hands of God and puts it into the hands of a human; something mankind has been able to live with for centuries and hasn't posed a practical problem since Roe v. Wade. But when coupled with the euthanasia movement that advocates for the right of those with a terminal illness to die via assisted suicide or just being killed if they're comatose, leads to the slippery slope of letting the government decide who gets to live.

If taken to its ultimate conclusion, the argument for the termination of life at both ends eventually results in the government deciding who needs to die for the benefit of society as a whole. The question then becomes one of how close to the euthanasia policies of Nazi Germany do Americans want to get. We've already reached the point where abortion has become a social policy tool as it's become the primary recommendation for crack addicted pregnant women and welfare mothers living in the country's slums as a tool to control the rift-raft.

Culture Wars

Thus we have another foundation stone for the culture wars that currently rage across the land and a reason why the politically correct were so adamant in their support of Bill Clinton, no matter how egregious his behavior. It also goes far in explaining why it is so difficult to get candidates for the judiciary approved by the

Senate and the disparagement of any and all prospective judges who deviate from politically correct norms.

Supposedly judges on the appellate level are supposed to read the Constitution and acknowledge that our Founding Fathers had a reason for why they wrote it the way they did when they make their rulings. Again, from the perspective of the politically correct, this creates an inconvenience since the correct ruling according to the written provisions of the Constitution might not produce the right result in the name of social justice.

They'd rather have judges who make it up as they go along to where the federal appellate system is nothing more than a super legislative body. This is why the late Supreme Court Justice Thurgood Marshall is lionized by the politically correct. By his own admission, he felt that the Constitution said whatever he felt it should say in order to obtain the result he wanted.

In its more absurd application, this means that the Supreme Court can effectively imply that the Constitution itself is unconstitutional as it did when it ruled that the upper houses of state legislatures had to be organized according to population equality. Since all but one state legislature has been structured similarly to the Congress, the Court's ruling that state upper houses had to change from geographic representation to population equality inferred that the US Senate's allocation of two Senators per state violated the principle of equal representation.

Thankfully the Supreme Court cannot rule the express language of the Constitution unconstitutional, which is why President Bush and the Republicans began pushing for a Constitutional Amendment in 2004 outlawing gay marriage. Even though the Defense of Marriage Act that the Democrats 2004 Presidential nominee, John Kerry, voted for and Bill Clinton signed into law leaves it up to individual states to determine, a ruling by 5 Supreme Court Justices can still make gay marriage legal. Ergo, the proposed Constitutional Amendment precluding them from doing so.

The problem now, in terms of legalized gay marriage, is that it takes only one state to effectively make it legal for the whole country, something the Massachusetts State Supreme Court did by a 4 to 3 vote. Since that ruling, gays have flocked to Massachusetts to get married just like people used to flock to Reno, Nevada to get divorced when every other state made divorcing couples prove cause. If it ever happens that Roe v. Wade is overturned, the one state that opts to legalize abortion will get to be the abortion capital of America and the procedure will remain legal for all, providing they have the money to make the trip.

However the battle being fought by the politically correct is to make sure this never happens by opposing every prospective strict constructionist proposed for the federal bench. Part of this conflict is the issue of 'transference' where one party decides that if they're going to make it up as they go along, so will the opposition. This means that Democrats and all the special interests they're allied with assume that whomever President Bush submits for a judicial seat will behave like Thurgood Marshall.

This is why they've blocked the nomination of Alabama's former Attorney General James Pryor despite the fact that he was the one who enforced a federal court order requiring the Chief Justice of the Alabama Supreme Court to remove the Ten Commandments from the Courthouse steps. Pryor did this despite his own personal beliefs as a devout Catholic because it was the law.

Still, Democratic Senators aren't willing to take the chance that he would act on his beliefs counter to Constitutional principles so they opposed his nomination under the bogus claim that he's 'too extreme' to be a federal judge. In the process they've effectively established a religious test for federal judges. Catholics who actually believe in the tenets of their faith need not apply. Nominal Catholics who give only lip service to their faith, that's OK.

Along similar lines is the Democrats opposition to other Bush nominees to the Federal Court of Appeals. One was blocked because the NAACP opposed him despite their local Mississippi chapter providing him with a strong endorsement. The current Chief Justice of the Texas Supreme Court, a woman, is too extreme to sit on the Court of Appeals despite being approved by a Democrat dominated state legislature.

The same is true for an African American woman sitting on California's Supreme Court who additionally had to be approved by the majority of the state's electorate in an open election. They even succeeded in derailing the appointment of President Clinton's Assistant Solicitor General because he was born in Nicaragua and worked his way up the hard way. A 'conservative Hispanic' who seems like a good candidate for the Supreme Court is one big no-no.

What do all these nominees have in common besides the claim that they 'allegedly' don't represent the values of the American people? It's that they are all officially minorities who reject the core premises of the politically correct and exemplify the fact that minorities do not need the 'free pass' to succeed. Thus proving that many are more than capable of accomplishing this on their own through the traditional path of hard work and professional competence. The problem is that this also proves the lie behind the existence of the country's minority gatekeepers who help sustain the Democratic Party.

The Problem With Bill Clinton

Bill Clinton is quite possibly the ultimate adult child amongst the 'baby boomers' who came of age during the late 1960s. That's his appeal since he's one of the most self-centered narcissists ever to be elected to the White House. Add this to his marked propensity towards pathological lying and one has the makings of one of the most corrupt administration in American History. Something that's well documented by countless sources ranging from trial transcripts and the *Wall Street Journal* with its six detailed volumes of his administration's transgressions, to a host of books covering all aspects of his and Hillary's life.

How despicable his eight years in office were is a matter for historians from the next generation to debate. But Clinton's obsession with promoting his 'legacy' and the positive propaganda surrounding it is slated for a shredding as the con that it was once succeeding generations get a hold of it. As long-time and famous newscaster David Brinkley put it amongst the comments he made on TV at the end of last election he covered during his distinguished career: 'Bill Clinton doesn't have a creative bone in his body'.

Now this might be a little harsh because Clinton was good for business, at least as long as it ponied up campaign contributions. With a lot of GOP help he did reform welfare, something Democrats in Congress now want to see die in 2005 due to its sunset provision, and succeeded in achieving some budget restraint to break the growth in federal spending that led to the budget surpluses late in his tenure. However that was about it as the rest of his legacy was mostly smoke and mirrors with many negatives related to national security.

The truth is that Bill Clinton was brought up amongst Hot Springs Arkansas's middle to upper middle class at a time when Hot Springs was a neutral Mafia vacation spa. His 'Uncle Buddy' owned a chain of auto dealerships including the one his stepfather ran while his mother was a registered nurse. At the same time, his uncle was the dominant force in Democratic politics when Arkansas was clearly a one party state and one of the country's most corrupt.

Given this, the 'spin' that he was just a small town boy from little 'ole' Hope, Arkansas doesn't hold water. His family moved before Bill entered school. Nor does his recent claim during various television interviews surrounding the publication of his book, that his record of 'improper behavior' is the result of growing up in an alcoholic family with an abusive father. There have been plenty of kids who've grown up in similar circumstances and became alcoholics themselves who've never reached the heights of 'improper behavior' that Clinton did. The fact is that Clinton learned how to get anything he wanted through the adroit manipulation of people and the record is that he'd do so without any particular moral qualms.

As far as 'conservatives' were concerned, the initial 'red flag' was the documented extent that he went to avoid military service and later disparagement of all things military while in the White House. This included letting the military run down like it did under Carter, slicing the number of Army combat divisions in half, and hardly ever meeting with hardly any of the CIA Directors during his term.

Then there was his sojourn as a law professor at the University of Arkansas where he didn't deem it necessary to grade the final exams he gave. The excuse he reportedly used was that he simply 'lost them' and then gave everyone a B+ to close the books. Because grades do matter in law school and carry consequences following graduation, some of his students no doubt had earned 'As'; others, students being students, probably shouldn't have gotten anything higher than a 'C'.

Thus Clinton's cavalier attitude, they weren't his grades after-all, towards his responsibilities as a law professor effectively screwed most of his students and rendered the concept of being rewarded for one's efforts moot. Ergo, we have another example of entitlement mentality at work, ie: it's who you know and where you are and not what you do that counts, an attitude that would carry over into his governmental career.

Next he married Hillary and got elected as Arkansas's attorney general and later to four terms as governor. This is where the 'fun' started with Hillary's stupendous career as the world's greatest trader of cattle futures on Chicago's Mercantile Exchange—something I was doing at the time as both a registered representative with NYSE member firms and as a registered commodity futures trading advisor.

However I didn't do as well as Hillary in the cattle pits because at the time, they were choppy markets and rarely developed clear price trends that one could ride. I also obeyed the rules and unfortunately spent lot of time working with various price models using raw data from USDA cattle reports and other sources—none of which was the *Wall Street Journal* since that paper's coverage of the cattle market was minimal at best on a big day.

hile I was approaching the subject as a professional, Hillary popped into one of Refco's brokerage offices and deposited a grand into an account. The next day she walked out with a check for five grand. Since each cattle contract represented 40,000lbs of beef live in a feed lot and the daily price limit before everything shuts down for the day is 2 cents per pound, she would have had to take a position of at least 10 contracts to net out five grand overnight.

The required exchange minimum deposit per contract was, as I remember it, was $800. This meant that under the rules that were usually strictly enforced, she needed at least $8,000 to produce her miracle overnight profit, probably more since cattle prices rarely moved the limit on any given trading day during the late 1970s. (I still have my price books that I used in developing my models) Then there was the $100,000 she later earned trading cattle without any apparent capital commitment on her part, something that *USA Today* finally showed should have required an almost $70,000 investment to do.

Additionally no broker in his right mind would ever let a client, especially one who was a lawyer, trade on 'house money' to that extent. Despite the above, Hillary sat before the assembled Washington press corps and declared that she accomplished her feat honestly by studying the *Wall Street Journal.* Following this charade with the now First Lady, the press went home and wrote their stories taking her explanation at face value, no questions asked—which makes one wonder about the veracity of the mainstream media.

The truth is that a 'bunch of good old boys' had decided that Hillary needed financial help and compensation for being a 'Wellesley grad stuck in the wilds of Arkansas'. Centering around the powers that be at Little Rock's Tyson Foods, Hillary was brought in on a cattle price manipulation scheme run by Refco with profitable trades made by Refco's floor brokers periodically journaled over to her account.

At the time Refco was both the largest producer of feedlot cattle and futures trader in Chicago. To maximize the price of their 'fat cattle' going to slaughter, Refco actively manipulated cattle futures prices using outside clients from their brokerage subsidiary to hide their hand. Therefore Hillary and her friends at Tyson Foods never really had any money at risk, and neither did Refco considering that profits disbursed to Hillary et al were offset by gains on slaughter prices.

Eventually Refco got caught by the Commodity Futures Trading Commission and forced to close down the futures side of their business, bringing Hillary's trading activity to a halt. Now under the rules, since she was profiting from a free ride created by a price manipulation scheme, Hillary was supposed to give up all her trading profits as was everyone else including her buddies at Tyson Foods. Fortunately for her, Refco stepped up and paid the $600,000 plus fine and in the process took everyone else off the hook—Hillary got to escape scot-free.

While Hillary was making the family fortune when Bill earned only the pittance the State of Arkansas paid him, overlooking the room and board that went with it, the chronic 'bimbo problem' that has plagued him ever since started. This has led to a few 'admissions' under considerable duress in the case of Paula

Jones and Monica Lewinsky, but also to the number of inferences pertaining to other sexual harassments including allegations of rape that a number of investigators have attempted to put together.

Whether Bill Clinton actually raped anyone, only a jury can determine and at this point the issue would be academic due to the statute of limitations. One point that has been brought up relative to these allegations is that who wants to run the risk of charging the attorney general and later governor with a felony in a state like Arkansas. The more egregious issue has been the National Organization of Women's vehement rush to his defense while they're the first in line to vilify any corporate CEO who's accused of emulating Bill's behavior.

There is also the matter of Bill Clinton's alleged drug use. When running for President he was asked if he'd ever smoked pot, and he responded by saying that he'd never inhaled. Terrific, given the license practiced by his generation and cavalier attitude, of course he'd smoked pot as did former Vice President Gore who's admitted buying it for his own use in Vietnam.

Finally there were the coke parties that Bill supposedly attended with regularity, or as his brother put it when arrested for dealing, Bill Clinton's nose was like a vacuum cleaner. (trial transcript: US v. Roger Clinton) To create a balancing offset to these allegations, naturally, the Democrats and their politically correct allies have to find 'proof' that George W. Bush also used coke. Thus the continuum of unsubstantiated allegations since the 2000 election that they're still keeping alive through the 2004 election.

None of this had anything to do with Clinton's impeachment trial and the special prosecutor, nor was this ever vigorously pursued by the press except for a few stalwart reporters at the *Wall Street Journal*. The initial issue was the Whitewater Investigation, a process that was started by a pair of savings and loan investigators working out of Kansas City trying to clean up the mess after regulators had seized Little Rock's Madison Guarantee Savings Trust for insolvency.

As these two worked through thousands of loan documents, they discovered irregularities pertaining to something called the Whitewater Development where the S&L's president, Jim McDougal and his wife Susan, had an equal partnership with the Clinton's. The problem was that a chain of loans between several McDougal influenced S&Ls around Arkansas had enabled the Clinton's to purchase their interest in Whitewater without putting up any real cash, nor would they since the loans involved were all non-recourse.

So far, no real problem for the Clintons. Of course, being equal partners with the McDougals, Bill and Hillary were entitled to half the tax write-offs produced by the real estate project that the Clintons naturally used. This was what triggered the initial criminal investigation because taking tax write-offs exceeding the amount of actual money invested in a tax shelter was fraud against the federal government, ie: tax fraud. When added to the $50 per pair deduction they took for used underwear donated to charity and other items, the IRS had quite a case against them.

The reason both Clinton's eventually avoided prosecution was that they settled up with the IRS upon entering the White House. This is what Hillary meant when she stated that they'd lost thousands on Whitewater. However they actually made money on the deal from the bogus tax deductions and the profits from 'house number 8' that Hillary foreclosed on every time someone was late with a mortgage payment and then resold without reporting the capital gain. No, it was not until paying the back taxes, interest and penalties that the Clintons netted out in the red.

The problem for the special prosecutor was that once the IRS had been satisfied, there no longer were grounds for prosecution and thus the 'exoneration' in the Starr Report. Having President Clinton's Attorney General Janet Reno passively but aggressively hinder the various investigations didn't help. In fact, that almost seemed to be why she remained in his administration as she continued to over-rule recommendations from both the then Director of the FBI and her own assistant attorney general that the Justice Department pursue prosecution.

As the Whitewater scenario was playing out, more problems emerged starting with the fact that Clinton had fired all the US Attorneys moments after taking office. This action instantly froze every federal investigation that was then in progress, which is why such preemptory firing has occurred only once—when Bill Clinton wanted to forestall the US Attorney's examination of his involvement in Whitewater.

Next came 'travelgate' and other matters surrounding Hillary's behavior where there is some question regarding her veracity. When quizzed by investigators about her missing box of billing records that could have proven that she had either falsely billed clients for legal work she never performed or committed real estate fraud by submitting false property valuations in another S&L insolvency, she dodged the question. She stonewalled the issue by ignoring the subpoena for almost two years until one day the billing records miraculously appeared. Once again she 'skated' from the consequences.

Another matter that hasn't seemed to bother the politically correct much was when Bill 'rented out' the White House for campaign contributions when he was short of money to finance his 1996 re-election. Unseemly though it was, it wasn't a criminal issue. That was left to his Commerce Secretary Ron Brown who 'sold seats' on his trade missions to China and other countries. This was clearly quo quid quo for campaign contributions and many companies took the President up on the deal including infamous Enron, just like his use of cash to provide African-American preachers with 'walking around money' to purchase get out the vote efforts in the black community.

Included in the morass were the cash contributions to Clinton's re-election committee and the Democratic National Committee made by Indonesia's Riady family and sub-entities of the Peoples Republic of China. In return for the cash, the Clinton Administration waived all kinds of rules pertaining to the sale of 'dual use' technology to Red China at the expense of American National Security. Additionally he tried to sell the former Long Beach Naval Base to a subsidiary of China's 'Red Army'. A point several investigators, including Dr Jack Cashill and former Representative Bob Barr who headed the House Impeachment Committee, have discussed at great lengths in their books.

What finally triggered the impeachment proceedings, though, was only the tip of the iceberg. Between Paula Jones's vigorous pursuit of her sexual harassment suit against the President and the Lewinsky affair, President Clinton crossed the line in his word parsing and 'obstructed justice' by committing perjury. This is a felony as Martha Stewart and other CEOs brought before the bar following the corporate financial scandals of the late 1990s can attest to.

The position taken by the Republicans who pushed the matter was that the chief magistrate of the United States shouldn't be going around committing felony perjury. The fact that he was found guilty of felony perjury is a matter of public record since the presiding judge in his cases reached that conclusion when she fined him 80 grand and yanked his bar license. Furthermore, the federal government declined to pay the bulk of his legal fees resulting from all the investigations—a sign that it didn't buy into Clinton's claims of innocence.

However there was only a snowball's chance in hell of throwing him out of office because Senate Democrats were never going to acknowledge that Clinton's behavior was really that bad, claiming that censor or some other slap on the wrist was appropriate. It was probably just as well, although not one Democrat has suffered for their lack of moral courage, proving once again that popular expediency frequently works. Had Clinton been expelled from office as a result of the impeachment trial, Al Gore would have assumed the Presidency and probably would have won re-election in 2000—just in time for 911.

The politically correct couldn't even go this far. From their perspective the Whitewater Investigation and all its accompanying items was all about sex. The spin promulgated by them was that $70 million was spent to 'pick on poor Billy', their hero, and that it was all the product of a vast right wing conspiracy to get him. Their point has been that what Bill did with Monica isn't a criminal offense and they're right, but to ascribe the total picture to simply a government intrusion on one's private behavior conveniently misses the point.

The fact that over the course of the broad investigation that centered around Whitewater, some 20 to 30 individuals involving the original S&L fraud and violations of federal elections laws ended up in prison because of it. This included Hillary's former law partner and Bill's Assistant Attorney General, Webster Hubbell. who finally pled guilty to stealing from his clients after receiving at least $100,000 in consulting contracts to keep his mouth shut about Whitewater. Altogether this works out to roughly $2.5 to $3 million per conviction, less if one counts Bill's perjury conviction—a reasonable figure considering what it cost LA County to prosecute OJ Simpson.

So why the vehement myopia on the part of the politically correct when it comes to Bill Clinton's behavior and the answer has to be related to the fact that he reflects their values, or at least the values of their youth. There isn't anything Bill has done that they haven't done. Whatever self-serving motives behind his behavior, the same have been typical of the politically correct. Bill Clinton could justify self-indulgence without any thought of self-restraint because he's in fact answerable to no one but himself in his own mind. To a great extent this is the ethos of the politically correct and they cannot condemn it in others without condemning it in themselves.

The Need for Demonization

There's an old adage amongst lawyers that if one doesn't have the facts, then argue the law and vice versa. This seems to be equally true of the politically correct. Besides arguing the facts involves more work and is often inconvenient. An equivalent approach is to demonize one's enemy in hopes that people won't get around to seeing how sleazy you are. Eg: Bill Clinton was a 'draft dodger' so George W. Bush must be one despite his honorable service as a fighter pilot in the Air National Guard. A record that is again being attacked during the 2004 election to the extent that fictitious documents were used by CBS News to prove 'W' had ducted his legal obligation.

This is also why the Democratic nominee for the White House in 2004 declares that Republicans are liars every chance he gets. Given the extreme vitriolic charges that we haven't seen since Jefferson invented dirty politics emanating from Kerry's camp, this hasn't been unexpected and by calling Republicans liars he's able to disparage any truthful remarks about his own record even before they surface since they must be lies too.

This often works better because it plays on the emotions of the crowd. Under this premise, Lenin and later Stalin, along with the spiritual successors, made anyone having private property the 'enemy of the people' since the acquisition of private property could only come through theft and influence peddling, which in Tsarist Russia was often the case. Today, in an American context, the Democratic ticket is doing the same thing when it rants about there being two nations with the Bush Administration favoring the rich at the expense of the 'poor middle class'—historically pure socialist rhetoric.

Later, when production goals set in the sequence of five year plans couldn't be met for practical reasons, those who'd pointed this out were labeled as saboteurs and promptly shot. Reality couldn't be allowed to interfere with the utopian vision. Thus anyone suggesting that human nature and the laws of physics might 'disprove' the assumptions behind the creation of 'heaven on earth' had to be eliminated before a regime based on the world as it is, replaced the ideologues. Ergo, the 2004 pledge by Democrats that we need to take back our country from classic whig liberals.

This was equally true of Nazi Germany only it was the Jews that interfered with the establishment of the master race because of their deviant behavior. At least that's what Herr Goebbels claimed and the majority of the German people believed him for their own psychological reasons. In fact the whole thrust of Nazi propaganda was designed to make those Germans who felt lesser than under normal conditions, feel that they were a part of something grand.

To accomplish this, the enemy, be it the Jews or communists or the old guard who'd engineered the 'stab in the back' resulting in the Versailles Treaty, had to be demonized. A trick also employed by Mao's Red China when he launched his 'Cultural Revolution'. In the case of Pot Pol and the Kmer Rouge, the demon obstructing the establishment of the 'perfect communal society' turned out to be anyone who knew how to read and write.

Recent examples include references to pundits Ann Coulter and Laura Ingraham as 'blond bimbos', something that's hard to prove when they're both ivy league graduates with law degrees from two of the nation's best law schools. Additionally the former made law review and clerked on the Court of Appeals while that latter clerked for the Supreme Court.

This has been followed up with efforts by fascist liberals attacking *the Fox News Channel* for being in 'cohoots' with the GOP. They, including several of the more leftist members of Congress. have even gone to the FCC to obtain relief from the channel's 'fair and balanced reporting'. The problem is that the channel is 'fair and balanced' and being unused to that, the politically correct are objecting to the fact that the public might learn that left of center propaganda isn't always the truth.

More egregious is the recent attack on John Kerry's fellow swiftboat officers who started running a few TV ads questioning Kerry's representation of his war record and reminding voters that Kerry slimed his fellow veterans as war criminals during testimoney before Congress in 1971. Instead of forthrightly defending his behavior, he's had his campaign vilify the 'vets' again—some of whom had defended him against war crimes charges when Kerry ran for reelection to the Senate in 1996.

The issue isn't whether the charges are true or false, it's that his fellow swiftboat officers who served with him must be made the enemy to destroy their creditability. Naturally no mention is made of Kerry allies, including Iowa Senator Tom Harkin who once claimed to have flown combat missions for the Navy over Vietnam until his military records showed that he never flown south of Okinawa.

So far they've spent upwards of $100 million to disparage George W. Bush every way imaginable. Nor made an effort refraining from calling republicans liars from the stump every chance Kerry can get. Despite that most of the $100 million has been provided by three men juxtaposed to the collage contributing to the swiftboat veterans campaign and $200,000 in seed capital from a Republican supporter from Texas, the chronic politically whine is that their effort is a Bush direct smear campaign.

Of course, as part of the process of disinformation, Democrats have tried to turn this into something it isn't. When 268 of his fellow officers who served in combat on the navy's swiftboats that patrolled Vietnam's southern rivers began their ads questioning his judgement and pointing out his proclivity towards hyperbole without substantiation, John Kerry's response was to whine that they were questioning his patriotism.

The same was true when Republicans in Georgia went after Senator Max Cleland, a decorated special forces officer and quadriplegic, during his 2002 re-election campaign. The point raised by Cleland's opponent was that the good senator had sacrificed the interests of national security when he voted against the 2002 homeland security bill because he wanted union rules and civil service benefits for the new cabinet department's employees counter to long standing practices.

Again the real issue was Cleland's judgement and priorities, not his patriotism. But this didn't stop Kerry from using Cleland's experience as a perceived pattern of GOP attacks on all Democrats' patriotism, proclaiming far and wide that the republican attitude that any criticism of the War on Terror was 'unpatriotic' was an attack on American's right of dissent. This wasn't true, but the whine has served its purpose in diverting attention away from the real issue of on his judgement relative to national security during his years as a United States Senator.

The politically correct's behavior isn't new and encompasses George W. Bush's 2000 campaign to become President of the United States and Ronald Reagan's years in the White House. The roots of this though, go back even further to the more leftist vilification of anyone having the audacity to disagree with them by pointing out the fallacies of their whine with facts as far back as the 1960s. As Stalin once put it, no one had a right to a political opinion that was different than his.

Fortunately by the time Ronald Reagan appeared on the scene, the violence the more leftist politically correct were accustomed to using to force its opponents into silence had disappeared. Still Reagan was disparaged as a dumb actor beholden to his advisors for what he thought, said or did despite evidence that his world view had been well thought out over a period of decades and that he often went against the advice of even his closest advisors.

Since Americans listened to him and agreed with his vehement opposition to communism, coupled with his campaign to send it off to the dustbin of history, the politically correct had to demonize him by calling him stupid and rendering him and the values he stood for as 'uncool'. All this despite the fact that he'd graduated from college at a time most Americans weren't even graduating from high school and that he'd been a very successful governor of California before his election to the White House.

The vilification didn't stop here as the politically correct went out of their way to describe the Reagan Years as the 'decade of greed' because his 'awful policies' that almost destroyed the country. Overlooked is the fact that his policies produced the exact opposite and that many of the politically wouldn't have a pot to pee in today, especially in Silicon Valley, if it weren't for his Presidency. However much of this propaganda is accepted as fact even to this day by these types.

What was and still is important, is that the Ronald Reagan's basic message ran against the grain of an entitlement society and that there was in fact something special about America and what it represented. The politically correct can't stand this because it refutes the notion that an imperfect world can be fixed if only the right thinking elite have their way under the auspices of a benevolent United Nations that would keep crass self-serving Americans under control.

When Bill Clinton appeared and loaded his cabinet with the 'right people' constituting an appropriate cross-section of color, everything seemed to be returning to normal. The centrist rhetoric of Clinton's campaign was written off as something necessary to get elected. Once in office 'ole Bill' went around saying the right things, plus Hillary was allowed to form a committee whose goal was to nationalize healthcare and the environmental movement was allowed to have its way.

As things began to turn south during his administration and the Republicans first gained control of the House of Representatives in 1994 and then the Senate in 1996, the politically correct were left with a need to believe the facade and deliberately ignore reality. If they didn't, the classical liberal Whigs would take over. However hope was on the way because they had a perfectly acceptable candidate available to replace Clinton once he won the 2000 Presidential Election—good old Al Gore.

From the perspective of the politically correct, Al Gore was the ideal candidate having served eight years as Vice President and buying in to all their fantasies without the baggage of Bill and Hillary, although they're still enthralled with the fiction she has made herself into. Something Dick Morris, Bill Clinton's campaign strategist for 25 years, makes perfectly clear in his book *Rewriting History* when he discusses the 'Hillary Brand'—sort of like Martha Stewart Living.

Given that he had represented Tennessee in both the House and the Senate, they could package him as a man of the people despite having grown up living an upper class lifestyle in Washington DC's best neighborhood while his father served in the Senate. Plus Gore was a Harvard grad. Hell, he'd even written a 'best selling' book about the environment and what had to be done to fix it.

The problem was that Al Gore's basically a lightweight no matter how he's packaged. Turns out, according to Laura Ingraham in her book *Shutup & Sing*, that his college board scores weren't quite as good as George W. Bush's and his superior grade point average wasn't enough to offset the impact of the grade inflation that crept into academia starting with the class of 1969. Which was Gore's class, Bush and I were from the Class of 1968. Even his literary best seller turned out to be long on hyperbole with a heavy load of junk science and short on fact.

In fact there wasn't much to suggest that Al Gore was up to the job of being the 'main man' besides the superficiality of his resume. He did serve in the Army and pulled a seven month tour in Vietnam, but he did this as a glorified private, which is what a specialist four really is, not as the officer one would expect a Harvard graduate to become. Instead of having a real job in his combat engineer battalion, he wrote the battalion newspaper, a nothing job that from my own experience the troops in the field could care less about.

About the only thing that seemed to stand out about his military service were his frequent runs to the coast of South Vietnam to buy the pot that he smoked. Therefore it was no wonder that when he ran for the White House, little was made of his war record, juxtaposed to the major effort to hype John Kerry's decorated service during the election of 2004. A war record that's deteriorating in the eyes of the electorate today due to close scrutiny because he's over-hyped it for years.

Returning to civilian life, Al Gore tried law and divinity school, flunking out of both with an academic record worse than my old collie's when he attended class with me as I earned my MBA. (At least 'Angus' got attendance points with his 'F incompletes') At this point the illustrious great leader of the politically correct became a hack reporter with a small town Tennessee newspaper before his father, the former Senator Al Gore sr., engineered his election to Congress.

Like Gore, George W. Bush was an Ivy League graduate—Yale. But unlike Al Gore, Bush spent 18 months on active duty going to flight school to earn his wings. He then served the rest of his military obligation as a fighter pilot in the Texas Air National Guard where he flew interceptor missions over the Arctic Circle as part of the Air Defense Command. Just like many of his fighter pilot peers in the regular Air Force and incurring more personal risk than regular Air Force officers manning missile silos in Montana.

After earning his MBA from Harvard, another rather difficult task, 'W' went back to his roots in Midland Texas and became a modestly successful Texas oilman before buying baseball's Texas Rangers and turning that franchise into a successful organization. Finally he ran for the governorship and surprised everyone by winning two terms. Not only that, he was one of Texas's more successful governors and left his mark on the state by getting the Democratically dominated state legislature to adopt many of his policies.

When it came to the Election of 2000, this more substantive resume made him a real threat to the politically correct and their aspirations. Not only that, he knew what he believed in as a result of his developing faith in Christianity. Something he has made no bones about referring to when he needs spiritual guidance, as have most American Presidents. Worse, he was saying the things Ronald Reagan said and he didn't equivocate.

If there was anything that could have made the politically correct answerable to no power greater than themselves go ballistic, this was it. Not being able to refute him in open debate, they turned to two tactics. The first was to 'promise' more than Bush did in order to blur any difference between him and their man of the people Al Gore. The second, in case expediency didn't work, was to demonize him as being un-American and having views that didn't reflect the values of the American people. Out went all the Hollywood intellectual lightweights to make the rounds of the late night talk shows to declare that George W. was 'stupid' and posture that since he was born with a 'silver spoon', his administration would only benefit the rich, etc.

Finally the election came down to a recount of the vote in Florida's most democratic counties where local election officials, democrats all, were fishing for votes by counting anything that might remotely have a mark on it, no matter how miniscule, that could suggest a vote for Gore. This was the famous 'hanging chad' fiasco and for the life of me I cannot understand how someone can mark a punch card ballot without making a least some kind of perforation.

Concurrently they were doing this while challenging the legitimacy of military absentee ballots as if service in the armed forces overseas axiomatically cost one the right to vote. A bigger chutzpah was that this was all being supervised for Al Gore by his campaign chief and former Clinton Commerce Secretary William Daily. He was the second son of Chicago's Richard Daily sr. who'd run Illinois's Cook County Machine for years while serving as the city's mayor.

Everything Bill Daily had in life he owed to Chicago's crooked elections where even the dead were enfranchised as long as they voted for his father. Yet there he was expounding on the importance of 'clean elections' where every vote counted, something unheard of in Chicago's Republican precincts during his father's reign. It had to have made more knowledgeable people ill to hear him, but the politically correct seem to be impervious to embarrassment when their cause is at stake.

Finally the US Supreme Court stepped in and brought the fire drill to a halt. Ruling that laws in place before an election, laws and procedures that both parties had mutually agreed to long before the election, were rules of the game. The Court established that the Constitution precluded retroactive changes to the benefit of any one side and Bush finally won Florida with its electoral votes pushing him into the White House.

This infuriated the politically correct because they tend to hate rules that prevent them from getting what they want, something that goes all the way back to their behavior as adult children in the 1960s and 70s. Rules are to inhibit the behavior of the other guy, like having Republicans adhere to the Federal Election Laws regarding campaign contributions while Bill Clinton had the right to violate them with impunity. From their perspective, if things aren't going their way, then the rules should be changed. This is just like the Blue-Gray football game where the losing side gets to receive the ball after they score, juxtaposed to the normal procedure.

Thus began the 'legend of the stolen election' that was decided in Bush's favor because five of the justices voting in his favor had been appointed by Republicans and were thus obligated to repay the favor. This was a gross disparagement of the Court because it is hard to image that it would think this way, but it does exemplify politically correct thinking where 'if we're willing to do it, so is everyone else'—justified immorality.

The ultimate irony of the Election of 2004 is that just about every news organization in the country with a liberal bias has gone down to Florida and repeatedly recounted the votes. Despite all these recounts under myriad criteria as to what was actually a vote, none of the liberal media has found any evidence that the election would have turned out any differently. The only way Gore could have won was if his henchmen were allowed to bring in boxes of blank ballots and declared that they were all votes for Gore.

Despite this truth, the politically correct still won't shut up about the 'stolen election', vowing to mount any legal challenge they can think of in 2004 to ensure that it won't happen again. A vow that augers poorly for the veracity of their potential behavior when the ballots are counted in 2004.

The Election of 2004

With this background it's not surprising that the Election of 2004 will be recorded as the nastiest we've seen since Jefferson cut loose in 1800. We've already seen the beginnings of this during the Presidential Primary season when one presidential wannabe accused George W. Bush of everything he could think of before self-destructing in Iowa. Another candidate, former House Majority Leader Dick Gephart, based his campaign on calling President Bush 'a miserable failure' without ever substantiating his claim. And it has continued to get worse.

On the Senate floor we've been subjected to Massachusetts Senator Ted Kennedy's howling claim that the War in Iraq was concocted in Texas for political gain, and West Virginia Senator Byrd, who once was a member of the Ku Klux Klan, hasn't behaved any better. Then there is Senator Tom Daschle of South Dakota clutching his hands like Uriah Heap in Dicken's *David Copperfield* while explaining why every Bush proposal is inadequate without ever offering proposals of his own.

Over in the House, Minority Leader Nancy Pelosi keeps raising the number of jobs that have been lost since Bush took office. She's now up to three million despite the fact that the actually number has declined to less than 1 million since the economy began recovering from the recession that Bush had nothing to do with. In fact we're still listening to all the trash talk about how this is the worse economic environment since Herbert Hoover, regardless of how ridiculous that assertion is.

Collectively, throughout the politically correct throng we hear the constant refrain that the Bush Administration is beholden to special interests. That Haliburton and Enron et al have purchased Bush's White House with campaign contributions. They ignore that Enron heavily supported his opponent, then Governor Ann Richards, during his first run for governor in 1994 and that the company contributed significantly to Clinton's 1996 re-election thanks to trading seats on the Secretary of commerce's trade mission flights for campaign cash.

Maybe Democrats just want to smother any reference to the support Enron's corporate leadership provided them in light of the precipitous collapse of the company and the major issue they made of that. Nor do they particularly want to remind anyone that Enron's campaign contributions did the company little good as it conspicuously received no help from the Bush Administration when it was going down due to financial fraud.

In fact the Bush Administration has methodically prosecuted everyone, including Enron, who created the corporate accounting scandals that occurred under the Clinton Administration—another ignored item that undermines the politically correct argument that the Bush Administration only represents corporate interests.

Notice too that special interest only refers to private enterprise. Within the politically correct rhetoric there is never any reference to all the public interest groups that have purchased the Democratic Party lock stock and barrel over the years. Particularly the unions since the socialist John Sweeney was elected to head the AFL-CIO in 1996 as laid out by Linda Chavez in her recent book. These are defined as benevolent groups who merely protect average Americans from the racipious grasp of the country's big corporations, ensuring that the environment is adequately protected and we all have clean air.

No mention is made that these groups collectively represent real money for the lawyers and associated minions who make their living off of the contributions public interest groups collect and the lawsuits against anyone and everyone with deep pockets they pursue. Since many cases require the defendant (government and/or private parties) to pay the legal fees for both sides involved in 'public interest group' lawsuits, any effort to reign them in is meet with opposition by Congressional Democrats. (By the way, the American Legion opposed this practice by resolution at its 2004 National Convention)

Despite the successful effort of Arizona's Senator John McCain to restrict the availability of 'soft money' in federal elections and coordinated independent advocacy efforts on behalf of candidates, we're now seeing groups like MoveOn.org run ads comparing the President with Adolf Hitler others and they are not being facetious. MoveOn.org is for the most part financed by one of the world's wealthiest man and advocate for the legalization of drugs, George Soros, and two others.

In fact they've succeeded in injecting a dangerous element into our political process because they're outside the regulated political process and subject to emulation the next time around. Throw in the liberal icon Michael Moore, who's touted as the country's great documentarian despite the fact that he's a college dropout, with his heavily dubbed over films purporting to be factual representations, and we're well on the way to the propaganda politics that tore apart Germany's Weimar Republic. If nothing else, it deliberately sows the distrust that Democrats turn around and decry despite being its creators.

So we're now faced with a campaign where two heroes of the American left are running for office because they, not the Bush Administration, reflect American values irrespective of voting records that make this claim a statistical absurdity. At the head of the ticket is the most liberal US Senator and the fourth most liberal has become his running mate. In fact the Kerry/Edwards ticket is even more 'liberal' than a Ted Kennedy/Hillary Clinton one. Thus it's not possible that two individuals at least two, if not three, standard deviations from the mean position taken by the other 98 US Senators as evidenced by their voting records, can reflect mainstream American values no matter how extensive the spin.

Next there is the 'deju vu' use of PT 109 with Kerry's band of brother's from his Vietnam swiftboat. It's almost as if he volunteered for swiftboat duty on the rivers of South Vietnam after reading PT 109 and decided that he too needed an equivalent entry on his political resume. Unlike JFK, though, Kerry has a solid anti-defense voting record that he is taking great pains to avoid mentioning during his presidential campaign as though he was the 'phantom senator' for 19 years.

John Edwards, the Vice Presidential candidate on the ticket, made his millions collecting his 40% cut from the jury settlements awarded his clients when he won cases based on junk science. For him to declare that he's the defender of the 'little guy', after his primary run was financed almost exclusively by the trial lawyers of this country, represents the height of hypocrisy. Like Clinton, his poor boy roots are a bit overdone. True his dad started his working career as a lowly mill worker in South Carolina, but the item left out of the John Edwards political resume is that his dad quickly rose through the ranks to become the mill's general manager.

That's not going to stop them from talking about the 'two Americas'—one for the rich represented by George W. Bush and the rest of America represented by the two of them. In the process they're going to cut the annual federal budget deficit in half in less time that Bush thinks he can do it, avoiding the fact that the deficit will shrink that much on its own as a standard economic cycle unfolds.

To make matters even better, John Kerry will personally create 10 million new jobs, something the economy is quite capable of doing on its own without his help. Then for victory in Iraq, we're going to bring in the French and significantly reduce our troop levels by July 2005. Nothing like telling the insurgents how long they have to hold out before the United States surrenders on the installment plan.

Most of this of course is hogwash, but it's what the politically correct want to hear so they get it by the shovel-full. Add this to the defamation campaign and its almost like the crowd cheering Il Duce in the 1920s. The reality is that the only people Kerry and Edwards represent are the politically correct and those gate keepers who suck in the money like the civil rights entrepreneurs. These are the people whose livelihoods are at risk from Classic Whig Liberalism and they will fight with means fair or fowl to maintain that status quo.

Addendum: Military Service

During the election of 2004 there have been numerous claims and counter-claims regarding each of the presidential candidates' military service during the Vietnam era. In the case of President George W. Bush, charges that he received special treatment to get into the National Guard and then failed to fulfill his military service obligations go back to his first campaign for the Texas governorship in 1994.

Throughout the last months of 2003 and the first half of 2004, these charges have built up a head of steam with the Chairman of the Democratic National Committee claiming that President Bush had been a deserter and 'AWOL in Alabama' in 1972. Declarations by other Democrats have been even worse as part of a concerted campaign to tear down the Commander-in-Chief during a time of war.

Following Labor Day 2004, CBS News finally got the 'evidence' they'd been looking for to 'prove' these charges and ran an exposé on *60 Minutes* with their chief anchorman Dan Rather presenting the story. Unfortunately for them, all the purported documentary evidence that they built their story around quickly proved to be forgeries. Ergo, the *60 Minutes* report was a fraud.

Had the mass media really been interested in President Bush's National Guard service they would have discovered that his sojourn was anything but 'dishonorable'. First to get into the Air National Guard as a potential fighter pilot in the late 1960s, one had to have 20/20 vision without a stigmatism, be big enough to fly fighter jets without being too big to fit into them, and pass a battery of pattern analysis tests. One also had to be a college graduate. At this point the vast majority of the waiting list to get into the guard and almost half the regular officers commissioned by the Navy/USMC in June 1968 would have been culled out.

Next, because President Bush received an honorable discharge with the rank of First Lieutenant, he had to have passed officer candidate school. To get his wings, as he did, he needed to successfully complete flight school—something that over 20% of pilot candidates fail to do. Following that, he needed to become qualified to fly F102 interceptor jets. Altogether this constitutes two years of continuous active duty, leaving four of his six year contractual obligation to serve in a guard fighter squadron.

Two of these four years George W. Bush did spend with his squadron, racking up almost 400 flight hours over 64 mandatory training days. Once pre and post flight activities, plus various administrative activities, are counted, this represents a lot of active duty time flying for the Air Defense Command in some rather dangerous airplanes. Had he been in the active Air Force, this would have covered the period he would otherwise have spent in Vietnam, but one should keep in mind that the earliest he would have arrived in-country was sometime in September 1970 when the war had clearly wound down.

The last two years, 1972-73 and the ones that the Democrats complain about, Bush earned 56 retirement points per year of the 50 per year that he was obligated to acquire. Then he received an 'early out' to go to Harvard and get his MBA—a routine procedure considering the massive reduction in forces that occurred at the time and one that reduced the active duty requirement for thousands of junior officers. One should also note that the Democratic Candidate, John Kerry received the same benefit in order to run for Congress.

Conversely President Bush's 2004 opponent was commissioned in the US Navy Reserve in 1966 and ultimately ended up as a junior officer about a destroyer for seven months off the coast of South Vietnam. Then at his own request, John Kerry was assigned to swift-boat duty on the Mekong Kong Delta where he served just over four months before being sent home thanks to his third purple heart.

Upon discharge to the reserves, he next organized his 'Vietnam Veterans Against the War' and concurrent with his 1,000 man march on the Capital he testified before the Congress about how all of his fellow officers promoted and sanctioned the commitment of 'war crimes' by their subordinates. Then as a naval reserve officer he went to Paris to conduct his own 'personal' diplomacy, which is against the law and construed by many as 'giving aid and comfort to the enemy'. That's his public record.

The issue raised by his fellow swift boat officers over the summer of 2004 was that despite Kerry's three purple hearts, bronze and silver stars, he was 'unfit for command' based on their personal knowledge from associating with him in combat. The point they raised was that Kerry, as a self-promoter par excellence, tended to inflate his after action reports with tales of enemy action that never happened and thus sent false information regarding enemy activity up the chain of command.

One of these tales resulted in Kerry's bronze star. Apparently, Kerry with three other boats were patrolling up a fairly wide river when a command-detonated mine went off sinking one of the boats. While two of the boats opened up with all their firepower as per standard operating procedures pertaining to immediate reaction responses, Kerry retreated in his boat before coming back to rescue a special forces officer who'd fallen off his boat into the water.

At the same time the other boats had recognized that they were merely shooting up the brush and hadn't received fire so they started rescuing the survivors of the boat that had been sunk. The problem was that Kerry's after-action report did mention receiving fire from the VC, etc. and when it reached the Admiral's staff, someone wrapped it up in standard boiler plate so that bronze stars were awarded all around.

The swift boat veterans also question the validity of Kerry's first purple heart. Seems that when he'd first arrived in country, he'd gone out in a sampan as part of his in-country orientation with another officer and a sailor. As they patrolled along the shore, they saw shadows in the brush and opened fire, nothing unusual from my experience. None was returned. Still to make sure they were alone, Kerry fired an M-79 grenade launcher towards the shore and was nicked by a piece of shrapnel from his own grenade in the process—one that barely broke the skin and was treated with ointment and a band-aid.

When Kerry requested a purple heart for this, he was turned down by his commanding officer and no entry was made in his service records at the time. Three months later, with a new commanding officer and doctor, he finally got his purple heart. The reason this smells to me was that I had been a company executive officer with the Marine Corps in Vietnam.

From my own experience I know that it is automatic to make the various entries in a wounded Marine's service records and forward information regarding the award of a purple heart up to HQ Marine Corps through the daily unit diary. Navy procedures were similar. Ergo, Kerry's first purple heart was self-awarded.

There are also questions surrounding what he did to earn his silver star and one of his other purple hearts. The premise according to the swift boat veterans is that the circumstances of that heart are less than creditable, just like his first purple heart. From what little that has emerged pertaining to the silver star action, the concept of heroism above and beyond seems to be missing.

One version has Kerry chasing a lone sniper into the woods and killing him. If true, this indicates a lack of judgement since the VC used snipers this way to suck Americans into ambushes. Additionally Navy lieutenants commanding swiftboats have other responsibilities. Ergo, Kerry's behavior that got him the silver star was juvenile and indicative of a lack of judgement. Had he been one of my platoon commanders, he would have received an 'ass chewing' instead.

Epilogue

Centuries had passed since the great empire had reached it apex and the citizenry had long ceased taking responsibility for its defense by joining its once powerful legions. In fact they'd collected by the hundreds of thousands in the empire's capital city expecting the elite to feed them 'three squares' daily without cost to themselves.

However the elites, who'd once considered it an honor to personally assume the burdens of building the empire's great civic facilities, were no longer financially in a position to do so thanks to decades of increasing tax burdens and the overwhelming growth of the empire's bureaucracies.

This had been compounded by the rise of a new state religion with the accompanying removal from the tax rolls of all of its facilities and officials. Thus economic activity had been shifted from the generation of wealth through commercial activities to the temporary retention of wealth by joining the new tax-exempt institution.

Finally out in the hinterlands of what had once been the land of Celtic barbarians, the people could no longer bear the burden that the government imposed upon them. So that when they looked to the hordes attacking from east of the great river, they concluded that stopping them wasn't worth the effort. Thus the western half of the Roman Empire disappeared from history.

Reading List for the Political Correct

Introduction:

Coulter, Ann; <u>Slander: Liberal Lies About the American Right</u>; 2002, Crown Publishers, New York, NY
Revel, Jean-Francis; <u>How Democracies Perish;</u> 1983, Harper & Row, New York, NY

Chapter 1:

Berlin, Ira; <u>Generations of Captivity: A History of African American Slaves</u>; 2003, Belknap Press of Harvard University Press, Cambridge MA
————; <u>Many Thousands Gone: The First Two Centuries of Slavery in North America</u>; 1998, Belknap Press of Harvard University Press, Cambridge MA
Coulter, Ann; <u>Treason: Liberal Treachery from the Cold War to the War on Terrorism</u>; 2003, Crown Forum, New York NY
Fischer, David Hackett; <u>Albion's Seed, Four British Folkways in America</u>; 1989, Oxford University Press, New York NY

Chapter 2:

Hayak, Friedrich A.; <u>The Road to Serfdom: A Classic Warning Against the Dangers to Freedom Inherent in Social Planning</u>; 1944, The University of Chicago, Chicago IL
Payne, Stanley G.; <u>The Spanish Civil War, The Soviet Union & Communism</u>; 2004, Yale University Press, New Haven CT
Pearson, Jack E. (editor); <u>The Norman Shield: Training & Reference Manual of the Sigma Chi Fraternity</u>; 1963, The Sigma Chi Corporation, Evanston IL
Sowell, Thomas; <u>Knowledge & Decisions</u>; 1980, Basic Books Inc., New York, NY
————; <u>Preferential Policies: An International Perspective</u>, 1990, William Morrow, New York, NY

229

_____; The Quest for Cosmic Justice; 1999, The Free Press, New York, NY

Chapter 3:

Allen, Louis; Burma: The Longest War 1941-45; 2000 (1984), Phoenix Press, London, England
Atkinson, Rick; An Army at Dawn: The War in North Africa 1942-1943; 2002, Henry Holt & Co, New York NY
Blair, Clay; The Forgotten War: America in Korea, 1950-1953; 1987, Doubleday (Anchor Press) New York NY
Davidson, Phillip B; Vietnam at War: The History 1946-1975; 1988, Presidio, Novato CA
Fall, Bernard B; Hell in a Very Small Place: The Siege of Dien Bien Phu; 1967, J.B. Lippincott Co, Philadelphia PA
_____; Street Without Joy; 1972 (1961), Schocken, New York NY
_____; The Two Viet-Nams: A Politcal & Military Analysis; 1967 (1963), Frederick A. Praeger, New York NY
Linn, Brian McAllister; The US Army & Counterinsurency in the Phillipine War, 1899-1902; 1989, The University of North Carolina Press, Chapel Hill NC
_____; The Philippine War: 1899-1902; 2000, University Press of Kansas, Lawrence, KA
Nolan, William Keith; Battle for Hue: Tet 1968; 1983, Dell Publishing, New York NY
_____; Battle for Saigon: Tet 1968; 1996, Pocket Books, New York NY
_____; Inside Cambodia; 1990, Presidio, Novato CA
_____; Inside Laos, The Story of Dewy Canyon II/Lam Son 719, Vietnam 1971; 1986, Dell Publishing, New York NY
Palmer, Bruce jr; The 25-Year War: America's Military Role in Vietnam; 1984, The University of Kentucky Press, Lexington KY
Prados, John; The Blood Road: The Ho Chi Minh Trail & the Vietnam War; 1999, John Wiley & Sons, New York NY
Turley, G. H.; The Easter Offensive: Vietnam, 1972; 1985, Warner Books, New York NY
Westmoreland, William C; A Soldier Reports; 1976, Doubleday & Co, Garden City NY

Woodruff, Mark W; <u>Unheralded Victory: The Defeat of the Viet Cong and the North Vietnamese Army: 1961-1973</u>; 1999, Vandamere Press, Arlington VA

Chapter 4:

Bowden, Mark; <u>Black Hawk Down: A Story of Modern War</u>; 1999, Atlantic Monthly Press, New York NY

Friedman, Norman; <u>Desert Victory: The War for Kuwait</u>; 1991, The Naval Institute Press, Annapolis MD

Henderson, Charles W.; <u>Marshalling the Faithful: The Marines First Year in Vietnam</u>; 1993, Berkeley Books, New York NY

Kyle, James H.; <u>The Guts to Try: The Untold Story of the Iran Hostage Rescue Mission by the On-Scene Desert Commander</u>; 1995, Ballantine Books, New York NY

McCrcoklin, James H.; <u>Garde D'Haiti: Twenty Years of Organization & Training by the US Marine Corps</u>; 1956, The United States Naval Institute, Annapolis MD

Paxton, Robert O; <u>The Anatomy of Fascism</u>; 2004, Alfred A. Knopf, New York NY

Ros, Martin; <u>Night of Fire: The Black Napoleon & the Battle for Haiti</u>; 1991, Sarpedon, New York NY

Schweizer, Peter; <u>Reagan's War;</u>

Summer, Harry G. jr.; <u>On Strategy II: A Critical Analysis of the Gulf War</u>; 1992, Dell Publishing, New York NY

Schwarzkopf, H. Norman; <u>It Doesn't Take a Hero: General H. Norman Schwarzkopf: The Autobiography</u>; 1992, Bantam Books, New York NY

West, F.J. jr; <u>The Village</u>; 1972, Harper & Row, New York NY

Wetterhahn, Ralph; <u>The Last Battle: The Mayaguez Incident & the End of the Vietnam War</u>; 2001, Carroll & Graf Publishers, New York NY

Chapter 5:

Bearden, Milt & James Risen; <u>The Main enemy: The Inside Story of the CIA's Final Showdown with the KGB</u>; 2003, Random House, New York NY

Coll, Steve; <u>Ghost Wars: The Secret History of the CIA, Afghanistan, and Bin Laden, From the Societ Invasion to September 10, 2001</u>; 2004, Penguin Press, New York NY

Frum, David & Richard Perle; <u>An End to Evil: How to Win the War on Terror</u>; 2003, Random House, New York NY

Gold, Dore; <u>Hatred's Kingdom: How Saudi Arabia Supports the New Global Terrorism</u>; 2003, Regency Publishing, Washington DC

Hourani, Albert; <u>A History of the Arab Peoples</u>; 1991, Harvard University Press, Cambridge MA

Hoyland, Robert G.; <u>Arabia & the Arabs: From the Bronze Age to the Coming of Islam</u>; 2001, Routledge, London UK

Keegan, John; <u>Intelligence In War: Knowledge of the Enemy from Napoleon to Al Qaeda</u>; 2003, Alfred A. Knopf, New York NY

Lewis, Bernard; <u>The Crisis of Islam: Holy War & Unholy Terror</u>; 2003, The Modern Library, New York NY

Moore, Robin; <u>The Hunt for Bin Laden: Task Force Dagger; On the Ground w/ the Special Forces in Afghanistan</u>; 2003, Random House, New York NY

Rashid, Ahmed; <u>Jihad: The Rise of Militant Islam in Central Asia</u>; 2002, Yale University, New Haven CT

Standish, John F.; <u>Persia & the Gulf: Retrospect & Prospect</u>; 1998, Curzon Press, Richmond Surrey, UK

Chapter 6:

Atkinson, Rick; <u>In the Company of Soldiers: A Chronicle of Combat</u>; 2004, Henry Holt & Co, New York NY

Fenn, Elizabeth A.; <u>Pox Americana: The Great Smallpox Epidemic of 1775-82</u>; 2001, Hill & Wang, New York NY

Hannity, Sean; <u>Deliver Us From Evil: Defeating Terrorism, Despotism, & Liberalism</u>; 2004, Regan Books, New York NY

Mayor, Adrienne; <u>Greek Fire, Poison Arrows & Scorpion Bombs: Biological And Chemical Warfare in the Ancient World</u>; 2003, Overlook Press, New York NY

Moore, Robin; <u>Hunting Down Saddam: The Inside Story of the Search & Capture</u>; 2004, St. Martin's Press, New York NY

North, Oliver; <u>War Stories: Operation Iraqi Freedom</u>; 2003, Regency Publishing, Washington DC

West, Bing & Maj Gen Ray L. Smith; <u>The March Up: Taking Baghdad with the 1st Marine Division</u>; 2003, Bantam Dell, New York NY

Zinsmeister, Karl; <u>Boots on the Ground: A Month with the 82nd Airborne in the Battle for Iraq</u>; 2003, St Martin's Press, New York NY

Chapter 7:

Bobbitt, Philip; <u>The Shield of Achilles: War, Peace & the Course of History</u>; 2002, Alfred A. Knopf, New York NY

Brendon, Piers; <u>The Dark Valley, A Panorama of the 1930s</u>; 2000, Alfred A. Knopf, New York NY

Dunn, Susan; <u>Sister Revolutions; French Lightning, American Light</u>; 1999, Faber & Faber, New York NY

Feldman, Noah; <u>After Jihad: America & the Struggle for Islamic Democracy</u>; 2003, Farrar, Straus & Giroux, New York NY

Gibson, John; <u>Hating America: The New World Sport</u>; 2004, HarperCollins, New York NY

Horne, Alistair; <u>A Savage War of Peace: Algeria 1954-1962</u>; 2002 (1971), History Book Club, New York NY

Chapter 8:

Bird, Richard M.; <u>Tax Policy & Economic Development</u>; 1992, Johns Hopkins University Press, Baltimore MD

Breen, T.H.; <u>The Marketplace of Revolution: How consumer Politics Shaped American Independence</u>; 2004, Oxford University Press, New York NY

Chavez, Linda & Daniel Gray; <u>Betrayal: How Union Bosses Shake Down Their Members & Corrupt American Politics</u>; 2004, Crown Forum, New York NY

Dilts, James D.; <u>The Great Road: The Building of the Baltimore & Ohio, The Nation's First Railroad: 1828-1853</u>; 1993, Stanford University Press, Stanford CA

Hoff, Trygve J. B.; <u>Economic Calculation in the Socialist Society</u> 1947, Liberty Fund, Indianapolis IN

Hughes, Jonathan; <u>American Economic History</u> (3rd ed); 1990, Harper & Collins, New York NY

McGaw, Judith A.; <u>Most Wonderful Machine: Mechanization & Social Change in Berkshire Paper Making, 1801-1885</u>; 1987, Princeton University Press, Princeton NJ

Von Mises, Ludwig; <u>Socialism</u>; 1932, Liberty Fund, Indianapolis IN

Chapter 10:

Andrew, Christopher & Vasili Mitrokhin; <u>The Sword & the Shield: The Mitokhin Archive & the Secret History of the KGB</u>; 1999, Basic Books, New York NY

Cashill, Jack; <u>Ron Brown's Body: How One Man's Death Saved the Clinton Presidency & Hillary's Future</u>; 2004, WND Books, Nashville TN

Collier, Simon & William F. Sater; <u>A History of Chile: 1808-1994</u>; Cambridge University Press, Cambridge UK

Conquest, Robert; <u>Harvet of Sorrow; Soviet Collectivization & the Terror—Famine</u>; 1986, Oxford University Press, New York NY

Courtois, Stephane et al; <u>The Black Book of Communism: Crimes, Terror, Repression</u>; Harvard University Press, Cambridge MA

Fitzpatrick, Sheila; <u>Everyday Stalinism: Ordinary Life in Extraordinary Times: Soviet Russia in the 1930s</u>; 1999, Oxford University Press, New York NY

Getty, J. Arch & Oleg V. Naumov; <u>The Road to Terror; Stalin & the Self Destruction of the Bolsheviks, 1932-1936</u>; 1999, Yale University Press, New Haven CT

Johnson, Paul; <u>Modern Times: The World from the Twenties to the Eighties</u>; 1983, Harper & Row, New York NY

Klehr, Harvey, John Earl Hays & Fridrikh Igorevich Firsov; <u>The Secret World of American Communism</u>; 1995, Yale University Press, New Haven CT

McGerr, Michael; <u>A Fierce Discontent; The Rise of the Progressive Movement in America: 1870-1920</u>; 2003, The Free Press, New York NY

Sudplatov, Pavel & Anatoli, w/Jerrold L. & Leona P. Schecter; <u>Special Tasks</u>; 1994, Little, Brown & Co, New York NY

Stone, David R.; <u>Hammer & Rifle, the Militarization of the Soviet Union: 1926-1933</u>; 2000, University of Kansas Press, Lawrence KA

Chapter 11:

Dornbusch, Rudiger & Sebastian Edwards (ed); <u>The Macroeconomics of Populism in Latin America</u>; 1991, University of Chicago Press, Chicago IL

Holland, Tom; <u>Rubicon: The Last Years of the Roman Republic</u>; 2003, Doubleday, New York NY

Ingraham, Laura; <u>Shut Up & Sing: How Elites from Hollywood, Politics & the UN Are Subverting America</u>; 2003, Regency Publishing, Washington DC

Morris, Dick; <u>Rewriting History</u>; 2004, Regan Books, New York NY

About the Author

Craig P Boulton experienced first hand the leftist campus turbulence as an NROTC Midshipman before graduating from the University of Rochester (Class of 1968) with an AB in Economics. Following active service as a Marine Corps officer and a tour of duty in Vietnam, he entered the securities industry as a stockbroker, financial analyst and ultimately branch manager before retiring in 1994. Concurrently, he was an elected GOP party official in Northern California for 14 years.

During the course of his career, he held licenses as both a principle with the Municipal Securities Review Board and General Securities Principle. Along the way he earned his MBA in Finance and Information Resource Management(Beta Gamma Sigma) from California State University, San Bernardino and a MA in Economics from California State University, Los Angeles before later becoming a Chartered Financial Analyst Charter. While on active service at Quantico, Va. He pursued graduate studies in economics at George Washington University in the economics of planned economies.

This is his fourth book having previously published *Twenty Years of Wall Street on Mai Street; Student Turns Professor;* and *Cutting Through The Fog of The Investment Wars.*

0-595-33402-4

www.ingramcontent.com/pod-product-compliance
Lightning Source LLC
Chambersburg PA
CBHW061347280526
45784CB00001B/173